The Blue Ridge Anthology

Poetry and Prose by
Central Virginia Writers

Charlottesville Chapter
Virginia Writers Club, Inc.

Cedar Creek Publishing • Bremo Bluff, Virginia
www.cedarcreekpublishingservices.com

Library of Congress Control Number 2007921260

ISBN-13: 978-0-9790205-4-4
ISBN-10: 0-9790205-4-9

Printed in the United States of America on acid-free paper

Table of Contents

PROSE FICTION

POETRY

PROSE NONFICTION

ON WRITING AND PUBLISHING

Introduction

Central Virginia writes. Conventional wisdom says that every literary anthology needs an overarching theme. This is the theme for *The Blue Ridge Anthology:* Central Virginia writes. We are blessed with so many writers in this region who pump out *New York Times* best-sellers regularly and/or whose writing receives critical accolades in the form of national awards that we tend not to realize that beyond those stellar writers is an army of other accomplished and developing writers of significant talent living and writing in the area surrounding Charlottesville, Virginia.

This anthology of poetry and prose, which was compiled and sponsored by the Charlottesville Chapter of the Virginia Writers Club, celebrates those writers by combining works by talented writers of all stages of development and of a broad range of writing topics and forms between two covers. In this volume, you will find work not only by a Pulitzer Prize winner and former national and Virginia poet laureate, Rita Dove; a former premier creative writing program academician and Virginia poet laureate, George Garrett; and a stellar best-selling author David Baldacci, but also works by a good representation of the published literary community of Central Virginia and by writing contest winners and developing writers who have vaulted the bars of selection and professional editing to appear in this book.

Among the eighty-eight works by forty authors we have collected for your reading pleasure, you will find a scope of writing categories that stretches from poetry, short fiction, nonfiction, and essays on writing and publishing to excerpts from works in progress, memoir vignettes, song lyrics, discussion of screenplay writing, and historical essays. Although many of the pieces deal with Central Virginia itself, some spin off to as far away as Brazil, Argentina, and the cold forests of Russia and as close in as the inner spaces of the mind.

At the heart of the anthology collection are all of the winning entries in the 2006 annual contest of the Charlottesville Chapter of the Virginia Writers Club as well as some of the winners of the 2005 contest, a few of which went on to win honors at the state level. All of these winning pieces are identified in the table of contents. To these we added invited material from published national- or local-level Virginia authors, selections from works presented at Club programs, and selected nonwinning entries to the Club's 2006 contest.

The genesis of this anthology extends back into the murky past of the Charlottesville Club, the territory of which extends several counties in all directions from Charlottesville and over the Blue Ridge Mountains as far as Staunton, Virginia. Club leaders for years past have had an ongoing dream of showcasing the breadth and depth of writing ability and categories of the Club's membership, which is representative of the high volume of active creative writers in Central Virginia. When I became president of the Club, I saw the benefit not only of such an anthology in showcasing the talent of our members but also as the centerpiece for an educational program that could be transported to the outer boundaries of our Club territories and to school venues as well.

We, as a Club, were very fortunate that my own expression of interest in publishing an anthology was met with just the right kind of expertise needed to accomplish this task. In our Club secretary/treasurer, Linda Layne (who also is executive director of the Virginia Writers Club), we had an expert in book production who was willing to volunteer her talents and time gratis to this project. Similarly, professional freelance book editor Gary Kessler, who had previously served as volume editor for an even more complex and voluminous international writers Web site anthology, stepped forward to provide editorial and book organization support. Two past presidents of the Club (and, not incidentally, Club and state contest winners in their own right), Sally Honenberger and Mike Zbailey, rounded out our committee of five on designing and launching the anthology project. Sally served as contest selection editor for fiction, with VMI English professors Kurt Jose Ayau and David Rachels serving as anthology selection editors for fiction. Albemarle artist-in-resident and University of Virginia educator Hilda Ward was our selection editor for poetry, and newspaper community editor Marian Courtney Styles was selection editor for nonfiction. To all of these talented and dedicated writing community personages, I extend the heartfelt thanks of the Club membership and leadership for bringing this anthology to reality.

I also wish to thank all of the contributors to this volume, not the least to our illustrious invited contributors, for showing their support for the developing writers in Central Virginia in the best way possible—by sharing their written talents with other writers and with readers. It is only fitting that I close this introduction with a poem by our poetry editor, Hilda Ward, which describes well what the process is for all of us who write because we must.

Enrique Herrera, President
Charlottesville Chapter,
Virginia Writers Club, Inc.

"On My Way to My Muse"

by H. E. R. Ward

On my way to my Muse
I must clean off the kitchen table
And put the dishes in the dishwasher
And put a load of clothes in
On my way to my Muse
I must get my favorite pen
And find a special journal
And finish writing out the bills

And pick up my messages
So I can have silence
On my way to my Muse
I must get rid of all my doubts
And my share of not being good enough
And not being organized
And not being ready for success
And so on my way to my Muse
I must call for a session to remove my doubts
And get a massage to relieve my tension
So I know that I am the best I can be
And so I try to reach out to my Muse
And I find my hands are not quite clean enough
And my space is not clear
And I haven't finished my chores
And so I write her a letter
And ask her to forgive me
And to come again when I am ready!

PROSE FICTION

"The Contract"

(An excerpt from a work-in-progress)

by George Garrett

Not counting that kind and helpful servant girl, that tall and slender, fair-haired young woman with the hearty ghost of a Westcountry accent still haunting her voice, and with eyes as cold and hard as polished brass buttons; not counting her, for she is not fool or ninny enough to believe anything whatsoever the man in the green cloak might promise; and she does not expect to see the antic fellow again, perhaps in all her lifetime, unless and until he needs something, her aid and comfort, once more; not counting herself, then, there are the three others who have been following him on this rainy summer afternoon, two up to no good, though as yet planning not much serious harm or mischief for him. (Though he cannot know that.)

One of these two is a large and memorably fat man, a man not at all unknown, not only in these parts of the city, but also in the larger world of England, where, fat or thin, tall or short, no matter, at least his name is known on and for several counts about which we shall speak soon enough. More to the point, however, he is known at sight in half the taverns and alehouses of this part of London, and so he feels he must hang back with his companion, not shadowing Greene too closely and certainly not following directly behind him into the warmth and comfort of any tavern hereabouts.

You might justly wonder why, if there are two of them together lurking behind the homeward wanderings of Robert Greene, the other one, a man of no known trades or masters, going by the name of Paul Cartwright at least for today, for here and now, meaning he has called himself many other names and will do so again, God willing—who, being newly come to London, himself, and newly in the employ of the fat man, is not yet known hereabouts by name or appearance or reputation. Trouble is that this Paul Cartwright, if that was in truth the fellow's name now or ever, is himself easily memorable. You would not forget him if you had ever seen him or spoken to him. You would, first of all, generally note and remember the great size and shape of him, a man tall enough and broad enough in shoulders and abeam, to find a place among the queen's yeomen of the guard if that way of life were his hope or his pleasure. The yeomen scorn all who are less than at least six feet in height and (believe it or not) have no difficulty in these days filling their ranks, with tall and sturdy young men. But even among them there be not so many so large—at least a head higher than six-feet—and as well-shaped as this fellow. Indeed, by his bearing, real or affected, and by his clothing and the way he chooses to wear it, by the tilt of his high-crowned, broad-brimmed hat, by the easy way he hangs a sword and a dagger, for simple comfort and quick and ready access, not for show or style, he must have been a soldier once upon a time. Stout fellow he is, then, large boned and heavy with meat and muscle, thick neck like a tree trunk, topped off with a florid face, quick to take color. A man slightly awkward on account of a limp, some kind of wound or injury to his left hip or thigh or both.

If it were not for the ragged scar, mostly now concealed by his beard, he might well be called handsome, as a fine draught horse is deemed handsome. And he might have found himself in uniform and armed and posted at the entrance or doorway of some inner chamber of the queen's court, where he would see (without turning his head or even his eyes to watch) the grand and the great, the men and the women who rule this island kingdom, even the queen herself, pass by, go in and out under his huge protection.

Other than these yeomen and a hundred or so gentlemen pensioners, this queen, out of her rigorous frugality, has no standing army, only a militia of mostly country bumpkins and the like, that can be mustered to fight in the wars that come and go like high clouds overhead. She does not know much of the military science, of the brutal arts and crafts of warfare. What she does know, what she understand beyond the capacity of other living monarchs and of most of the common people in this world, far and near, past and present is the imagination and how, like a simple and predictable machine, a kind of child's toy, it does its subtle work.

Thus.

She has built no new fortifications, not counting some work up on the Scots Borders at Berwick-On-Tweed, nor even kept the forts that she inherited, large or small, in adequate repair. The old castles (still powerful military structures) crumble away all across England and are replaced, or are being so, by great houses, made half of glass windows and almost utterly indefensible. Foreign powers take note of the elegant houses and imagine—since it would be true of them in any case—that England is too rich and much too powerful to need the expensive trappings of conventional security. There must be some kind of secret that gives the queen and her kingdom this astonishing self-confidence. So also many of her own people, even among those who in fact know better, imagine, thus *believe* the myth.

Likewise at the court, the yeomen, plentiful only here and in the Tower, by their size and by the number of them in halls and at doorways, give the imagination permission to believe that not only the court itself, but all of merry England is always and in all ways guarded and well protected.

Merry England?

Ah, that's another story of and for the imagination. Not here at this time to tell it. Except to say, by sleight of hand, like a mountebank or a magician, the old queen has managed, over the many years of her reign, to convince her people, against hard evidence and what they can see with their own eyes, that the droughts and famines and wars and troubles that have plagued every day of her reign, day by day, are no more than false illusions and that in truth—and who will choose to contradict her?—she and they are enjoying a long time of peace and prosperity.

Bless her mind and her magic, then, her own acute imagination, and let us now move on with our own tale.

But first another observation: that even though she can, when she elects to do so, imagine a future, or several versions, in large and small, for her kingdom, she cannot imagine (nor could anyone, gypsy or witch or prophet or whatever) that more than four hundred years after every living soul in London and in all of England and all the known and unknown world is dead and gone, travelers will still find old soldiers, yeomen of the guard, wearing her uniforms, protecting the Tower and still performing ancient drills and ceremonies that began with her reign.

Now back to this hulking and handsome fellow (as he truly would be if he were not so crudely scarred from eyelid to lips and chin) who is not now and never will be a yeoman. Who may yet prove to be, or may have elsewhere been a felon, risking the quick dance on thin air at Tyburn gallows. Chances are that anyone who sees him, even in this city where bedlam is redundant, will remember him and be able to bear witness to his presence.

Which serves to limit the use and the ability of Paul Cartwright to serve as a stealthy shadow.

Which, come to think of it, may be the logic of Henry Chettle—who is the fat man—in hiring Cartwright in the first place. He wants the quarry, the prey, in this case Robert Greene, to have every chance to know that he is being stalked. And if Greene is too drunk or obtuse to notice, others will certainly notice and be quick to tell him the bad news.

Bear in mind that we have not so much as mentioned the most striking aspect of Cartwright's appearance, not merely a large, full beard, but a whole crow's nest of bold, bright, red hair. Rare enough in England in these days.

Thus.

Put this emphatically red-haired giant to work following the lead of another lively, and much smaller, red-haired fellow, this gifted and n'er-do-well Robert Greene, then join the two redheads together, as if linked by an invisible chain, and you will have lost advantage of secrecy. If nothing else, the two men are bound, sooner or later, to see and to take some note of each other. Which, as I have already said, may very well be what the fat man has had in mind from the very beginning.

Chettle in truth wishes Greene no harm. Indeed he wishes that the man be well, in good health and long life and prosperity, if only so that Greene can live long enough to pay back the money that Chettle, not without good lawful reasons, believes that Greene owes him and about which Greene takes a different view. What the fat man wants, at least for the time being, is simply the opportunity and occasion to talk with Greene, a calm and peaceful dialogue. What the fat man fears is not Greene, who is, rich or poor no matter, an educated gentleman of a kind. No, Green is decent enough, at least when he is properly cornered. What the fat man fears—as do many others in this troubled city, people who know nothing of Greene, is the brother-in-law of Robert Greene, a ruthless and altogether dangerous man, a notorious criminal they call by his nickname—Cutting Ball. Who will gladly send you out of this world and into a better one for a few pennies or simply because it might please him to do so at the time. Who, for more cause than family pride, has taken a strong liking to Greene and can be counted on to stand firm for him in any dispute.

Except, perhaps, one in which Greene is in no real or imminent danger and in which Henry Chettle's interests are represented by a red-haired giant, new to this town and looking likely to be more than a match for the celebrated Cutting Ball.

The man (Cartwright, he means) is not without a mind. And here he suggests a strategy that will at least keep Chettle and himself out of the rain. Suggests they enter the Saracen's Head soon but separately. Suggests that Chettle keep clear and, if he can, well out of Greene's view. Greene will be preoccupied with his cards or dice—whatever he chooses to use for robbery here, and will also take note of Cartwright. Chettle will move out through the kitchen to the back door. Where he will shortly be joined by Robert Greene, fleeing with Cartwright from a quarrel—and others for whom Greene's trickery and conny-catching customs will have been easily exposed. Greene runs for the kitchen and the back door. Where he finds Chettle, the fat man, waiting to help him flee from the enraged giant. These two will run for their lives, curses and shouts behind them, through a maze of footpaths and alleyways emerging at last close by Dowgate and the river. Which is where we find the three of them next, at a tavern called the Turk's Head, favored by seamen, where they are now drinking burnt and sugared sherry wine to celebrate their mutual escape.

Escape from what? Greene, though a little bleary already from this strong drink, is not so foolish as to believe he wasn't fooled by the two of them. He is, after all, the chief scholar and critic of the ancient arts and crafts of trickery.

"Well, then, Mr. Chettle . . . ."

"Call me Henry, if you please."

"And you, sir?"

"Cartwright's the name. But you can call me what you please. Let us not stand on ceremony."

"Odds are that you imagine we have gathered here not so much for the sake of the sack and sugar, though it is as good and strong as any you can find this side of the river. Chances are you surmise that I have followed you, caught you, and brought you here, together with the help of my sturdy man, Cartwright, to collect some or all of the debts that you owe me."

"My mind is open to a number of possibilities, though, I must admit your notion has crossed my mind."

"Perish the thought," Chettle said, finishing off his cup of sack in a large swallow and signaling the tapster for more for all of them.

"Look here," he continued. "I want my money back, of course, That is primary."

"True," said Greene. "And it is for me too."

Cartwright allowed himself a skeptical sigh and shifted his weight on the bench. But Chettle wore a serious expression.

"I could swear out a warrant and have you sent to a debtor's prison. Could cool your heels for a time in the Fleet."

"Yes, you could do so."

"But while that would please me and satisfy my mundane need for justice, it would not help me to recover my money, would it?"

"No, sir. It would not."

"And I could unleash this man I have with me. Free him to break a bone or two or put out one or the other of your bloodshot eyes. That would be a lesson to you, but still no nearer to my money."

"Perhaps we could pause a moment to speak, to negotiate, as they say, the validity of your claim . . . ."

"No, sir. Absolutely not. Consider that suggestion completely out of the question. Do you understand?"

"Yes, sir."

"Finally, Greene, you may imagine that if we come to quarrels and blows, you can call upon your bloodthirsty brother-in-law, Cutting Ball, and that will be the end of it. Don't think of it. My man here is at the least a good match for yours, and if Cutting Ball has horse sense, he will not risk a confrontation for any reason."

"Probably not."

"What I have in mind is not to injure you in any way, but instead to give you more money, here and now, an advance against work to be done for me, thus more money which will enable you, in due course and time, to pay back the money and the interest that you owe me."

"I'm not certain I understand you, Mr. Chettle."

"Henry, please."

A pause while the cups, brimming with sweet sherry were served to them.

Then Chettle continued: "See here, Greene. You are a writer, not without gifts (though you have pissed away too much). And I, sir, am a publisher, among other things. You need employment, especially this summer while the stages are closed and the actors are loose on the land. I need pamphlets and such to keep my trade alive and well through this difficult season. I need someone who can yark up a text or a pamphlet in short order and at short notice. And you, sir, are a master of short notice and short order."

"How shall we manage this?"

"My man, Cartwright here, has on his person a legal document, one which we can simply sign and seal—Cartwright will witness. It lawfully provides that I shall here and now present you with a sum of money, an advance payment for work to be done at my hire, and that I will likewise, provided the work for hire is done and delivered on time and deemed acceptable, at the conclusion of this happy arrangement, I shall forgive and write off all your earlier debts to me."

"Sounds much too good to be true."

"If, on the other hand, you should fail to deliver on time, or should deliver shoddy and unacceptable work, or, God forbid it, something should happen to you, death or disability, then you hereby agree that I shall be the rightful owner of all your written work—poems and plays and books and pamphlets—past, present, and future, as it pleases me."

Another pause as the three looked at each other. Greene raised his cup in toast and drank it dry.

"Let me see the money."

The giant, Cartwright, produced a large purse and poured out a shining splash of gold coins.

An hour or so later, he guesses, Roberto—as he sometimes styles himself these days, finds his way home in a driving rain. He is burdened, both arms occupied, with good food and drink from the tavern's kitchen and also with some gifts for his wife and his child, Fortunatus. For Dolly a bright ribbon for her fair hair and a little jeweled ring for her little finger. For his son and heir a wooden sword and a tin windmill that turns in the breeze like a real one and will delight all the three of them and bring some laughter into his bleak chambers.

He is still half cup-shotten from all the sack and sugar he drank with Chettle and Cartwright. Sweating despite the cool rain, and his vision doubled and hazy. But happy also, still dazzled by the little scene in the host's upper chamber above the tavern, where by decent candlelight, with pen and ink and blotting sand furnished by the host, who, it seems likely, has presided over the signing of more than one legal document in his life as a tavern keeper. Signed, sealed, and delivered, one copy for Chettle and a copy for himself. He looked at it closely, as if he were really reading it, but the words winked and wiggled and he had no idea what it might be that he was selling and signing his name for. Knew only, and cared only, at this instant, that he had, in gold, more money jangling in his purse than he had earned in many months.

God bless all printers and publishers. And look, Lord, with special favor, on your fat and greedy servant, Henry Chettle. And not to forget Chettle's servant, this large, crude, dangerous creature who contributed a stern and threatening look to the ceremony of signing the contract. A look that was a kind of contract in and of itself, promising without another spoken word that, should Green fail to fulfill his obligation, he would be as doomed as a pig in the middle of Blood Month.

Lord, likewise, for Jesus' sake, guard and protect this, thy worthless servant, Robert Greene.

Adding something from the Book of Common Prayer: *Lord God, who seest that we put not our trust in any thing that we do, mercifully grant that, by thy power, we may be defended against all adversity; through Jesus Christ our Lord.*

Halfway up the slick and rickety outside stairs to his chambers, in Master Issam's old house, Greene is laughing out loud. First from the bitter pleasure of imagining that perhaps the plague will take him long before Chettle and Cartwright, separately or together, can do him any harm. Or, perhaps the plague will take them too. Meantime, he and his wife and son can live well enough and well beyond their means.

More seriously, he pictures what will happen in the moments just ahead when he arrives at the landing and kicks at the door to let them know he's there. Will kick at the door, and soon it will be unbolted and opened. Revealing Dolly, holding a flickering candle and possessed by an anxious look. Which anxiety will fade and vanish instantly, as if by magic, when she sees the man she loves coming safely home at last. Who left here empty-handed, hours ago, has now returned proudly with what profit he has somehow won from this wicked world.

Her smile of welcome will be brighter than the little flame of her candle.

And, somewhat later, happily full of food and drink, and with Fortunatus at last sound asleep, and the two of them now as naked as when God first made them, he will have her hold a candle close so that he can upturn his purse and pour cold coins on each other in baptismal and parodic ceremony before they snuff out the candle and fall across the bed, bound in each other's arms.

"Second-Hand Man"

(From *Fifth Sunday,* 1985)

by Rita Dove

Virginia couldn't stand it when someone tried to shorten her name—like *Ginny*, for example. But James Evans didn't. He sets his twelve-string guitar down real slow.

"Miss Virginia," he said, "you're a fine piece of woman."

Seemed he'd been asking around. Knew everything about her. Knew she was bold and proud and didn't cotton to no silly niggers. *Vir-gin-ee-a* he said, nice and slow. Almost Russian, the way he said it. Right then and there she knew this man was for her.

He courted her just inside a year, came by nearly every day. First she wouldn't see him for more than half an hour at a time. She'd send him away; he knew better than to try to force her. Another fellow did that once—kept coming by when she said she had other things to do. She told him he do it once more, she'd be waiting at the door with a pot of scalding water to teach him some manners. Did, too. Fool didn't believe her—she had the pot waiting on the stove and when he came up those stairs, she was standing in the door. He took one look at her face and turned and ran. He was lucky those steps were so steep. She only got a little piece of his pant leg.

No, James knew his stuff. He'd come on time and stay till she told him he needed to go.

She'd met him out at Summit Beach one day. In the Twenties, that was the place to go on hot summer days! Clean yellow sand all around the lake, and an amusement park that ran from morning to midnight. She went there with a couple of girl friends. They were younger than her and a little silly. But they were sweet. Virginia was nineteen then. "High time," everyone used to say to her, but she'd just lift her head and go on about her business. She weren't going to marry just any old Negro. He had to be perfect.

There was a man who was chasing her around about that time, too. Tall dark Negro—Sterling Williams was his name. Pretty as a panther. Married, he was. Least that's what everyone said. Left a wife in Washington, D.C. A little crazy, the wife—poor Sterling was trying to get a divorce.

Well, Sterling was at Summit Beach that day, too. He followed Virginia around, trying to buy her root beer. Everybody loved root beer that summer. Root beer and vanilla ice cream—the Boston Cooler. But she wouldn't pay him no mind. People said she was crazy—Sterling was the best catch in Akron, they said.

"Not for me," Virginia said. "I don't want no second-hand man."

But Sterling wouldn't give up. He kept buying root beers and having to drink them himself.

Then she saw James. He'd just come up from Tennessee, working his way up on the riverboats. Folks said his best friend had been lynched down there and he turned his back on the town and said he was never coming back. Well, when she saw this cute little man in a straw hat and a twelve-string guitar under his arm, she got a little flustered. Her girlfriends whispered around to find out who he was, but she acted like she didn't even see him.

He was the hit of Summit Beach. Played that twelve-string guitar like a devil. They'd take off their shoes and sit on the beach toward evening. All the girls loved James. "Oh, Jimmy," they'd squeal, "play us a *loooove* song!" He'd laugh and pick out a tune:

I'll give you a dollar if you'll come out tonight
If you'll come out tonight,
If you'll come out tonight.
I'll give you a dollar if you'll come out tonight
And dance by the light of the moon.

Then the girls would giggle. "Jimmy;" they screamed, "you outta be 'shamed of yourself!" He'd sing the second verse then:

I danced with a girl with a hole in her stockin',
And her heel kep' a-rockin',
And her heel kep' a-rockin';
I danced with a girl with a hole in her stockin',
And we danced by the light of the moon.

Then they'd all priss and preen their feathers and wonder which would be best—to be in fancy clothes and go on being courted by these dull factory fellows, or to have a hole in their stockings and dance with James.

Virginia never danced. She sat a bit off to one side and watched them make fools of themselves.

Then one night near season's end, they were all sitting down by the water, and everyone had on sweaters and was in a foul mood because the cold weather was coming and there wouldn't be no more parties. Someone said something about hating having the good times end, and James struck up a nice and easy tune, looking across the fire straight at Virginia:

As I was lumb'ring down de street,
Down de street, down de street,
A han'some gall chanced to meet,
Oh, she was fair to view!

I'd like to make dat gal my wife,
Gal my wife, gal my wife.
I'd be happy all my life
If I had her by me.

She knew he was the man. She'd known it a long while, but she was just biding her time. He called on her the next day. She said she was busy canning peaches. He came back the day after. They sat on the porch and watched the people go by. He didn't talk much, except to say her name like that:

"Vir-gin-ee-a," he said, "you're a mighty fine woman."

She sent him home a little after that. He showed up again a week later. She was angry at him and told him she didn't have time for playing around. But he'd brought his twelve-string guitar, and he said he'd been practicing all week just to play a couple of songs for her. She let him in then and made him sit on the stool while she sat on the porch swing. He sang the first song. It was a floor thumper.

There is a gal in our town,
She wears a yallow striped gown,
And when she walks the streets aroun',
The hollow of her foot makes a hole in the ground.

Ol' folks, young folks, cl'ar the kitchen,
Ol' folks, young folks, cl'ar the kitchen,
Ol' Virginny never tire.

She got a little mad then, but she knew he was baiting her. Seeing how much she would take. She knew he wasn't singing about her, and she'd already heard how he said her name. It was time to let the dog in out of the rain, even if he shook his wet all over the floor. So she leaned back and put her hands on her hips, real slow.

"I just *know* you ain't singing about me."

"Virginia," he replied, with a grin would've put Rudolph Valentino to shame, "I'd *never* sing about you that way."

He pulled a yellow scarf out of his trouser pocket. Like melted butter it was, with fringes.

"I saw it yesterday and thought how nice it would look against your skin," he said.

That was the first present she ever accepted from a man. Then he sang his other song:

I'm coming, I'm coming!
Virginia, I'm coming to stay.
Don't hold it agin' me
For running away.

And if I can win ya,
I'll never more roam,
I'm coming Virginia,
My dixie land home.

She was gone for him. Not like those girls on the beach: she had enough sense left to crack a joke or two. "You saying I look like the state of Virginia?" she asked, and he laughed. But she was gone.

She didn't let him know it, though, not for a long while. Even when he asked her to marry him, eight months later, he was trembling and thought she just might refuse out of some woman's whim. No, he courted her proper. Every day for a little while. They'd sit on the porch until it got too cold and then they'd sit in the parlor with two or three bright lamps on. Her mother and father were glad Virginia'd found a beau, but they weren't taking any chances. Everything had to be proper.

He got down, all trembly, on one knee and asked her to be his wife. She said yes. There's a point when all this dignity and stuff get in the way of Destiny. He kept on trembling; he didn't believe her.

"What?" he said.

"I said yes," Virginia answered. She was starting to get angry. Then he saw that she meant it, and he went into the other room to ask her father for her hand in marriage.

But people are too curious for their own good, and there's some things they never need to know, but they're going to find them out one way or the other. James had come all the way up from Tennessee and that should have been far enough, but he couldn't hide that snake any more. It just crawled out from under the rock when it was good and ready.

The snake was Jeremiah Morgan. Some fellows from Akron had gone off for work on the riverboats, and some of these fellows had heard about James. That twelve-string guitar and straw hat of his had made him pretty popular. So, story got to town that James had a baby somewhere. And joined up to this baby—but long dead and buried—was a wife.

Virginia had been married six months when she found out from sweet-talking, side-stepping Jeremiah Morgan who never liked her no-how after she'd laid his soul to rest one night when he'd taken her home from a dance. (She always carried a brick in her purse—no man could get the best of her!)

Jeremiah must have been the happiest man in Akron the day he found out. He found it out later than most people—things like that have a way of circulating first among those who know how to keep it from spreading to the wrong folks—then when the gossip's gotten to everyone else, it's handed over to the one who knows what to do with it.

"Ask that husband of your'n what else he left in Tennessee besides his best friend," was all Jeremiah said at first.

No no-good Negro like Jeremiah Morgan could make Virginia beg for information. She wouldn't bite.

"I ain't got no need for asking my husband nothing;" she said, and walked away. She was going to choir practice.

He stood where he was, yelled after her like any old common person. "Mrs. Evans always talking about being Number 1! It looks like she's Number 2 after all."

Her ears burned from the shame of it. She went on to choir practice and sang her prettiest; and straight when she was back home she asked:

"What's all this number two business?"

James broke down and told her the whole story—how he'd been married before, when he was seventeen, and his wife dying in childbirth and the child not quite right because of being blue when it was born. And how when his friend was strung up he saw no reason for staying. And how when he met Virginia, he found out pretty quick what she'd done to Sterling Williams and that she'd never have no second-hand man, and he had to have her, so he never said a word about his past.

She took off her coat and hung it in the front closet. She unpinned her hat and set it in its box on the shelf. She reached in the back of the closet and brought out his hunting rifle and the box of bullets. She didn't see no way out but to shoot him.

"Put that down!" he shouted. "I love you!"

"You were right not to tell me," she said, "because I sure as sin wouldn't have married you. I don't want you now."

"Virginia!" he said. He was real scared. "How can you shoot me down like this?"

No, she couldn't shoot him when he stood there looking at her with those sweet brown eyes, telling her how much he loved her.

"You have to sleep sometime," she said, and sat down to wait.

He didn't sleep for three nights. He knew she meant business. She sat up in their best chair with the rifle across her lap, but he wouldn't sleep. He sat at the table and told her over and over that he loved her and he hadn't known what else to do at the time.

"When I get through killing you," she told him, "I'm going to write to Tennessee and have them send that baby up here. It won't do, farming a child out to any relative with an extra plate."

She held onto that rifle. Not that he would have taken it from her—not that that would've saved him. No, the only thing would've saved him was running away. But he wouldn't run either.

Sitting there, Virginia had lots of time to think. He was afraid of what she might do, but he wouldn't leave her, either. Some of what he was saying began to sink in. He had lied, but that was the only way to get her—she could see the reasoning behind that. And except for that, he was perfect. It was hardly like having a wife before at all. And the baby—anyone could see the marriage wasn't meant to be anyway.

On the third day about midnight, she laid down the rifle.

"You will join the choir and settle down instead of plucking on that guitar anytime anyone drop a hat," she said. "And we will write to your aunt in Tennessee and have that child sent up here." Then she put the rifle back in the closet.

The child never made it up to Ohio—it had died a month before Jeremiah ever opened his mouth. That hit James hard. He thought it was his fault and all, but Virginia made him see the child was sick and was probably better off with its Maker than it would be living out half a life.

James made a good tenor in the choir. The next spring, Virginia had her first baby and they decided to name her Belle. That's French for beautiful. And she was, too.

"Labor Day"

by David Baldacci

I am old enough now to have forgotten that the Jerry Lewis Telethon is broadcast over Labor Day weekend. But how could I ever lose the memory of coffee cans filled with money that my sister and I carried into Channel 6's studio and dumped into the old aquarium with the cracked glass taped over? The tally board, with its constant, dizzying whirl, encouraged by Jerry yelling, "Do it, come on, do it!" The phone banks staffed by celebrities and just regular folks. Jerry so bubbly and spry on Saturday morning, but then wearing down through the hours until by Monday he is rubber-legged, the crimson eyeballs of a drunk, stumbling through his routines, singing with Sammy and Frank, chatting with regional beauty queens who hold giant community checks, playing (for the umpteenth time) the straight man for clean-cut youngsters, all with impish eyes and perfect Hollywood teeth. And then the serious, sad moments of children trapped in wheelchairs and clunky braces that make them lunge and jerk when they move, some mumbling their lines, terrified at being on national television, like any child should be, and others with voices so big and confident coming out of those tiny mouths, those weakened lungs, you'd swear it was all dubbing.

All those Labor Days, eight summers in a row, my sister and I collected MD dollars, politely sipping lemonade from elderly ladies who filled up our coffee cans. Years later I married, and now, for the last ten years, I have had slowly evaporated from my thoughts: Jerry. Until the end of this summer, until this Labor Day.

The last time I saw Jerry he looked thicker everywhere, especially in his neck, which has disappeared somewhere into his shoulders. He is a big man, when he always looked so small next to Deano.

But won't Jerry always be the skinny one with the picket fence teeth, the Moe Howard coiffure and Mr. Ed laugh? How old can Jerry be now? Over sixty? I knew he had heart problems long ago and required, I think, a bypass. How could Jerry Lewis ever grow older than about thirty-one? Why does a rail-thin comedian barely thirty need his heart arteries replaced? Is Jerry wearing out right before us all?

Jerry visited my wife and me on our honeymoon in Aruba during a brief rain shower. My beautiful new wife and I sat in our little tropical suite, feeling our sunburn and moodily contemplating another fall, winter, and spring of work, three seasons of toil ahead; she examined a lizard running up the wall, and I sat there and watched Jerry roar across the stage, Mr. Tally Board right behind him crunching hard currency, making sick kids rich with hope, allowing Americans to do what they do best: just give money. I thought back to 1970 and to the old rusted Maxwell House coffee can my sister and I lugged to Channel 6; how we tossed all those pennies and nickels, dimes, quarters, a few Kennedy pieces, and some dollar bills into that aquarium. Thirty-one of the fish on Mr. Tally Board would always belong to us no matter how disillusioned and cynical we might have eventually become. It was a burst of how utterly good humans can feel about anything, and it has remained a test for how far I have fallen from that plateau since. Yet, how easily the Telethon can make me twelve years old again; my own fountain of youth in Aruba. I was selfish, I didn't share it with my wife; and that our honeymoon. I felt I was off to a bad start.

This year, the year I will rediscover Jerry, we are spending Labor Day at a beach house in North Carolina. We have done this the last five years. A group of us, made up of family and long-time friends, rent one of those lumbering salt-treated wood, low-maintenance mini-hotels with soaring ceilings, fans, lots of fans (though the wind has never once stopped blowing all the years I've gone) and decks and decks, more decks than fans, if that is possible. The house is cradled between two meager sand dunes, a twin house sits next door, and, in fact, as you look in either direction, the same house, the very house we are staying in, replicates itself over and over as though spit out from an enormous North Carolina-based cloning machine. And the beaches, what exactly happened to them? The sand is barely ten feet wide now at low tide; at high tide one can dip his feet into the Atlantic from the upper deck of the rental house. "Don't cut the grass," the real estate agent tells you in a serious, warning tone, as though you might actually be contemplating the kidnapping of her children. "It facilitates erosion of the beaches." "But it's over," you want to say. "The Atlantic has reclaimed its property. Erosion isn't a strong enough word, try . . .'vanished.'"

Everyone moves their belongings into the house, cautiously sniffing out prospective quarters, cocking invisible legs, eager to mark territory. Each person has at least three bags, my wife four plus cosmetic tumbler with the mirror glued to the inside lid. Far more clothes that we could ever hope to wear in a week, even if all we did was constantly strip and reclothe ourselves.

"My God, is the wind always this strong?" asks my cousin Linda. She clutches her floppy straw hat, and presses her small son, Ricky, against her big hips. Linda, a first-timer here, looks at each of us, accusingly, like someone in the room has stolen from her and she's waiting for a confession.

"Actually honey-pie, we only come down here for the wind," says her uncle Harry Butler, my uncle too. He lives in D.C., has for years, works for the Department of Energy, and hasn't had much to do since Carter left office; he's thinking of early retirement. He's one of those older guys always with a grin on their chubby face, cracking jokes relentlessly, flirty with the young women, goofy to the point of eventually everyone feeling embarrassed for him, and for his wife, Sybil.

"Honey-pie, you don't look to me like you're going to blow away," he says, clearly eyeing Linda's anchor hips. "Why if you lived in Washington, *Foggy Bottom* Washington, you'd appreciate wind, you'd long for simple dry heat like you get in an oven, no humidity. Today is the first time in three months my undershorts have been dry this time of day, isn't that right honey? I mean you should know if anybody does."

Uncle Harry pinches Sybil, his straight man for life, his Bud Abbott. She laughs on cue, a bit wearily, but she's a loyal player. We all do, except Linda, who still looks sore, and except for Ricky, who looks apprehensively at the other kids, all regulars, who haven't finished sizing him up yet.

"Grandpa has great, big pee-pee stains on his underpants, I've seen them," points out Lucy Butler, Harry's youngest grandchild at four years old, who has perked up at the mention of Harry's underwear. She spreads apart her tiny hands to show us all the dimensions of the leakage. "Grammy has to SHOUT it out," she adds with her cute, oval face, surrounded by brown locks, looking up at Harry, so proud of the information she has shared with us. A nervous giggle moves across the room, mostly from the young boys; the grin slowly melts from Harry's face, his eyes have a startled, hunted look. I take the opportunity to carry our luggage into one of the nicer bedrooms.

It is Saturday morning, and the noise of dishes crashing, showers running, and the smell of coffee perking makes me roll over and press the snooze button. I think, "Why do people shower before going into the ocean?" I hear Rhonda, a friend of my cousins', yell for someone to fix the DVD player. I imagine Rhonda with curlers all askew, sleep drooping from pale eyelids—she is definitely not a beach person—stomping around the living room in her floor-length sweatshirt that tries to hide the fact that she is no longer young, no longer exercises but only works, eats, and sleeps like the rest of us. I wonder why she has driven four hundred miles to a house on the Atlantic Ocean with an army of adults and children to watch a batch of old movies she carries in a black duffel bag, which reads: "Everything's A Lie, Believe Me!"

I feel around for Ann, but she is already up; my wife is one of those interesting combinations: an early riser only while on vacation. I think I hear her voice in the kitchen. I pull on my baggy, knee-length beach shorts and rainbow tank shirt and slip on my Air Nikes. At thirty-four, I'm still unwilling to pursue recreation dressed as an adult. I take my five minutes in the bathroom, and then I walk down the stairs to the main level where the efficient kitchen and sprawling living room are located. Rhonda sits on one of the crate-style sofas wearing a bulky black sweatsuit, barefoot, twirling her straight brown hair with one pudgy finger. The TV is off. I spot Ann in the kitchen, a juice cup in her hand. My wife has aged much better than I have, though she is seven years older. She seems to grow leaner each Labor Day. The years, though, are beginning to gnaw at the simple beauty of her face, scribbling a maze of tiny wrinkles into the corners of her eyes and around the edges of her mouth. The skin is stretched tightly over her chin, like a flower bud waiting for warm weather. Her legs are long and slender, almost too thin. Blonde hair, recently permed, is sprawled across her head in that carefree look so popular these days. Yet, the constant chemical blast is taking its toll and thinning what used to be luxuriously thick hair that I loved to run my hands through. The more her hair thins, the more perm and *special* styling at exorbitant prices is required.

My own hair has thinned considerably in the last two years, though due to genetics rather than a beauty parlor conspiracy against women. The more hair I lose, the bigger the tennis shoes I buy as if I can compensate for the loss on one end of my body with added ballast on the other. I don't have a paunch yet, but my muscle tone has ebbed. I still may be able to outrun my wife, but I'm not certain. I imagine our future together: I roll around in a wheelchair spitting up liquid vegetables from my wasted frame, while pencil-thin Ann runs marathons and has encounters with young, well-dressed men.

Ann is a lawyer and she has the precise ways and analytical bent of mind so common to the breed. At first, it was exciting to be married to someone with a successful career who took such good care of herself; every aspect of her life under such tight control. A renaissance woman was what I had married, and fortunate to do so. Lately, though, her gesticulations annoy me, the legal words she drops so casually, more second nature to her than we are to each other, tend to cause my mind to drift. Just recently, I think of having relationships with other women, though I doubt if any of that will ever go beyond the walls of my imagination. I wonder if she is growing dissatisfied with me, with my ineptness in those areas she considers so important, with my slowly decaying body, and the fact that she will always earn much more money than I will. When we first started out, that was one of the most special parts of our love, especially for me. She certainly wasn't marrying me for my fortune, so it had to be for my other fine qualities, whatever they might be. But as the years have gone by, the fact of her superiority to me in this regard has become a strain. We don't talk about it, each probably afraid to hear the other's views, preferring to be ignorant rather than hurt, or alone.

We're still childless, with no immediate plans to change that. She says it's her career, the demands, and that it's not time, not right for her yet, that her clock still has ticks left. Really, she was vague about the whole thing. I think it may be her first marriage, a short-lived embrace, the memory of a still-born child the only thing to survive from its ashes. I also think she's afraid of bloating up like her mother. Perhaps she's flirting with anorexia so to have a buffer if she does get pregnant. I have told her before that I want a family, yet a quiet desperation has been overtaking me the last year; an urgency I have not voiced, out of fear of her response.

"What's the problem?" I ask Ann, looking across at Rhonda, then back at her.

"VCR's on the blink. Rhonda wants to sue; she wants me to represent her." Ann has little patience for people like Rhonda, who want the world to be constantly attentive to their problems, the dilemmas of their existence, but at the same time, proclaiming a desire for complete privacy and independence. "I told her she has no oral or written contract, no representations from anyone, that she's not even paying anything to be here, so no consideration either, but try to tell her that."

"Uh-huh" I say, the legal mumbo jumbo holding no interest for me. I walk past Rhonda, who's still twirling her hair. I work with a bald guy who constantly digs at a small crater in his scalp with that same motion Rhonda is using. His left shirtsleeve is always torn because the motion causes his elbow to worry the fabric, like when you make a new belt hole by twisting a knife into it. I wonder if I will eventually dig a crevice into my head.

I shouldn't, but I feel sorry for Rhonda; her duffel bag sits in the corner, its zipper teeth grin at me. I go over to the VCR. Like with just about everything I own or use everyday, I can operate a VCR, but I have no idea how it actually works. The *African Queen* sits half-way in the intake slot. I turn the machine on and give the tape a little bump. I suspect Rhonda is watching me. The machine whirs and the *African Queen* sails into Sony harbor. I click on the TV and press the start button. So far so good. Maybe I can do something here. We get the FBI warning, with its criminal penalties for doing anything with this videotape except to sit back and enjoy it. Then the distributor's logo soars across the screen in big beautiful colors, completely overwhelming the drabness outside our rented beach house. Then the studio music starts, the creaky, jerky explosion of instruments so common back then, which seems so corny today, all of which makes me feel sad for a moment. I'll wait for the movie to start then toss the remote to Rhonda, let her admire my technical genius in silence for a moment, and then I'll head into the kitchen for some breakfast. Yet, right before I do this, white streaks—like the "flack" you see during dogfights in those old WWI newsreel films—start firing across the screen. The credits jump, Katharine Hepburn's name resembles hieroglyphics, and I miss Bogart's altogether. People walk by with little jerks of motion like battery-powered toys running down as the pixels on the screen seemingly commit electronic suicide. Then a crunching sound emanates from the machine, and Rhonda screams "Turn it off, turn the goddamned thing off before it ruins my tape." I quickly do so and turn to her with the tape guts of the *African Queen* in my hand. All I can think to say is, "Whoops." The *African Queen* has *sunk* a little ahead of schedule.

I stand there, embarrassed, for a moment, while she looks at me like I'm the biggest idiot she's ever seen. After what I feel is an appropriate time, I look back at the TV. I think I'll do this just for a moment and then hit the kitchen for coffee. That's when I see Jerry. He's with Ed McMahon. Why does it strike me that they've worked together before? Some connection they make in my head? Then I realize it's because, at some point, true or not, they both had reputations of being drinkers. That coffee cup Jerry carries around with him on the Telethon; years ago, my mother had told me about that cup. Jackie Gleason carried one too when he came out from behind those billowy curtains in Miami, sweating and breathing heavy from being so funny. "Coffee doesn't stay warm that long," my mom would say. "But other things do." She said this with a raised eyebrow and never elaborated. But now I think, so what if he takes a pop every now and then? He's entitled. I'm not sure about Ed McMahon, though, but I've never been a big fan of his anyway. Ed's made millions from doing what I don't know except being in the right place at the right time. But then who wouldn't settle for that if they could get it?

"What are you doing?" my wife asks.

"I'd forgotten the Telethon was on. Look, there's Jerry, and Ed McMahon from the *Tonight Show.*" I sit down on the floor in front of the screen. "See that? The Tally Board's already up to six million." I could remember when that would be a record haul for the entire Telethon.

"Do you want some breakfast?"

"Honey, come over here for a minute." I motion her with my hand; I hear her small sigh as she approaches. The Muscular Dystrophy poster child is on. A little girl named Cindy. The steel shafts around her twisted arms and legs give her a mechanical half-robot look.

"Look, that's the MD poster child. Her name is Cindy; she's an orphan. She lives in a state home somewhere down South, Georgia, I think Jerry said."

"She's so young," Ann says in a depressed tone. "Do you want any breakfast? I'm going down to the beach in a few minutes, and then you're on your own."

"There's an 800 number you can call to talk to her. You can call between 7:00 and 9:00 tonight."

"Okay" she says, "okay." I feel her fingers in my hair. She touches my bald spot, and I think of that crevice starting up; my skull will have depression holes that soon will be exposed to the world. The same holes that suck cars and homes and people down into the

Earth like you see in Florida. Florida! That's where Jerry said Cindy is from. How sad to be trapped in a state that lives by the outdoors, by the warmth of its sun, where you can run and play and age your skin all year round, and being unable to sprint through the heated sand, splash in the warm waters, your hair dripping wet but already being dried by that red ball of fire. An orphan, stricken with this terrible disease, forced to exist in something called a state home, a place she can't possibly enjoy, can't possibly want to be, but can do nothing about. Of course she would make a great poster child. What heart could she not break? What wall of hatred, of apathy, could she not crumble? I wonder what a state home is. What do children with steel for legs and arms do there? What fun could they possibly have?

"In a little while," I tell her. "Go ahead."

"Bobby, you watch enough television at home. This is vacation."

"I watch videos at home," I correct her. "This is the Telethon, this is different." Cindy stumbles off the stage, her gracious smile fading from view as the camera swings away from her. Back to the Sunshine State, back to desperate lingering in the shadows. The Telethon will be on next year, with Jerry, but where will Cindy be? I run to get paper and pencil to write down the number to call her. Rhonda is laying flat on the couch, her eyes shut; the shipwrecked *African Queen* lies on her belly. When she is like this, she says she is meditating. A small snore escapes her lips. She needs someone in her life, I think, besides Humphrey Bogart, besides Buddha.

"Open a window," Uncle Harry says to one of the boys. Harry sits at the table, his paper in front of him; a bowl of bran cereal that resembles tiny rabbit pellets at his elbow. He is always reading something, the paper, magazines, newsletters, almanacs, books on the most arcane subjects, billboards, matchbook covers, bumper sticks; he watches the news with intense energy; he reads product labels for nutritional content and then buys the corn dogs. It seems not a scrap of knowledge can be allowed to pass him by.

The kitchen table is long and low, with benches down both sides. Between meals it will be used for paddle ball. Even now the kids are waiting for Harry to finish, the plastic net balanced in Freddy and Sam Jr.s' hands. Both boys are overweight, which seems to be the norm these days. So many obese children, their parents' bad habits transmitted to their offspring earlier with each passing generation. Soon all humans will be nothing but blubber, our skins a slimy transparent oozing cholesterol yellow. My children will not be fat, I vow, not until they're ready to have kids of their own. Not until they're like me.

My brother Nelson has six children; three from a previous marriage, none of them here. Nelson and his second wife Lucy arrived late last night. The kids from his first marriage are staying with their mother; he and Lucy's with my parents, they tell us. They both look tired, but expectant, hopeful. I like all of Nelson's children, more than I like Nelson as an older brother. Nelson is forty-seven and looks his age. He seems to have arrived at the point where he awaits death almost anxiously, thinking, with a thin smile, that things could not be worse. Our parents are in their late sixties. How will they keep three cyclones under control and content? I ask Nelson this.

"They love having them, Bobby. Keeps 'em young. Besides, Lucy and I need some time alone, it gets to you. Nothing's your own space any more. But I guess you can't understand that."

"Why don't you ever leave them with Ann and me?"

He looked surprised. "I didn't think you liked kids, Bobby."

I write down Cindy's number and put the paper in the pocket of my sweater. I turn the Telethon off but not before I hear Jerry yelling in a deep bass, a grown-up, determined voice, so unlike the nutty professor, so unlike Cinderfella, "Do it, come on do it. Yes!" Mr. Tally Board spins new wealth for research; Jerry emotionally climaxes on national television. I watch the empty screen for a few minutes, the impression of Jerry standing there on the stage appears to be embedded into the gray glass. Rhonda's snores mix with the cyclonic bursts of Atlantic wind, and I put my sweater on, suddenly cold.

The table is cleared now. Harry has drifted to the upstairs john to finish his knowledge fix and pass his rabbit pellets. I go over to stand by the patio door; the screen is up and the wind hits you full force there, funneled into the room, the whole strength of the universe being strained through the tiny holes of the screen door of our rental house in North Carolina, of all places. You hear every kind of sound in that wind: the waves exploding on the receding beach, always receding, like my hair, like any chance for happiness for the slumbering Rhonda, covered with a Hollywood quilt; the cries of children sprinkling sand down each other's shorts, tiny anuses twitching to reject the grit, the first in a long life yet to come; the high-pitched voices of the women sprawled facing the sun, talking of men and their shortcomings, by far the weaker sex as even men will readily admit these days; the ladies speak with a certain satisfaction as if they had known the truth all along, and were proud of how long they had deceived us; of splashes of sea gulls and the occasional ship's horn; and the swirl of multicolored kites as they zoom and dip in the unpredictable wind that has temporarily freed them from the vast, saddened lethargy of the Earth.

For a moment, I hesitate at the door. All those sounds, forces in themselves, attract me, pulling me down to be with them. But then I want to return to the Telethon. To over twenty years ago, with my sister, Nancy, now dead, as we pour our waterfall of copper, silver, and green into that aquarium. My young, vibrant parents beam behind us, Nelson, nearly a man himself, hovers nearby, bored with the entire process, instead, eyeing the legs and bosom of the Channel 6 women, oblivious to the harvest of good we had reaped on the world. Nelson, a petty man with six children who adore him, who will excite and disappoint him, who will give him grandchildren, who will watch him grow old, who will care for him, bury him, mourn him, and then remember him, at least for a while. A car accident robbed my sister of the chance to become a woman, to become a mother. Barely two years after our metamorphosis into good, caring people, our hearts poured into that cracked bounty at Channel 6, we buried her, and mourned her, and now simply remember her from fading photographs with the serrated edges, dates imprinted on the back, so many years ago, too many to recall clearly, and from dim memories of bouncing balls and laughing laughs, wiping tears and gushing secrets. I believe my mother longs for Nelson's oldest daughter to reach Nancy's age when she died, to give her one more chance to complete the maternal process, to assist a young girl into precious womanhood. I can only wait.

As I turn to go back upstairs, Aunt Sybil carries a small glass of liquid into the living room. The house is almost deserted now, the younger women are on the beach, including Ann, the paddle game replaced by radio-powered cars on the concrete driveway; most of the older people have gone into the little souvenir towns nearby to hunt for just one more seashell ashtray, their wants steady and low-key. Rhonda is still there, in deepest meditation, and I watch Aunt Sybil sit down with her glass. Of course it's liquor, bourbon probably; the wind has revealed that to me as she passed. I see that it is only eleven o'clock. I suppose Uncle Harry is napping or perhaps still snugly wedged into the toilet seat contemplating what to make of the rest of the small pie slice of life he has left to ponder. Aunt Sybil reads her magazine, turns on the TV, a flash of Jerry! then gone. She finally settles on an old Lassie show, the one with the tow-headed boy, his mother, the woman who would later rocket skyward in *Lost in Space,* as she works the hand-crank telephone on the kitchen wall. Older people have these walls, built up over time, far outdistancing even the latest in engineering design with its mathematical intricacies and computer-driven souls.

Harry and Sybil, Sybil and Harry, interchangeable. Four kids; five grandchildren, with more to come; and now all they seek are independence and distance from one another. Sybil finds hers in the bottom of an oversized shot glass, channel hopping; Harry in embarrassing (and ever-young) humor and as an addicted tracker of all the knowledge in the world. And as I look down at my hundred-dollar Air Nikes and my black Beach Laguna shorts with the fluorescent green stripes, I wonder how far away Ann and I are from them. How are we different except for having brought no one else into the world, except for having no one to remember our thoughts and our simple, loving caresses, our dreams, our ridiculous faults? Our longing for more than life will ever give us?

"I'm gray," my wife says, "gray and a little blue." Lately, she has been talking like that, in colors, as though she's been taking a philosophy course or studying modern painting. I've given up trying to follow it.

"Actually," I reply, "you're a bit red. Too much sun, the first day." I smile at her as she lays on the skinny North Carolina beach, her slender figure nestled into a two-piece shiny black swimsuit. Big sunglasses look up at me; sand is caked around her feet, compressed between her long toes. She doesn't bother to smile back.

"It's cloudy, there's hardly any sun."

"I've told you a hundred times, clouds don't stop the UVs; nothing does." I hurl a small seashell into the surf, instantly reversing probably a thousand years of travel. There's a big undertow here, a real nasty one, especially this late in the season. It'll pull you parallel to the beach for awhile, so gradual you don't even notice until you look up and see nothing remotely familiar. Then, you're out in a hundred feet of water, heading for the shipping channels, but you'd never last that long. It's dangerous, this water all around us. Last year a guy right next door to us drowned. They closed the beaches that day because of rough water—the white caps were probably running four feet—but this guy went out anyway. We watched from the kitchen as they pulled him out, his limp body covered in seaweed, while Uncle Harry recited to us the national drowning-while-on-vacation statistics.

"Let's walk for a few minutes," Ann says.

She stands up and kicks at the flakes of clinging sand. Her shoulders are slightly freckled, like miniature pennies scattered across her skin. While she lifts her hair and pins it into a bun, I can see her nape. It's white blonde—the same color her hair was when she was little—and fuzzy, like you see on babies and on the sides of a young girl's cheeks, open and expectant, fully knowing that changes are ahead. Cindy would still have such markings despite the MD; the MD couldn't stop her from being a little girl, couldn't stop the anticipation of the fuzzy spread. Yet when you grow up, the small hairs are pushed back and eventually are hidden forever, behind metric tons of hair spray, and artificial curls and waves. We walk.

"I can't believe you were sitting in there watching TV," my wife says. "You've never done that before. I hope you're not starting to get like Harry."

"It was the Telethon; it's not like I was watching a damned porno flick." She takes my hand, squeezes it.

"Okay. Okay, it just wasn't like you, that's all. You're usually the first one on the beach."

"Getting old I guess." I hear her sigh. Of course, she is thinking this means she is *already* old with the way the world works. Did I mean to imply that? I think back to Cindy, and I am ashamed to conclude that, yes, I probably did.

"You know what I'm thinking?" she says. I shake my head and watch a school of porpoises play a game of tag about twenty yards out.

"Next year, I'm thinking we should go to Europe on vacation. Instead of two one week trips, let's go to Europe for the full two. Then the next year, we can go to Asia; we can pick a different part of the world each vacation." I nod my head while I consider this.

"Well, I only get two weeks each year. What about coming down here?" Her lips curl into stiff pieces of metal and she lets go of my hand, crossing her arms as we walk; she looks like a priest stalking along to some holy chant.

"Well, I get *four* weeks, but I always spend two of them just sitting around the house."

"You sometimes visit your mother."

"In Wheeling? I can drive to Wheeling in two hours. That's not a vacation. That's not Europe."

"Well, travel, it sounds okay, but it's pretty expensive."

"We come here every year and, with the rent and food, and beer, and gas, and all the little trinkets you manage to buy, we probably drop a couple thousand. That's round-trip business air fare for one right there."

"For one," I say.

"We've got money, Bobby, at least that's something we've got. Besides, there're good packages available."

"I see you've already looked into this."

"It takes planning, lots of it; someone had to do it." She stalks on.

We do have money, a good amount, for two people who work every day for a living, who came by it honestly. But how do I remind her that that money's for raising a family? I thought we had decided that, but thinking back to our last conversation two years ago, I realize we had decided nothing.

"Look, Ann, we haven't even really started out yet."

"It's been ten years, Bobby."

"Right, so what, my parents have been married for forty-six, longer than we've been alive." I take a deep breath. "My God, we haven't even started our family yet. We've got all that to look forward to yet. But all that takes money." She stops stalking and turns to look at me but says nothing. Then she looks out at the water.

"Do you know how old I'll be when that child turns ten? Fifty-two. And that's if we had one nine months from today. She'll be in fourth grade, and I'll look like her grandmother at the PTA meetings surrounded by all those thirty year olds."

"You look great, you're in terrific shape, you look like you're twenty now."

"And who's going to care for them? It's a twenty-four-hour-a-day job. I've got fifteen years at my firm, I'm on the management committee; I'm a trial lawyer. You think I can take six months off and then just go part-time? I'm locked in Bobby."

"I can take care of them."

"And what about your job?"

"Screw the job, we're talking about our children." She shakes her head.

"That's real easy to say, Bobby. Now! You can barely look after yourself. I mean look at how you're dressed. Do you think you're ready to be a father?"

"Well, maybe I wear this stuff because I don't have any kids to buy this shit for; maybe I'd like the chance to. What you're saying isn't what we decided." I am raising my voice to her, not the first time.

"We didn't decide anything, and I never said I even wanted children. It's always been you. Why is this so important to you? Nelson treats you like shit, his kids act like he's Santa Claus all year round and then laugh at him behind his back. Kids can be cruel, Bobby. I know it may be hard to believe, but it's not a great world out there to bring children into. It takes a huge amount of work; it dominates your life, and eventually the children always come between the husband and wife. I'm sorry, but that's the truth. You have to realize if we have kids, it's not just you and me anymore, it's us and them, it's 'we.' We can't just pop into town for dinner, or go to the ball game, or run up to New York when we feel like it, or stay in bed late on the weekends. We won't have a good night's sleep for the next four years; we'll be cleaning mountains of poop away; we'll end up paying hundreds of thousands of dollars for doctor bills, school, clothes, cars, and the kid will grow up to hate us anyway. It's not all it's cracked up to be, it's not a fairy tale Bobby; it's not Ozzie and Harriet.

"I'm getting old, Bobby, we both are, you as good as just said that. And what have we done? Worked all our lives? I've made partner, that's it for me. You've moved as far in your company as you're going to. So, what? We buy houses, fix them up, spend a lot of money, live in them for awhile, and then sell them and move on. We buy a new car every three years. We eat out too much. How many really good friends do we have? We've never met any of our neighbors; we're just passing through. What things do we enjoy doing together? My father's dead, my mother's about ready to go. Your parents are getting up there; I mean, we're next in line, we are walking up to the turnstile, how much time do we have left?"

"I'm only thirty-four," I say, and then regret having said it. My relative youth seems so unimportant, so pale in the face of what she is saying.

"Is this it? IS THIS IT?" She swings her arms around pointing out the sun and the beach and the water and the sky and the people and the kites and the wind, and, I think, me. She drops on the sand and starts to bawl like when her father died, a force that comes from so far down your lungs and gut you wonder how you ever survived with something that volcanic inside.

"Goddammit, I've had my child!"

I drop down beside her, pull her to me; she tries to push away, but I cling, like the sand on her feet, I cling. I think of her nape, the pull of her smile, I think of Cindy's steel legs and the number I will call tonight. I think how my wife's face must have looked when her child is born dead, her hope for memories, for love and care in life, over, before it started. I hold Ann with all my strength.

* * *

It is one minute to eight, and I am hidden away in one of the downstairs bedrooms, the boy's room, with litters of toys, clothes strewn about, the smell of dirty underwear and sweat so peculiar to teenage males. A bottle of cologne sits on the dresser, like a tiny amulet, what all the occupants of this room are striving for amidst the electronic games, radio cars, baseball cards, and *Playboys* stuck under flimsy mattresses. "Don't hurry," I should tell them. "Don't bother." But that's the sort of advice that's never shared.

It is eight o'clock now, and I dial the number Jerry has given me. I hear voices outside the door, but the light is off, and the noises soon trickle away. Jerry's phone rings somewhere.

"Hello?" I say. "Hello Cindy? This is Bobby, Bobby Cameron."

"Hi, my name is Cindy Malone," the same little voice next to big Jerry says to me. I think of the smile, the even rows of tiny teeth, her nose still just a nodule of cartilage, so much growing yet to do.

"Listen Cindy, I'm in North Carolina. I don't live here, I'm on vacation. I saw you on the Telethon."

"I'm the Muscular Dystrophy poster child this year."

"I know you are, sweetheart."

"Please give to the Muscular Dystrophy Association. We need all your support."

"I know you do," I say, my voice slowing as I listen to the tape whir at me. "I'll give. I collected thirty-one dollars for you, before you were even born. My sister, Nancy, and me." Outside, firecrackers are going off, booms and whistles fill the breezy air; the boy's room is lit by bursts of M-80s, twirls of sparklers. I watch a string of crackers go off, like white Christmas lights.

"If you would like to make a pledge, and you have a touchtone phone, please press one and a volunteer will assist you. Thank you very much, it all helps, you know, it will all do good. I love you. Good-bye."

I punch the one, and after a moment, a voice comes on the line. I consider pledging our entire life savings, but don't. I give thirty-one dollars. I tell the woman it's from Nancy Cameron, fifteen years old, from Richmond, Virginia. I give her my home address to mail the voucher to. I say it twice so the person will get it right. Then I ask if Cindy is nearby, if maybe I could talk to her. But she's not there. Back to Florida probably, back to the State Home. I ask the voice what a state home is. Whether it's just in Florida. But the voice doesn't know what I'm talking about.

"Say hello to Jerry for me. Tell him Robert Cameron from Pennsylvania thinks he's doing a great job, that he looks better than ever." The voice says she will. "And tell Cindy good-bye for me, give her my address, you have it, tell her it's okay to write to me if she wants. Here, here's my number where I'm at now. Tell her to call me if she wants, to call collect." The voice says okay, sure, anything to get me off the phone. I hang up and stare out at the sky over North Carolina. It is dark again; the fireworks over. I should get up, go to be with the others, But I just lay there, waiting to fall asleep, waiting for the phone to ring. I am sure someone will come for me, eventually.

* * *

There is a hang glider outside. While I am walking on the beach, I look up and he hurtles by; at first I thought it was a large kite. Then I see the person hanging on the little bar, tucked womblike under the wings; he is trapped in a cross-current, slung up and down parallel to the beach by the same force that has ripped him from the ground, allowed him to frolic so far above us. I see his face as he fights against the pull; there is fear in the tightness of his mouth, the nut-shaped bulge in his cheek. His eyes would probably show the fear more clearly, but they are hidden behind thick goggles. He is being thrust dangerously close to the houses, but I have no way of reaching him. I can only watch as he is slung back up the beach and then back to me again, like he is connected to a wire being swung by some playful giant. The boys eventually discover him and follow his path from the ground; one tries to pitch him a rope, but he is too high up, the wind too strong. I go up to the top deck to see if there is a way to help him, but there is none. I call to him, but he cannot hear me over the Atlantic.

Ann comes to stand beside me. We watch together as he is dragged back and forth along the beach, always stopping at the same place, never progressing an inch further than before. He must be growing tired, I think. I take her hand, she slips her other around my waist. The police are called, but they too stand on the beach looking up, powerless. I think back to the hulk of seaweed dragged from the ocean that year, death so close to all of us; we're surrounded by its tentacles; no one will ever be above it. Ann is right, the turnstile grows nearer. But we all have choices to make while we can, while we are still able to think, to feel. I hope he won't be blown out to sea; they will never find him, his family will never know.

I turn to Ann and kiss her, on the cheek, the same way I planned to kiss Cindy, if we ever met. "I think Europe sounds good" I tell her. "I think it's time we started to do things like that."

As we watch, the current weakens and the glider is free; we see him furiously work his straps and he sails over top of us, across the houses, over the dwarf trees, over the little souvenir towns, over the reeling North Carolina landscape; in a few seconds he is gone.

"Happy Labor Day" I tell my wife. We go inside, up to our room, where we will be free from the wind.

"Five Days in the Life of Jacob"

(From the novel in progress, *When Lucky Underwear Is Not Enough*)

by Deborah Prum

Day One
November 21, 1994—Monday

My name is Jacob Knudsen. I am training at Duke University Medical Center to be an intensive care pediatrician. I see people at their most vulnerable times. Can there be anything more difficult than watching your child suffer? The pain is like being eviscerated with a dull knife. I can tell you that first hand.

I am a content man. However, I don't know that I will ever feel unfettered joy again outside of heaven. On the morning of the last day I felt truly happy, I had slept in until 7:30. Normally, as a third-year pediatric resident, I was expected at the hospital by six. But the night before, my twelve-hour shift had turned into a twenty-hour marathon. My attending had had mercy on me. "Come in by 8:30," he said.

My wife, Andi, inadvertently had slept in, too. Not a believer in alarm clocks, she always depended on me to wake her.

As I stood in the bathroom peeing, she rushed through. "Jacob, gotta run. Listen for Eileen. If Maclain is late to school one more time, they're going to arrest us. I just know it."

Andi lives a life of high drama. Breathless hyperbole is a way of communication for her. When we first met in college, I always took her literally. When Andi said she had to read a hundred books for a course, I expected to see a required reading list several pages long.

After I brushed my teeth, I stood outside Eileen's door, listening. I didn't dare open it for fear of waking her. I wanted to sneak in my shower before dealing with diapers and bottles. Eileen was the namesake of Andi's favorite cousin, Leenie. A miracle child, our dear daughter arrived after three miscarriages.

As I stepped into the shower, I reviewed the names of the twelve cranial nerves: olfactory, optic, oculomotor, trochlear, trigeminal, abducent, facial, glossopharyngeal, vagus, accessory, hypoglossal. I liked to use down time to go over basic facts I learned in medical school.

Wait. That was only eleven. Which one had I missed? I felt a little panicky. I went through the list one more time as I tipped my head to get below the shower. At six feet, six inches, I always had to bend to wash my hair. If we ever emerged from medical school debt, I'd make sure to own a bathroom where the shower nozzle loomed well over my head.

Vestibulocochlear. That was it. I could relax.

I noticed a layer of gray dust along the top of the shower stall. If they are short, even the cleanest people forget to clean that uppermost rim. Andi is not short, but also not tall enough to see the grime that accumulates. You don't tend to deal with what you can't see. I swiped my white washcloth along the ledge, then rinsed it carefully. Andi wouldn't be happy to know I used a facecloth as a cleaning rag.

I toweled off rapidly, all the while listening for the baby. How much could I accomplish before she woke up? I needed to be out the door by 8:10 to make it to the hospital in time. E. K. Powe, the elementary school, was right around the corner. Andi might make it back by eight. If Eileen stayed asleep, maybe I could manage a cup of coffee and a bagel.

I slipped past Eileen's door, avoiding the creaky floor board at the top of our steps. I listened. Silence. I could almost taste that coffee.

Eileen never slept past seven before. I turned around and pushed the door open. Our baby was still.

Holding my breath, I edged toward the crib. Eileen lay face down. Was that how we left her? I couldn't remember.

Her hand was what I noticed first. Her chubby hand, still dimpled at each knuckle. Her tiny finger nails—were they tinged blue?

I lowered the side rail of the crib and turned my child over. Her face looked blue, almost purple. Was she moving any air at all? I couldn't tell.

What happened next remains a blur to me. I know I started CPR on my own child. I know I called an ambulance. I know when Andi pulled up to the house, she watched as two EMTs and I rushed out the door with our baby.

I do remember Andi's scream—a raw primeval wail that cut through my heart. I didn't scream. I didn't talk. I kept breathing air into my child's body, kept pressing her little chest, kept listening for breath sounds, chest sounds, but except for my wife's cries, I heard no sound at all.

The EMTs took over CPR in the ambulance. We followed behind. I prayed as I drove, a simple, almost babyish prayer. "Oh God. Don't let this bad thing happen to us. Oh God."

In the emergency room, my colleagues surrounded me. They worked frantically, then furiously, then futilely.

Heroism. At first, Andi and I were surrounded by heroes, doing all they could, no holds barred. All the equipment, all the interventions, all the drugs.

Then, anger. The doctor shouted at the nurse. That nurse chastised a technician. Nothing worked. Nothing.

Then, flat line glowed on the screen. No one made eye contact with us.

The ER attending said, "I'm sorry. She's gone."

Andi screamed. She attempted to punch the doctor. He caught her arm.

She pushed him away, then threw herself across Eileen's body and cried, great convulsed, aching sounds.

The ER attending took my hand. "I'm sorry."

When I didn't answer, didn't even move, he said, "Do you want us to call family or friends?"

Twenty minutes later, our friends, Jane and Teek, arrived, their eyes wide and their mouths wordless. By that time, the nurse had escorted us to another room, a small place off of the hospital chapel—a sanctuary where people could grieve. I'd always avoided the room in the past. I never knew what to say.

Andi sat on a couch, holding Eileen, their faces touching. She kept murmuring something to the baby. I couldn't hear what. Jane rushed to them and stood, holding them. Two things struck me. Jane was so short that her height standing was roughly the same as Andi's sitting. In all the years we'd known each other, I'd never noticed that. Also, Jane is not a physically affectionate person. Usually, it was my Andi who did all the hugging. Yet, Jane had wrapped her arms around Andi and Eileen. Both women rocked and sobbed.

Teek fell to his knees next to the sofa. Then, he cradled his head in his hands and wept. I sat in a straight-backed chair across the room and concentrated on breathing in and out, in and out.

Later, after my wife and our friends left, a nurse came around. "Dr. Knudsen, we need you to sign a release so that we can do an autopsy."

I made an excuse. I had to check with Andi, I said. I told her I'd sign the release later.

Meanwhile, my baby lay all alone on a gurney. My first thought was that the rails were down, Eileen could roll off. I put up the sides and then waited for an orderly to come from the morgue.

Day Two
November 22, 1994—Tuesday

I am a Christian. Since childhood I had heard Bible stories about God raising people from the dead: the widow's son, Jairus's daughter, Lazarus, Eutychus. If you believe, you shall receive.

I was a desperate Christian. I had nothing to lose. I am a rule follower to the nth degree, yet I filched the key to the morgue. At two in the morning, I arrived at Teek's house and begged him to come with me. Who else could I ask? I couldn't take Andi.

We walked into the morgue: a cold tomb with green cinder-block walls, stinking with the odor of death.

I opened my Bible. "From Isaiah 26, 'But your dead will live; their bodies will rise. You who dwell in the dust, wake up and shout for joy.'"

Did Teek even believe in God? I didn't care.

We laid hands on my child. Then I prayed, "Lord Jesus, raise this child from the dead. I believe you can. I know you can."

Eileen lay still and waxy white. No chest moving, no eye fluttering.

"Oh God. What more do you want?"

No tears came to my eyes, but Teek wept.

Eileen stayed dead.

Day Three
November 23, 1994—Thursday

I lie on the heart pine floor of my living room. My cheek rests on the cool smooth soapstone hearth of my empty fireplace. I stare into the sooty cavern trying to imagine a fire, its warmth and fragrance, but cannot.

The wire frame of my glasses cuts into my temple above my ear. I don't adjust them. The pain is a welcome contrast to the numbness I feel throughout the rest of my body and soul.

Andi's parents, her cousin Leenie, and our friend, Tia, will be arriving tonight. I feel certain they will throw themselves into a fury of grief.

My son, Maclain, is at Jane and Teek's house, spending the night with their boys. Andi rests upstairs in a valium-induced sleep. If I bother to listen, I can hear her moan every few minutes. But I concentrate on not listening.

My lips press against the top of my knee. I smell fabric softener on my khakis. Mountain breeze. I wear khaki pants and a yellow or white buttoned-down shirt every day of my life, except for very special occasions, like funerals. Tomorrow I will wear my black wool suit.

I hug my legs so tightly to my chest, I can hardly breathe. I wonder if I can hug myself to death, can squeeze all the air out of my lungs?

A loud thunk. I don't look up. Our front door is warped. The only way to open it is to slam your knee against the door, as you turn the knob. On humid days, you have to lean with your whole weight in one final push in order to unjam it. The landlord refuses to fix it.

Teek stumbles in, wine bottle in one hand, a black book in the other. I barely glance at him.

"Jake, I'm here. Buddy, I'm here." Teek sits cross-legged next to me, the pointy part of his knee touching me. I edge away.

Teek slides closer so that his leg rests against my head. I don't move.

"I brought some wine. Have a drink." Teek pulls the cork out of the bottle.

"No."

We sit in silence for ten minutes. Teek drinks steadily, as I lay motionless.

"Jake. I'm not religious or anything. Or at least I don't think so. I know this stuff means something to you. I thought I'd just read. Okay?"

I can only sigh.

Teek opens the book. "'Blessed is the man who takes refuge in the Lord. . . . The Lord is close to the brokenhearted and saves those who are crushed in spirit. A righteous man may have many troubles, but the Lord delivers him from them all.'"

Teek places his hand on my head. "I'm sorry."

My cheeks and lips are moist. I part my lips let the saltiness rest on my tongue.

Day Four
November 24, 1994—Friday

I look down at my navy-blue tie. A crusty yellow stain covers the tip. I scrape it with my fingernail.

Eileen had spit up on me as I held her in my lap at church just last Sunday—the day before she died. The sermon mildly bored me—I can't even recall the topic now. I remember placing my chin on Eileen's head, breathing in that aroma of baby shampoo and baby scent. Maclain's head had held the same fragrance.

Now all I can smell is the sickly sweet perfume of flowers, piles of them laying across Eileen's tiny casket. They say your nose connects you to a specific memory more quickly and more accurately than any other sense.

So here I am, transported back to my own mother's midwinter funeral, many long years ago, the North Dakota soil too frozen to dig a grave. After the bitter cold and brief graveside service, my father and I watched as men slid her coffin into an above-ground burial vault.

The North Carolina clay is plenty warm and soft today. It is an open mouth, ready to swallow my child whole.

As Eileen is lowered into her grave, our pastor reads from Job: "Though Thou slayest me, Lord, yet I will trust in Thee . . ."

Wild with grief, Andi sobs. I reach to take her hand, but she throws herself against my chest, clutching the lapels of my jacket.

At home that night, I lie next to Andi, my heart beating in perfect sync to her low, slow breath sounds. How long will she have to take drugs to ease her into sleep?

I sigh. And then I sigh again, longer and deeper. Can I exhale all the air out of my lungs? Can I leave myself oxygenless and thereby free to die?

I have come to the end of myself. I feel weightless in this world. I have come to the end of myself. Yet, I do not know where I have arrived.

I love you, God. I hate you, God.

Yet, whom do I have but you?

Day Five
Four Years Later
February 14, 1998—Saturday

My name is Jacob Knudsen. I am an intensive care pediatrician at the University of Virginia. I see people at their most vulnerable times. Can there be anything more difficult than watching your child suffer? The pain is like being eviscerated with a dull knife. I can tell you that first hand.

It was Valentine's Day. At six, I was supposed to take Andi at six to Hamilton's, a new restaurant in town. Last night, it had taken several phone calls before we finally found a babysitter to stay with Maclain and our baby, Sudie. All day I'd felt optimistic that I'd escape the hospital in time.

Even though most of the department doctors were off at a conference in Utah (skiing, probably), my colleague Margot was on call for the night. We didn't have very many in-house patients. Best of all, the ones we did have seemed to be stable.

At 5:30, just as I was signing off on my last chart, Margot got a call saying her child had a high fever and was throwing up. She said she felt pretty sick herself and asked if I could cover for her.

Of course, I had to say yes. I still was hopeful. As an attending physician, I could take call from outside the hospital, unless there were an emergency.

Well, the emergency arrived at 5:40. I had walked as far as the parking lot, when my resident paged me: a two-year-old cystic fibrosis patient with pneumonia was crashing in the ER. The resident needed help.

I called Andi as I ran back to the hospital. "Can you meet me at Hamilton's? I need to stabilize a patient. I'll be there as soon as possible."

I walked into a chaotic scene. My resident, a first year, had not taken charge of the situation. The meds he ordered were not quite right. The nurses noticed and were squabbling with him in front of the parents.

Mrs. Doucet sat close to Caleb, whispering to him, maybe praying. On the other side of the bed, Mr. Doucet held his son's hand in both of his. When I came into the room, he said, "Caleb had this cold for a couple days. It didn't seem so bad."

I put my hand on Mr. Doucet's shoulder. "Let me take a look."

Caleb was in worse shape than I had anticipated. I decided to get advice from our pulmonary specialist, who also was at that conference in Utah. After making several calls, I finally reached him. He suggested a very aggressive course of drugs.

I spoke with Mr. and Mrs. Doucet. "We're giving Caleb antibiotics to fight the infection. We're giving him two other kinds of drugs, one to reduce the inflammation in his lungs and another kind to open up the airways."

"Will he be okay?" Mr. Doucet barely met my eyes.

"Caleb's situation is serious. His disease—the cystic fibrosis—hampers his ability to fight off the pneumonia. We are going to do all that we can." Oh, how I wished I could promise that everything would be just fine. But I knew full well that I could not.

Although still labored, Caleb's breathing became much better within an hour. I decided he was stable enough for me to leave. By that time, my third-year resident, Kendra, had arrived for her shift. Kendra was both confident and competent. I trusted her to manage Caleb's care.

I finally made it to Hamilton's by seven o'clock, all the while though, I thought about Caleb. Had I done enough? Was I missing something?

Andi asked about the health of the child, first thing. In all our years of marriage, she's been gracious. "I think he's stable. The pneumonia has affected both lungs. In combination with cystic fibrosis . . . the boy's got a difficult night ahead of him."

At 7:30, Kendra paged me. Caleb had gone into respiratory arrest. I rushed back to the hospital. We revived the child and kept him alive until midnight, at which time his little heart stopped beating.

I cannot tell you how difficult it is to inform a parent that their child has died.

They cried. I pulled up a chair next to them and cried, too. I asked if they wanted me to pray. The father nodded. I held each of their hands. "Oh Lord, please comfort these parents . . ." was all I could choke out.

As we three wept, I knew that if the Doucets asked God to comfort them, He would. And later maybe, they'd be able to comfort others in a similar situation. I also was certain that the pain of their loss would never completely leave them, not on this earth anyway.

Finally, the Doucets left. They had to go back home to be with their other children. Mrs. Doucet was still nursing her three-month-old baby, Rene, and the child had already missed one feeding.

I sat by Caleb, waiting for an orderly to come up from the morgue. No child should ever be left alone on a gurney, not even one whose soul is no longer here.

I staggered into my house at near 2:00 in the morning. I went straight to Sudie's room. I laid one hand on her head and one on her chest. I felt the breath moving in and out of her. I let tears run down my face as I remembered our baby, Eileen.

In my own bedroom, I looked down at Andi, only half-covered by a sheet. I pulled the sheet over her and kissed her head. She woke and asked about the boy. "Dead," was all I said.

Then, I climbed into bed and drew the comforter over the two of us. I closed my eyes.

In an instant, I am dreaming. I dream of holding great armfuls of chubby babies, maybe ten or twelve. I am trying not to drop them.

I think: Maybe I am in heaven now and everything is okay.

"Puncture"

by Kurtis Davidson

I. Mom

Last month I had to quit my job to start home-schooling him. Of course, I know all about the law that says public schools can't discriminate against any kid because of anything that's wrong with him. They want you to believe that every little boy is entitled to an education. But now the public schools won't take him. They won't even take my phone calls. And the private schools won't take him. It's gotten so bad that even the military schools, even the ones that are like juvenile detention centers, won't take him. After the so-called "generals" at the military schools talk to the principal of the public school, they won't even let us come for an interview. I tell the schools that no human being deserves to be treated this way, that every human being deserves to be treated with decency, and that's when they fall back on their technicalities.

II. Dad

It's the "New Europe" vacation, places you can't even pronounce, all these Slavias and shit. My brother-in-law set it up. He's a travel agent.

"It's cheap," he said.

"I've never heard of these places," I said.

"The places you've heard of?" he said. "You can't afford those."

So, for three years we saved money for a "special" family vacation, and now we're stuck with this shit. It isn't right. This is something they're supposed to tell you. But nobody said a word. All they said was, "Come bring your dollars, take a four-hour fucking tour of the Royal Puppet Factory, count the hairs on the chins of our beauty queens, and, oh, yeah, by the way, make sure that you lock up your kid at night." Except they don't tell you that last one. That's the part they conveniently forget to tell you.

III. Son

My mom told me that if I won't ask to go outside, then I can have as many video games as I want, but I can't keep the TV screen turned up very bright. I said yes without even thinking about it. Outside is way overrated.

Last month I got *Texas Hold 'em Snoop Doggy Style* and *Spring Break III: Attack of the Candirús*. I burned through them like *that*. But that's okay, because when kids come over, they're all, like, "Wow, man, you got *Snoop Dogg*?" and they get so preoccupied that they don't know that I'm bored with the games and that I'm thinking about *them*.

Mom won't let any of the kids from my old school come over, only kids from Poortown, because Mom says nobody cares about the kids from Poortown. I guess she's right, because there haven't been any complaints.

When the kids leave, they're just like everyone expects them to be after three hours in front of the TV. Their skin is all pale and their eyes are all glassy and they don't say much. Only they stay that way.

"Tools"

by Kurtis Davidson

Why do I kill them with hammers? I won't lie to you. I kill them with hammers because other tools haven't worked.

I tried pliers first, but they were no good. I clamped down and squeezed until my knuckles turned white, and I know it hurt them like hell, but they wouldn't die like that. They just screamed.

Wrenches were the same story.

The vice might have worked if their heads weren't so big.

Screwdrivers? A tantalizing failure. The killing was easy. I just stabbed them until they bled to death. But they took so long to die, screaming the whole time, that I couldn't take it. That and all the blood.

Once I tried using a tape measure. I know that sounds crazy, but when you've got to kill them, and you've got so many to kill, sometimes the crazy choice becomes the logical choice. I wrapped it around their necks and choked them, which at least kept them quiet, but the edge of the metal tape cut my hand, so I quit. Like I said, I'm not much on blood, and that goes double when it's mine.

The handsaw killed them well enough, but it took too much time and effort. And, of course, there was the screaming. And the blood. The term "arterial spray" doesn't prepare you for the experience. When you hear "arterial spray" on one of those true-crime TV shows, they might show you a mist of blood, but it's nothing like the real thing. You want to trust me on this.

Then I tried the electric saw, which I thought would be mercifully quick, but I couldn't reach them because I didn't have one of those long orange extension cords. Then, once I got an extension cord, I couldn't get near them because the saw made so much noise that they would run away. Maybe it would have worked with one of those bone saws that surgeons use—they just hum, right?—but where do you buy a thing like that? I made some calls, but the people at the medical supply stores just went all stupid on me.

By now you probably won't be surprised to learn that the cordless drill was a disaster, too. I knew I had a noise problem again, so I sneaked up on them and pinned them down before I turned on the drill, but the damn thing just wasn't powerful enough. They would get all tangled up with the drill bit, things would start smoking, there would be that pitiful screaming, and then, of course, the blood would spray.

So that's why I kill them with hammers. Life is trial and error. Life is a bloody mess. And I try not to get too bloody. Not if I can help it, anyway.

"Bouncing Back"

(1st place fiction, Charlottesville VWC, 2006;
2nd place fiction, State VWC, 2006)

by Gary D. Kessler

"Cause ya know what my momma always said, ..."

Lucille paused and lit up a cigarette, using the dashboard lighter, and nicked a long, hot-red-polished nail as she pushed the lighter back in.

"Damn. Broke another nail. Third one since we started this trip, and here we are . . . wherever we are . . . and Inez is all the way back there in Fincastle. I don't let no one other than Inez near these nails. Like my nails, Ralph? Candy Apple Supreme. Inez says it's all the rage over in Blacksburg. Well, I like it . . . a lot."

Lucille reached over and pulled the cigarette tray open. Ralph slapped at her hand with a "harumph" and hunkered himself over the steering wheel while Lucille rolled down her window a notch and tried to flick ashes to the winds. The force of the car's momentum drove them back inside, and Lucille patted the sparks dead on the flounces in her once-white blouse.

"Hells, bells, Ralph. Don't drive so fast. If you won't let an ash tray do the job God gave it, at least drive slow enough so's I can get the ashes outta the car."

Ralph sped up and squared himself more solidly behind the wheel, eyes firmly on the road, the veins in his neck standing out real strong.

"Anyway, as I was sayin', you know what my momma always . . . Ralph. Ralph, baby, wouldn't it have been a good idea to take that turn back there?"

The old Cadillac Seville just kept pointing straight down the road. Ralph's knuckles were white on the steering wheel.

"She always said, 'Lucille, you are just like a bouncing ball. No matter what happens, you just bounce right back. It's your gift, honey. Use it well.' That's what she always said, 'No matter what happens, you just bounce right back.' And it's just like my ex, Danny, said—my second ex, that is; Timmy was my first, as you well know . . . goodness gracious, Ralph, you almost hit that little ole lady at her mail box. I don't know what's come over you of late. My momma always told me that you'd snap one of these days. But she said, 'Lucille, you don't need to worry none, because you're just like an ole bouncing ball. You just keep on bouncing up, no matter what.'"

Lucille lit up again, and, for the first time, Ralph turned his eyes from the road and stared daggers at her until she flicked the cigarette out of her slitted window. Ralph's eyes went back to front and center and Lucille popped in a couple of sticks of chewing gum. She scooted a foot out of a sling-back high heel. She proceeded to prop it up on the Seville's dash and started poking around the edges of the hot-red nails with the edge of an emery board. Lucille's gum snapped, and Ralph took in a extra-large lungful of air and slowly let it out.

"What I don't understand is why you don't just stop at a gas station and ask for some directions. You said you thought we'd find the interstate more than a half hour ago. But I don't see no interstate. Do you see an interstate, Ralph? Do you? Now there's a gas station right up ahead there. We could stop there and you could ask directions."

Lucille snapped her gum again, and Ralph's knuckles got even whiter on the steering wheel.

"Well, there's probably another gas station up the road a bit. I agree that that one looked a little seedy. Bet they didn't even have a usable ladies room." Down went one foot and up went the other. Snap went Lucille's gum.

"Hey, look, there's another gas station. Pull over, Ralph. I gotta go. You need gas anyway, and you could always ask for directions to the interstate from here."

The Seville slowed down and eased over beside a pump. Lucille gathered up a bag from the back seat, opened the passenger door, and stepped out.

"Just be a minute, hon. A girl's gotta make herself pretty for her man, ya know." Snap went Lucille's gum as she tap tapped around the side of the building on her sling-back high heels in short strides restricted by her tight skirt.

Twenty minutes later, a door at the side of the building opened, and Lucille came tap tapping back toward the gas pumps. Halfway to the pumps, though, she came to a stop and just gawked. No Seville at the pumps. She swiveled her blonde beehived head in both directions. No Seville in front of the station or over by the air hose. No Seville over in front of what looked like a mom and pop diner next to the gas station. Her eyes went back to the gas pumps, willing an old red Cadillac Seville to materialize there. But there still was no Seville parked at the pump. What was parked at the pump was a beat-up old blue Samsonite two-suiter suitcase. Lucille's suitcase; sitting up on its hinges right in the road beside the pump.

Lucille's eyes narrowed and she surveyed the landscape again. Two men were plastered at the grimy window over at the gas station office, staring at her real hard. But when she met their stares, they looked embarrassed and their faces disappeared from the window.

Lucille stood there for several minutes, waiting for reality to set in. But the reality that was setting in wasn't the one she was looking for. At length, she gave a sigh, sat down on the suitcase, and dug around in her purse for a cigarette and an emery board. She remembered what her mother always said, and she'd just sit here and wait for Ralph to return and give her a perfectly good explanation for this.

An hour later, the sun was getting pretty hot and Lucille was still sitting on her suitcase beside the gas pumps. She'd smoked her last two cigarettes and filed all three offending hot-red-polished nails nearly to the quick. She was just fishing around in her empty cigarette pack one more time, without any real hope of finding anything, really, when one of the station attendants, the younger and better-looking one, approached her with shuffling steps and his eyes plastered to the ground like he was avoiding stepping in a puddle of oil or something, and she just waved him away with a devil-may-care lilting laugh.

"He'll be back in a few minutes. My husband's just gone on an errand. Everything's fine, hon. Thanks. I'll just set here a spell. Say, you don't happen to have a cigarette for a lady, do ya?"

Still not looking directly at her, his face beet red, the attendant pointed to Lucille's empty cigarette pack with one hand and the nearby gas pump with the other and then made a mushroom-cloud gesture over his head with both hands.

"Sure, hon," Lucille responded with her best happy camper laugh. "I get the picture. How about a stick of gum then?"

The attendant searched around in his pockets and came up with a grimy, crinkled, yellow-papered stick of gum, which he handed over to Lucille with a blush and an apologetic look, and then he turned and scurried back to the safety of the station office. He didn't disappear far into the building, though; Lucille noted that both men had their faces plastered to the window again, and both looked embarrassed and concerned. She assumed their concern was for her, and she arched her back, crossed her legs, and pointed her toes primly for their benefit.

It was getting on toward dark, and Lucille and her suitcase were still taking up space beside the pump. Luckily, business hadn't been very good and nobody had needed Lucille's pump yet. Lucille was a little shaken now. She'd just gone through the litany of what her mother had always said about her, and one of her momma's frequent sayings had just popped up for the first time. It's what she'd said about Ralph. She'd said—more than once—that Ralph had that impatient, wandering streak in him and that someday, if Lucille didn't watch out, he was going to up and leave her. Lucille had always thought that her momma was saying something about a weakness Ralph had at those times, but now . . .

It was at this low point in Lucille's mood that the younger station attendant materialized again with a paper cup full of hot coffee and a shy, sympathetic smile.

"Thanks, hon," Lucille responded with a warm smile of her own. "Coffee's good, but a girl gets hungry now and then too. Don't suppose you know where I can get a bite to eat, do ya?"

The young man grinned big and pointed to the diner next door, the end of which looked like it was leaning a little to the left from Lucille's vantage point but which was now lit up like a Christmas tree and doing pretty good business, if the number of cars parked outside was any indication.

Lucille sighed and rose from her suitcase. The young man picked the case up and backed toward the station office, never taking his eyes from Lucille. Knowing she was being watched, Lucille gave a little extra swing to her hips as she tap tapped on her sling-back high heels and inside her tight skirt toward the diner. As she got closer, she saw the "Help Wanted" sign in the diner window, and her spirits bounced up. Just like her momma always said to her, . . .

"Stepping UP"

(2nd place fiction, Charlottesville VWC, 2006)

by Jack Trammell

Museums were such a bore. Especially with Tutor McGeorge.

"The Greeks painted very realistic eyes on these statues, Jeremy, though the color has long since worn off, as you see . . ."

Jeremy stared at the statue. It was life-sized, white as chalk, a naked man with the most defining feature broken off, and, yes, he noted, the eyes were indeed hollow, colorless concave pools of smooth granite. They looked empty. So what? Who cared? Paint 'em again.

Tutor McGeorge pushed up his wire glasses. He cared. He opened his mouth as if to speak, and it made his snowy white beard tremble. He was clearly entranced by the supposed beauty of the statue.

"What happened to his male pride?" Jeremy asked, pointing.

McGeorge was Jeremy's private tutor. He whirled around, the frown creeping off his face and into his arm, which suddenly rapped a walking cane twice loudly on the marble floor.

"Jeremy. Do not mock that which you do not pretend to appreciate or understand. You belie your ignorance. Your parents are paying me to help you understand."

"I understand just fine. It's a three-thousand-year-old statue of a naked guy. But somebody broke his thing off."

"Enough!" McGeorge said. "We will not continue this lesson, if you persist—and then I'll have to tell Hal. Do you really want me to do that?"

Big Hal. Big deal. Actually, Hal would probably wonder about the statue, too. He was always telling Jeremy, "You're got to step up and discover your own truth." But in this case, even Hal would have to admit that the Greek guy would not be doing any stepping up.

"Shall we proceed, or not?" Tutor McGeorge asked, peering over the top of his glasses pompously. "We do need to see how the Romans later adapted this style and made it their own."

Jeremy shrugged. "Why not?"

"I caught him with pot again."

Jeremy's mother spoke the words like a computerized telephone operator—listless and monotone. Jeremy's father, a striking, quiet, and tallish man, who was a pharmacist by training but an overgrown college student by temperament, pursed his lips in response.

"Do they still call it that?" he asked. "He's a fifteen year old. We did all kinds of things like that when we were his age. He'll be just fine."

The suddenness with which she threw her purse on the rolltop desk beside the bed startled him.

"It's not fine," she said. "This is the third time it's happened. He's been kicked out of regular school, kicked out of reform school, and now he's going to get kicked out of private tutoring. For God's sake, what's normal about that? Did we ever go to reform school?"

"It was military school, and it wasn't right for him. You know that. He's meant to be an explorer, an inventor, an artist and creator—like you . . ."

His blatant attempt to mollify her surpassed her ability to ignore, and some of the anger melted from her face.

"Yes. Nonetheless, I don't want him learning how to paint in jail."

"Relax. He's not in jail. He's just a typical angry teenager who needs to grow up a little bit. He's got a support network in place to help him do that. Hal and Mr. McGeorge are part of that."

"So, what do we do about the pot?" she asked.

He hesitated, and then smiled sheepishly. "Do you still have it?"

"Of course not. I flushed it down the toilet."

He sighed. "Oh well, then . . . I guess we should tell Hal."

On the way home from the museum, an idea began to form in Jeremy's mind. It was only an idea, but it was a fine idea, the kind that could cause a person to withdraw and think of nothing else. He didn't even notice when Mr. McGeorge slammed the brakes on his 1979 Sterling coup and cursed at the garbage truck driver in front of them in decidedly untutor-like language.

"I changed my mind," Jeremy said. "Can we go back to the museum tomorrow?"

Tutor McGeorge didn't seem to hear him. "Get your green behemoth out of the way . . ."

"HEY!" Jeremy said loudly.

The brakes screamed again, and Tutor McGeorge's beard began shaking.

"Do not yell at me like that, cretin. We're in wild and violent traffic. Do you want us to become involved in an accident?"

"I said that I want to go back to the museum tomorrow."

McGeorge was shocked. "What?"

"Can we go back to the museum?"

"Of course we can. We've barely scratched the surface of the Roman era, and we really should see the visiting Byzantine manuscript collection. Do you know what illuminated manuscripts are?"

"Like *Playboy* magazine?"

Silence. McGeorge stared ahead, squinting, and then laid heavily on the horn. Traffic was clearly an issue at the moment.

"No. No, no, no. The Byzantines were much too refined for that sort of crass nonsense. No! It's not like *Playboy* magazine. But we can go back. I'm glad your interest has a pulse."

Jeremy smiled and then ducked when he saw the red lights on the garbage truck looming abruptly in front of them. For the moment, teasing McGeorge was not a good idea.

Hal was a psychologist who wore tennis shoes, had a small basketball hoop attached to his trash can, and loved to flirt with his not-so-beautiful receptionist, Mrs. Harmon. He was smart, but terribly disorganized, though most people who witnessed firsthand his smile and beach-boy hair couldn't help but forgive him. Jeremy liked him; maybe even respected him.

"Jeremy, why did you give Mr. McGeorge's poodle beer?"

Jeremy shrugged. "He looked like he was thirsty."

Hal threw a wad of paper at the hoop on the trash can, which missed and hit the wall.

"I like beer. But I don't think dogs do very well on it. Mr. McGeorge really deserves better than that, Jeremy. He's trying to help you."

"Help me what—go crazy out of my mind? The museum is like a morgue for dead ideas. Have you ever been there?"

"Yes, and it's not that bad. The ideas there are only dead if you choose to tune them out."

"That's McGeorge talk," Jeremy said.

"No it's not. You tell me what you're interested in, and I'll tell you how the museum is relevant."

Jeremy paused. Hal was an expert at mind tricks, and this smelled like a setup.

"Video games," he said slowly.

Hal threw his hands up, smiling, and rocked forward in his squeaky desk seat.

"See? What did I tell you? Video games are all about visual stimulation. The same neurons that fire through your synapses when you're playing Vice City are the ones that should be firing when you're at the museum. You're closing your mind. You're the one with dead ideas."

"McGeorge talk."

"Do you know what kind of video games Da Vinci would have designed? Whoa. Go check out some of his sketches."

Jeremy frowned. "You also told me I should be actively manipulating my own environment. It's not just about visual stimulation. Games involve active manipulation—not just mind tricks."

Hal jumped up from his desk, found an orange foam ball on his desk, and swished it through the miniature hoop into the trash can. "He shoots; he scores."

Hal was so easily distracted. He sometimes made Jeremy forget that *he* was the one diagnosed with ADHD. It was annoying, and in the end it distracted Jeremy, too.

"There aren't any Da Vincis in this museum," Jeremy said.

Hal retrieved the foam ball from the garbage can and then groaned when he shot and missed. The ball came to a rest between them, and Hal stared at it as if it were a dead mouse in the middle of the carpet.

"That doesn't matter," Hal said. "I want you to think of something you saw there—anything, it doesn't even have to be one of the works of art. Think of something you saw, and go back and look at it *again*. Think of this as a mental video game. We'll get the active part going. You're got the joystick."

"It's called a PS2 controller."

"Find something there, and tell me why it sucks; or tell me how you would do it differently. Better yet, show me why it bothers you, or how it moves you."

Jeremy nodded slowly. "Something that bothers me?"

"Yes. It's not just about what you like. It's also about what's unpleasant, unattractive, or even disturbing. Art, by definition, is messy."

"And art builds on art—I've heard my mom say that."

"Yes, yes, yes." Hal reluctantly slid out of his chair and retrieved the ball. He shot again, and the ball bounced around several times before falling through. He turned to Jeremy with a huge smile and held his arms up to signal a three-point basket. Jeremy rolled his eyes.

"So, will you go back?" Hal asked.

"Yes, I'll go back. In fact, I want to go back. I have an idea."

"What? That was way too easy . . ."

"No. I want to go back."

"McGeorge talk," Hal said.

Jeremy's father was pouring his third cup of coffee when the cell phone on his belt chimed. He ignored it momentarily, closing his eyes as he sipped a tiny bit of steaming dark roast blend. When the ringing continued, he set the mug down on the counter, unintentionally spilling his frustration and his coffee. The number on the LCD indicator was his wife's.

"Yes, honey, what's going on?"

"I think you'd better come down to the museum."

"Why? What's wrong? Did something happen to Jeremy?"

"Not exactly . . . But I think this may test even the bounds of your laissez-faìre parenting philosophy."

When Jeremy's father arrived at the front entrance of the museum—a monolithic cavelike opening pinioned by huge, square granite columns—a small crowd was awaiting him, including his wife, Tutor McGeorge, Hal, and a young woman who appeared to be a museum administrator. None of them looked happy.

"Don't look at me," Hal said, holding his hands up.

"I quit!" Tutor McGeorge said in a tremulous voice.

"He's *your* son," his wife said.

"Right this way," the museum person said darkly.

They entered the building and quickly turned into a short corridor lined with small offices. The museum person, a short, young woman with insanely red hair and glasses that made her appear to be important, pointed them in. Jeremy was seated in a swivel chair near her desk, and she dramatically spun him around to face his father.

"What do you have to say for yourself, young man?" she said.

Jeremy smiled at his dad. "Hi, Dad. How did they lure you out of the cave?"

"Jeremy, what have you done?" he asked.

"I took everyone's advice, and I got interested in something classic. I found my own truth."

His father shrugged and looked at the redhead. "What exactly happened? Will someone tell me what he did?"

The redhead pointed to the security monitor in the corner of the office, near the ceiling. He squinted. All he could see was what appeared to be an old Greek statue.

"I'm stepping up." Jeremy said proudly.

"Oh, Merciful Jehovah." McGeorge moaned.

Hal and Jeremy's mother covered their eyes.

"I don't see anything," his father said.

The redhead grabbed him by the arm, rather brutally, he noted, with a mixture of pleasure and shock, and pulled him out of the office, down the hall, and into the cavernous first gallery. A large crowd had gathered around the statue and flashbulbs were going off every second or two in spite of the museum rules forbidding photography. She pushed him through the milling patrons to the velvet cordon rope and pointed.

"See? Look at that."

He didn't see the significance and was fearful that she might slap him. "What?"

Behind him, Jeremy and the others caught up. Jeremy smiled broadly, leaning dangerously on the rope.

"Hal told me that ideas are only dead if you choose to ignore them. I decided to liven things up. A little modeling clay and a little imagination, and well, the rest took care of itself."

"It's a complete forgery," McGeorge hissed. "The Greeks never placed emphasis on size."

Then Jeremy's father saw it. It was enormous.

He nearly fell over. He couldn't help himself. He guffawed slowly and then ruptured into increasingly rapid laughter, so loud, in fact, that the murmuring crowd was surprised into silence. When he looked again, it actually hurt his abdominal muscles.

After several prolonged minutes of uncontrollable hilarity, he put his arm around Jeremy's shoulder. "My son . . ." he said slowly, with exaggerated dignity. Then he burst into laughter again. "My son."

"What are you going to do?" Jeremy's mother asked. "What are *you* going to do?"

"This is a serious matter," the redhead said.

When Jeremy's father finally stopped laughing a few moments later, he was forced to draw a deep breath in to even be able to speak.

"What am I going to do?" He paused and shook his head slowly. What I'm going to do is I'm going to remind Hal that Jeremy is finally stepping up . . ."

"I had nothing to do with this," Hal said.

"No more trips to the museum," McGeorge said.

"There may be charges pressed," the redhead said.

"He *will* be in jail learning how to paint," Jeremy's mother said, threatening to burst into tears.

But Jeremy's father had already pulled him into the snack kiosk at the front of the museum. He was buying Jeremy lunch.

A *giant* chili dog, no less.

"A Time to Die"

(3rd place fiction, Charlottesville VWC, 2006)

by Leonard Tuchyner

Within the Emperor's holy city was the Bondi temple. Within the Bondi temple were the Bondi gardens. And within the Bondi gardens was the Bondi playing field. Although there were hundreds of cities within the emperor's kingdom and within each city was a holy Bondi temple that contained its own gardens and Bondi playing fields, only the best players of the realm represented the emperor in the holy imperial city.

Senshi was such a player. At least, he had been. As he took his place on the practice field, his teammates looked at him with sideways glances.

The traditional bong was struck, announcing the approach of Master Gangi. The imperial champions knelt in unison and bowed their heads in respect to their teacher, the great Bondi master.

Master Gangi stepped into the traditional teaching deck and acknowledged his students with a slight but courtly bow.

The students raised their heads and eyes as they sat in seiza.

Senshi loved the practice field. He feasted his eyes on the flowering gardens surrounding and defining the playing area. There were artistically twisted trees of all sizes of different-colored blossoms. Strategically placed ornamental shrubs hinted of pathways that disappeared beyond view. The perfumes of blossoms and flowers were ever changing from week to week and from season to season.

Today, as he looked intently at his master, Senshi's heart sank in recognition of the somber black hooded robe, which usually signified that someone must die.

An anticipatory tear rolled down Senshi's aging cheek. It caught at a crease that spread from his mouth and flowed down the shallow crevasse. He loved his life but did not feel completed.

Master Gangi began to intone the death chant and then, with a tone of gentleness, said, "Master Senshi, will you please approach me."

Senshi rose on legs suddenly tired and trembling. He walked directly to the front and bowed before his master. The sensi reached inside his robes and pulled out a black sash, which he then placed over Senshi's shoulders.

"Before I pronounce judgment, is there anyone here who would speak against the wisdom of my decree?"

The world stood still for Senshi. He floated in a pool of hope and despair. Surely someone would speak in his defense. He could not die. Not now.

Through that pool, the sound of a man's voice penetrated. Despair retreated into a corner and glowered at him. Hope ballooned and filled Senshi's stomach, but the eyes of despair still burned through, like a persistent irritation. It was the voice of his friend, Torgu.

"I most humbly would speak words of defense for my friend, Master Senshi."

"Very well," Gangi said. "Speak your words."

"Senshi is still one of the best of us. If we lose him, we will suffer," Master Torgu said.

"I do not dispute that. But we will gain by other younger players who will exceed him. They will also gain by being with such accomplished masters."

"With all respect, Master, it is not Senshi's fault that his skills have eroded."

"Master Torgu, it is never useful to lay blame at the foot of the one who simply grows old."

"But I know Master Senshi can regain his old prowess and perhaps even exceed it."

Master Gangi's eyes smiled sympathetically. "If you can help bring such a thing about, I, of course, will welcome it. I do not wish for our beloved brother to depart from us. How could such a thing come to pass?"

"I have been noticing something about Master Senshi. He is not eating right. He has been too self-indulgent, and the food has made him sluggish. Too often do I see him enjoying milk, eggs, and honey. His salad bowl has the residue of heavy oils, and the crumbs of wafers stick like telltale sins on the sides of that vessel. If Master Senshi would eat only dark-colored vegetables, his old catlike reflexes would return, and he would build higher upon that which he has already mastered."

"Do you think so?" Master Gangi said, with hopeful but quizzical eyes.

"Oh, yes, Master. I believe it."

"Ah, miracles can be performed by belief. It is not permitted for any being to put himself in the way of faith. Would you be willing to take the responsibility of making sure that Master Senshi follows the diet you prescribe for him?"

"With the deepest gratitude, Master."

"Very well. Then, so shall it be done. Master Senshi, please hand me back the sash of death. You have received a reprieve."

With a heart that swam in the wine of relief, Senshi removed the black sash and folded it ceremoniously. With bowed head, he laid it in Master Gangi's outstretched hands. Then Senshi turned toward Torgu, a broad smile on his face. Though the thought of eating food that was meant for horses and rabbits was a daunting one, he knew he would make this work.

And so it was. Torgu became Senshi's guardian angel—and sometimes more like his guardian demon. Not one morsel of unapproved food passed Senshi's lips, except on one occasion when the erstwhile player picked up a piece of sweet bread that had fallen from another's plate. Before the pitiful little speck could begin to dissolve in Senshi's mouth, a Bondi stick hit him squarely on the back. The crumb of sweet bread exploded from his mouth like a missile, along with a mouthful of salivated digestive juices.

But lo and behold, Master Senshi's reflexes returned to his old catlike self. And in keeping with the purpose of all Earthly beings, he continued to learn, to experience, and to evolve.

But the ravages of time wait for very few souls. Senshi witnessed the death of Melira, his team's left forward. He remembered the days when she fluttered down the field like a crimson butterfly, her movements light and unpredictable. She would float past opposing players, using their own attacking energies to waft herself away from them. But then her beautiful wings seemed to become more ragged with each passing month. She began to throw her body, at times full tilt, at persistent pursuers. The tactic worked for awhile, but she came off the field of battle with increasing bumps and bruises, and one could almost hear her bones creaking in protest.

When Master Gangi announced that it was time for her to die, he saw a decided look of relief in her face and posture.

"Thank you, Master Gangi," she said as he placed the scarf of death over her shoulders.

In the week she was given to put her affairs in order, Melira gathered together the gifts and mementos she would present at her Day of Departure. On that day, she stood on the sensi's dais, for on that day she was the teacher. She delivered a message of gratitude and personalized it for each of her teammates and master coaches. Then they all filed up to her to receive their gifts and to offer words and blessings to their departing teammate.

"And to you, Senshi, I have made a salad, that salads will always be to you a blessed gift."

Senshi blushed as he and his comrades laughed and appreciated her gesture.

"And for you, Melira, I offer a song. We know that music and thoughts are some of the few things we can take with us in our departures:"

Lovely yellow and black caterpillar, why do you fold away from life?
Why, sir, to become a butterfly, which must be done out of sight.
Beautiful butterfly, with wings so bright, why do you fold away into the night?
Why, sir, can't you see? It is to take a freer flight
Out of the night. And into the light.

Melira bowed to Senshi with a tear in her eye, and he moved back to his place, never again, in this life, to see her in this form.

Torgu approached her next, and to him she gave a Bondi stick.

"Master Torgu, this stick was given to me by my parents when I was a little girl. It is too heavy for my style, but it is perfect for whacking errant masters across their backs when they try to eat what they should not."

And so it went. When all of the masters had said their good-byes, Melira bowed, turned, and disappeared down one of the trails of death.

Although from that day forth, Torgu never had to use the Bondi stick on Senshi's back, his prowess on the field began once again to dwindle. And there came again the day when Master Gangi called him to the front of the playing field and placed the scarf of death around his shoulders.

Again, Senshi did not feel he was ready to die, although his body was beginning to feel ragged and abused.

"Is there anyone who would speak against the decree of death?" Master Gangi asked.

Again, Torgu's voice was heard.

"I most humbly would speak words of defense for my friend, Master Senshi."

"Very well. Speak your words."

"I have noticed that there is one significant flaw in Master Senshi's play. He has mastered his body, and his stick has become its extension, as is the way of masters. But he has never understood that the stick itself has a spirit. Any stick for him has been adequate. And while his body was in its prime, his skills surpassed the flaw. But now he must find his own stick. He must let it speak to him, as much as he speaks to it. He will evolve, and his skills will become greater than ever."

Master Gangi smiled. The baleful eye of despair that once again had retreated into the shadows of Senshi's consciousness seemed to sigh in resignation. Senshi could hear it say, "I'll be back."

"Who will teach this to Master Senshi?" Gangi asked.

"I will undertake the divine task, Master," Torgu said.

And so it was. Master Senshi's game style changed in the most divinely subtle way. And there were those who said the stick would play while its master slept.

But alas, strong as he was in the way of the game, the ravages of old age eventually seemed to prevail. And for the third time, Master Gangi, himself a wizened old coach, called Senshi to his podium and draped the black scarf of death on his shoulders.

Senshi looked for the fear that had promised to return at each reprieve from death he had received in the past, but he could not find it. There was something there that had a similar face, but it smiled at him, as though it had been just fooling him those other times. He looked for the face of resignation, but Senshi could not find it either. Instead, he found acceptance, and it laughed at how it had teased him when it wore the costume of resignation.

"Before I speak the decree of death, is there anyone here to challenge my judgment?" Master Gangi asked.

Torgu's voice spoke out once more. "I would speak in defense of Master Senshi. His days of greatness have not yet begun. I have noticed a few things that Master Senshi has been ignorant of. With time and attention, all will be amazed at the kind of player he can yet become."

Senshi was sorry to hear his friend's words. He was tired and ready to leave his beloved field of play. But he saw the look of desperation on Torgu's face. He glanced at Master Gangi, and they exchanged a flash of sympathetic knowing.

"What are these things of which Master Senshi has been ignorant?"

Torgu went through a litany of very subtle facets, corrective exercises, and meditations that would improve Senshi's play. Some of them were so divinely exquisite that Master Gangi was truly amazed.

Master Gangi smiled at Torgu in a kind and sad way. He glanced again at Senshi, who nodded assent, in such a way that Gangi knew the assent was for Torgu's needs and not Senshi's own desires.

"Then, Master Torgu, go and perform your miracles once more."

And so it was. Senshi entered into the new program with the purpose and vigor that old age left to him. Indeed, he learned and improved in certain areas of play, so that his decline was slowed. But decline he did, and it was not very long before he was once more wearing the scarf of death.

When again Torgu spoke out for him, Senshi raised his hand in gentle protest and said, "No more, my friend. It is time. I must walk the trail of death. Strong as I am in the game, there is no power on Earth that can move the glass of time backward or stop even a single grain from falling. I accept Master Gangi's decree and ask that you do the same."

"In three days, then, we will have the ceremony of departure." Gangi made a gesture, and a low, doleful bong sounded from within the gardens.

As was the custom, Senshi continued to participate in the training program even to the final day. In fact, on that final day the emperor's team was playing against the team of a neighboring kingdom, and the emperor's prestige was at stake.

In deference to the departing ceremonies that were to take place in the evening of that day, Senshi was not expected to participate. The game did not go well for the emperor, and they were down several points.

The emperor's players sat in seiza in the last quarter contemplation break.

Senshi looked out over the Bondi field from his kneeling bench and listened to the sound of the quiet morning early autumn day. The deciduous trees wore robes of gold and red leaves that took turns flitting to the Earth singularly and in companionable groups. Song birds twittered their tunes back and forth to each other, while the raucous sound of two crows punctuated the symphony with their raspy voices. A gentle breeze, warm with sunshine and cool with autumn, added gentle movement to limb and leaf that played with the sunshine. The breeze brought all the familiar smells of earth, air, and water. It brought memories from his sojourn in this incarnation. And then a subtle memory that was not really a memory stirred in him. He arose and approached Master Gangi.

"Yes, Master Senshi, what wisdom have you brought to me?"

"I wish to take this opportunity to give my team their collective parting gift."

"Is it wise to interrupt their contemplation? Our honorable opponents are kicking our holy asses, and I want them to think about it."

"Most honorable Master, I wish to play in this last quarter. It feels right."

Master Gangi looked at Senshi in puzzlement. "Are you sure?"

"On the day of my death, I am closer to truth than ever was I before."

Master Gangi studied Senshi and then bowed deeply. "Then let it be so."

After the break, Senshi took his place on the playing field. Master Gangi saw a wizened old man standing in place, leaning on his Bondi stick as though it were a cane. Then the Bondi puck was thrown into play, and a golden glow emanated from the old man's body, and in its radiation, the old man disappeared. In his place was a young vibrant body. He had the physical attributes of youth, but his eyes were those of an old, wise person. He sprung and floated into action. And, oh, such brilliant action. Genius, poetry, and prowess incarnate. His glow of energy infused the rest of his team, and all felt a gladness not of this side borne of life.

The score rapidly rose to an even tie, with still much time to spare. But Senshi called for a time out. Then, as he stood there in the stillness of time, his knees bent, his body stooped, and he leaned once more on his Bondi stick as the glow dissipated. He turned and walked to Master Gangi.

"That is all I am permitted. The team will do what it will do now. It is not important who wins."

Master Gangi bowed and nodded his head in agreement and understanding.

Senshi stood on the teaching dais as he taught his departing lesson to his teammates and coaches. He saw not only the living players but also many who had already departed. He found it difficult, at times, to distinguish the living from the departed. But he knew that was common in the last hours and days before death. All, living and dead, were rapt in this lesson, including Senshi himself.

Finally, it was time to say good-bye to each individual on the podium and to exchange gifts.

When Torgu came to the dais, a gift clutched tightly in his hand, tears dribbled down the growing creases of his face.

"Torgu, my old faithful friend, I wish to tell you of my gift to you before you speak. I am simply going to leave and hope you learn the lesson of letting go. Were it not for you, I would have left this life unfulfilled, unfinished. You pushed me to heights only a friend such as you could have done. I am eternally grateful. Now I must leave. That is what I will do."

Torgu stared at him for a while, and then the drooped corners of his mouth began to turn up, and the wisdom crinkles around his eyes fanned out like sun rays, and the waning daylight glistened off his drying tears like fairy wings. Then he started to laugh. They laughed together and had to support each other in hugging arms. Then, with a final mutual bow, Master Senshi turned and walked the perimeter trail until he saw Melira beckoning to him. Then he disappeared to view, as his old teammate guided him to the next game.

"The Serengeti of the Heart"

(1st place fiction, Charlottesville VWC, 2005;
1st place fiction, State VWC, 2005)

by Sarah C. Honenberger

"No heartbeat." The doctor was mumbling, but Christie heard it, wondered if she was supposed to hear it, worried that he was avoiding the details on purpose because he wasn't at all confident she could handle bad news.

It took all her self-control not to repeat the phrase, though it echoed in her head and in the examining room, outfitted so beautifully in peaceful pastels with teddy bears and baby lambs. Looking around to keep herself from losing control, she felt again that hint of eternity peering at her from above. A son, a daughter, it didn't matter to her; she was so engrossed in the idea of The Baby she could hardly think straight.

No heartbeat was not in the vocabulary she and Isaac had been practicing since the doctor had confirmed the pregnancy. She pursed her lips to say the words, but she couldn't. It was too awful to say out loud, too awful even to contemplate, and yet the vision appeared; the baby, floating face up, eyes open, a vacant stare from the amniotic fluid that flowed through her veins, into and around the miniature version of Isaac, her enthusiastic and devoted husband, and back around to her own lopsided view of herself, fat and happy and full of anticipation.

Babies were a miracle. God would not destroy a miracle. Would he?

At the grocery store she bought lettuce and zucchini and asparagus. Green things would supplement her intake of iron, would keep her strong. Isaac had printed from the Internet a list of foods that strengthened a woman's system. The Baby needed her to be healthy. The Baby drew his strength from hers. She had an obligation, a duty. Even Isaac acknowledged this distinction. Fathers could eat whatever they wanted, but mothers had to do the right thing.

How was she going to tell him? Maybe the doctor was wrong. Or maybe the baby had simply been turning and the electrode had shifted, sliding away from the steady proof of life. It could be a mistake, a small insignificant error that would right itself without any action on her part, so that next month when she went, the heartbeat would be there, loud and clear.

After grilling the zucchini under the broiler of the toaster oven, she sprinkled the slices with Parmesan cheese. Extra protein. She put the platter with the dinner in the oven to stay warm. Sometimes if Isaac had to work late, he forgot to call her. When the phone rang, a short shriek erupted from her where she sat buried in the newspaper in Isaac's recliner. She hefted herself up and sprinted to the kitchen phone.

"Hey, babe." Isaac. "Are you elevating your feet?"

"I'm not even five months. It's too early."

"You should be practicing."

"Are you on the way home?"

"Why? Need pickles?" Isaac found the idea of cravings hysterically funny and took every opportunity to remind her she was no longer in control of her life. At first it had been heartwarming. Two months since the positive home pregnancy test and his sense of humor was wearing thin.

"It was a simple question," she said, staring at the miming newscaster on the silent television.

"I'm sorry." He sounded contrite, which made her feel terrible. She almost told him the doctor's warning over the phone. The burden of carrying around the horrific possibility suddenly weighed her down to the point of total despair.

"Are you okay?" He asked with a voice that trembled, she was sure.

Had he guessed somehow, from her tone, her failure to chirp on about her day and the painting of the nursery? "Did Dr. Averill call you at the office?" She asked too sharply, instantly apologetic for violating some unspoken rule not to even hint at disaster.

"That's right, you had your checkup today. What'd he say about the due date?"

She stumbled over the answer, finally managing to eke out *no change.*

Without commenting on her hesitation, Isaac continued, "Brian said with their first he took Maryanne for pickup rides over the railroad tracks. Apparently that brings on labor."

"We're a long way from labor." Her impatience with his jocularity belied the tears she'd fought back all afternoon, but she couldn't say what hovered on her lips. She'd wait until he was home. She'd tell him then, face to face. He'd see in her eyes that she needed him to be strong. He'd understand.

The morning traffic was already zipping by when she awakened, wrapped cocoon-like in the sofa's afghan, where she'd fallen asleep waiting for Isaac to come home. He was long gone, back to the store, selling furniture to people who could afford only payments, not whole sofas. With the sun's sharp fingers probing the spaces between the solemn furniture, she stood, stretched, and padded to the kitchen.

His note was stuck in the toaster. *Strawberry preserves from Aunt Maggie. She's worried you're not eating right. Says you should be fatter. Love, I.*

Christie held the note, not willing to throw it in the trash quite yet. How had she slept, knowing that The Baby might be dead, suffocated in the stuffy sinkhole of her uterus, no fresh air, no clear liquids or Tylenol to ward off disease? She stood in the kitchen, the crumpled paper in her hand, and cried. Tears ran in steady streams down her cheeks, staining the beginnings of her tummy, and dropping like warm rain on her bare toes.

"Damn, damn, damn, damn." Although she rarely cursed, the words flowed like the most careful harmony, slightly syncopated with hiccups from crying and speaking simultaneously.

When the backdoor bell rang, she wiped her face on the terrycloth sleeve of Isaac's robe before she moved trancelike to the door. "Yes?" she asked, keeping the chain on.

"I'm from Hartford Life. Your husband inquired, and I'm here to answer your questions."

She undid the chain. In silence he followed her past the dirty supper dishes to the living room and sat on the sofa that had been her grandmother's before she went in the nursing home. Covered in a yellow-flowered chintz, it didn't match anything else in the room, or the house for that matter—Isaac liked modern furniture, leather and teak, which they couldn't afford—but the sofa made it possible to entertain another couple without having to drag in the kitchen chairs. With a baby coming, they were on a tight budget.

The salesman's new shoes squeaked on the fake wood floors of the townhouse Isaac had bought before the wedding. What a planner he was, insisting on a closet big enough for a washer—*you won't want to be carting clothes to the Laundromat with a baby on your hip,* The Baby not even an inkling at that point—and on built-in bookshelves for all the books he was going to own once he finished at the community college.

Christie sat back in the recliner, keeping her distance from the stranger. He smiled, a fake smile, but that could be nervousness. Barging into someone else's house and having to talk about personal things with people he'd never met before must be hard.

"Life insurance," he held up a brochure with the company logo, a giant hand holding a house, "is the best protection you can have against tragedy." He paused and clicked his pen. To emphasize the point, she guessed. Put the worst possible spin on it, scare people and they would listen up, she assumed. She was listening.

"Oh," was all she could manage, but he didn't need any encouragement.

"Say, the primary breadwinner has an accident," he took a breath as if his brain were whizzing through a catalogue of accidents, searching for just the right one for this particular customer, "he slips when he's washing the car. Hartford would be there for you."

She envisioned a muscled little man in a bowler cap, Hartford embroidered on his jacket, whistling as he scooped up Isaac and carried him into the living room, spreading him out on the garden sofa, and propping up the rapidly swelling ankle with the pillows.

"Hartford," the salesman continued, "knows how to make things right. Why, once they received the death certificate, they'd send someone to complete the claim forms, scurry them through Adjusting, and within thirty days they'd mail you the first check."

"A person couldn't die from slipping on soapy water in the driveway."

The salesman's smile drooped. "It's a hypothetical."

"Like a doctor who can't quite hear a baby's heartbeat before it's born," she said.

"Exactly," the salesman nodded.

Not long after the insurance man left, Isaac called to check on her. A glorious colored booklet decorated the coffee table Isaac had made from shellacked two by fours. It took her eight rings to drag herself from the recliner to the kitchen phone.

"Were you asleep?"

"No."

"Sweetie, are you alright? You sound exhausted. I can barely hear you."

"Sorry," she made an effort to enunciate.

"Are you going in to work this afternoon?"

"I'm not sure."

"Are you on the schedule?"

"Yes." She closed her eyes. She was exhausted. The insurance man had recited a dozen scenarios, each worse than the last. She and her hypothetical husband and children were all dead. Insurance envelopes were littering the foyer under the mail slot, the money piling up in a totally unnecessary, useless jumble, while the plants died and the water was cut off and the spiders built webs in the corners. Maybe there were worse tragedies than a missing heartbeat.

Someone at Isaac's work was whistling in the background. He raised his voice. "Would you like me to come home and drive you over there? It's muggy today, the bus'll be hot."

"You're sweet, but I think I should do this as long as I can."

"That'a girl." She could just imagine him beaming at his colleagues over this plucky little wife who persevered despite all odds. He laughed into the phone. "I'll save you some Chinese."

"Don't you dare." In spite of herself, she laughed. He knew how much she hated Chinese food; pregnant or not.

The bus actually felt chilly after the baked sidewalks and the steaming Plexiglas booth at the bus stop. Although she usually chose to wait in the fresh air, she had had to sit. Her heart had flipped in wild arcs when a mother with a double stroller parked in the shade of the booth. The toddlers talked incessantly, chewing their fingers and mashing graham crackers in their tiny pink fists. The urge to gather them both in her arms took hold, and she had to turn her back to them. When she climbed the bus steps, she was crying quietly, patting her eyes surreptitiously with an old napkin from her purse.

There were lots of empty seats, but she waited until the mother with the two children had settled in the back before she sat, as far to the front as possible. Could a mother's heartbeat simply mask the weaker, newer sound of her baby's so that a doctor, distracted and busy, might not be able to distinguish it? Of course, that was it. She checked her watch. Plenty of time to telephone Doctor Averill from the flower shop. It probably happened all the time. No wonder he hadn't seemed concerned. The nurse could probably tell her.

Several stops later when the stroller rolled by to disembark, Christie put her hand on the mother's arm. "They're so sweet together. You must be very proud."

The mother smiled. "Twins are hard work. Well, not just twins, babies." She squinted against the afternoon sun outside the bus window. "It's fun, though. You'll see."

Shocked that someone could tell from the little mound of belly that had appeared almost overnight, Christie forgot all about getting off herself. She had to walk back four blocks to the "Forget Me Not" Flower Shop and Quick-Mart.

Her boss noticed something right away. "You shouldn't come if you're not feeling well."

"I'm fine. It's the heat. And I missed my stop."

"Take five and have a soda. The delivery van's not back yet anyway."

After she splashed her face with cold water, she wadded up the wet paper towels and made a compress. It slipped nicely into the sandwich bag in her lunchbox once she took out the grapes. One by one she plucked them from the stem and ate them, careful to bite them before she swallowed. Over five hundred people choked to death each year in the United States. An accident the insurance salesman had missed in his litany.

At nine, half an hour before closing, Isaac arrived with an iced mocha decaf.

"How's my girl?"

Mr. Malone had gone home, and Christie was finishing the bouquets for tomorrow's commuter buckets. "You didn't have to come."

"I wasn't doing anything else." But he put his arms around her as if he had come for that reason only. "We had to finish annual reports tonight at the office. I haven't even been home." His breath was soft on her neck, dry and warm.

After she untangled herself, she began to cart the buckets back to the walk-in cooler. "Your friend from Hartford came by the house today."

"I don't know anyone in Connecticut."

"The insurance man."

Isaac's forehead quilted into even creases, the skin tucked into neatly aligned furrows. "What insurance man?"

"He said he knew you, that you'd called and asked about life insurance."

"You let him in?"

It hadn't occurred to her to be afraid. The man was wearing a suit, had shaken her hand. He'd offered a business card, hadn't he? She must have put it on the kitchen counter after he'd come inside.

In a flash the meeting spun through her mind. He had talked almost constantly. Only a few questions, no trip to the bathroom, no undue absence when he could have rifled through her jewelry box—not that there was anything to steal of any value—and he had left the brochure with his phone number.

"He's selling life insurance, not casing potential burglaries."

"How do you know? If he's smooth, he practices a routine to throw you off. And you're so gullible. He could say anything and you'd be fooled."

"I'm not stupid."

Isaac pulled her to him. "I didn't mean that. I'm just worried about you. With the baby and all, you have to think twice, be extra careful."

She twisted free, slammed the cooler door, and grabbed her purse. As if she would do anything to jeopardize The Baby. How could he even suggest it? Hadn't she read the entire hospital handbook the day after the drugstore stick turned blue, before she'd even told her mother? Hadn't she checked the labels on every Onesie, every three-month sleeper, every baby blanket to be sure they weren't flammable? Hadn't she gone on the Internet and found out which brand of paint was nontoxic before painting the thrift store crib?

As she stomped ahead of Isaac to the car, she ran through the myriad of precautions she'd taken. It simply wasn't possible that there be no heartbeat. But how could she tell him now, after she'd been so careless as to let a strange man into the house?

In the car Isaac handed her the iced mocha. The perspiration on the plastic cup dripped on her skirt, but she didn't care. She watched the small circles dry and disappear as if they had never existed.

"Wanna drive out to the Bluffs and smooch a little?" he asked after he pulled round the corner onto High Street.

"You are such a romantic."

Without speaking he turned toward home. He drove stiffly, not even the least little hum. She'd hurt him, and it wasn't what she'd intended at all.

"I can make you a grilled cheese sandwich," she offered once he'd slid the deadbolt into place and they were standing in the unlit kitchen.

"Whatever you feel like. I'm not very hungry."

Working busily to keep herself from thinking about Isaac mooning about the bedroom, she slathered the bread with butter, checked the flame under the frying pan, and put pickles on both plates. The sizzle of butter in the pan was oddly comforting, a small normality in the wide void of fear in which she'd been drowning since the doctor's pronouncement. With the Hartford brochure in hand, Isaac shuffled back in, his boxers loose at his waist; no sympathetic weight gain for him.

"Smells good." He stood by the plates as she flipped the sandwiches. "Ah, the ubiquitous pickles."

It took him a minute to realize she was crying. Flinging down the brochure, he took the spatula from her and sat down, pulling her into his lap. "Hey? What's the matter? I shouldn't have said all that about the insurance guy. You made the right decision. With the baby coming, we ought to have some life insurance. Then you two would be taken care of if something happened to me."

She buried her face in his shoulder.

"Christie, sweetheart, it's okay. Nothing bad's going to happen. It's just we have to be prepared. You know, life doesn't always turn out the way you expect. Whatever happens, we'll be together. It's okay, now. Shhhh."

It was like leading him on to pretend everything was fine. The doctor had explained the odds to her on the phone when she had called from the flower shop. *Percentages and statistics. It wasn't for sure, they would know more next month.* But she couldn't wait a month, holding this in, trying to handle it on her own. And Hartford couldn't help.

Here was her Isaac who worked sixty hours a week and studied economics, desperate to earn his degree and move into management. This was the man who fixed the disposal the same day it broke and held her during scary movies and surprised her with iced mochas. She put her fingers on his lips and waited until he was silent so she could explain.

"The Road, The Rock"

(2nd place fiction, Charlottesville VWC, 2005)

by Valarie Massie Watersun

The quarter mile of one-lane dirt drive led past my front yard as long as I could remember. Grandpa Simmons said it had been there, in almost the same configuration, since the War Between the States, considerably longer than my thirteen years.

So when Daddy decided to widen the road, the decision was met with confused protest. Surely, if the drive had been adequate during the past century, there was no need to change it now.

True, highway Virginia 151, which took us east and west, had been paved and repaved endlessly, the asphalt sludging down onto our road like fresh cow flop. It was also true that a hard, wet winter often left us spinning wheels on a drive of slippery mud, too much like snot to be believed, river stone jutting up like Aunt Esther's plump wrists at the dinner table. And with three families living in Simmons Hollow, all using the same road, having to back out when you met someone coming or going was an expected occurrence.

Uncle Cockeye, Daddy's brother, who lived further-down the drive with his wife, Kim, and three daughters, was peeved at the idea. He called a family meeting and spent most of the time yelling at Daddy. He cussed about the bother of having the drive all tore up for weeks on end and then really went on about the expense. How dare my Daddy ask him to pay one third on a project he hadn't even agreed to?

Grandpa and Granny Simmons didn't say much at the meeting. I saw Granny motion Cockeye down one time, but he just glared at her and carried on. They seemed agitated, though, and I could tell they wished Daddy had taken up stamp collecting or some other such thing instead of this silly road crusade.

The only ones in the family who defended Daddy were Mama and her sister Esther. Esther had lived with us the six years since her husband died, and though she was sad a lot and ate too much, she was easygoing, agreeing to most anything. Mama liked the idea of fixing up the drive, I could tell. She had been listening to all Daddy's road plans with wide eyes, encouraging him all the way. At the meeting she stood up and pointed out all the advantages to having the drive widened and straightened.

No one seemed to care.

The meeting ended on a sour note; Cockeye swearing he wouldn't pay and Daddy swearing he'd do the road no matter what.

The very next morning, as it was Memorial Day and Daddy had the day off from his job at the garment factory downtown, he was out there on his tractor, scraper blade raised like a weapon. I watched him from the kitchen window as I ate cold cereal.

"Whoa, he's knocked down all the banks," I murmured to myself as I loaded my mouth with more cereal.

Mama, washing dishes at the sink, overheard me. "Well, you know, you gotta crack eggs to eat them," she advised.

I sent my eyes around the kitchen, noticing for the umpteenth time the split plaster on the walls, the unfinished wood floor. "Why's he really doin' it, Mama?"

She turned and fixed me with soft brown eyes, understanding my meaning. "Lord knows, child," she answered, sighing deeply. "It's just something Sheldon feels he's got to do." She dabbed at the table with a damp dish cloth. "It'll be nice when he's finished."

"He'd be better off doin' some of the work around here," I commented crossly. "Has he fixed the dryer yet?"

Mama turned away abruptly. "He hasn't been feeling too well lately, Stuart. You know that. Now, go on out there and help him before he has to come looking for you," she added, effectively dismissing me.

I felt stupid standing out on the tumbled dirt of the drive with nothing to do, so I started piling loosened bedding stone into neat mounds at regular intervals. Daddy worked methodically, guiding the tractor blade back and forth, smoothing out gullies, laying new drainage ditches, and pushing banked soil to one side.

Sunlight crusted my skin, and the newly turned earth steamed pungently under my hands as I plundered stone. Cars passing on 151 often distracted me, so I created a game in my mind, trying to guess their destination and purpose.

We worked this way until midafternoon, when, after a hurried lunch of roast beef sandwiches, Daddy and I drove the pickup into town to get diesel for the tractor. Memorial Day meant we traveled to three stores before finding one open that sold diesel.

"Oh hell," muttered Daddy, as we lifted the three-gallon cans from the truck bed.

"What's wrong?" I queried, looking around. I didn't see anything amiss, just a group of old men loitering around the front door of the market.

"Ain't nothing," he answered.

We filled the cans and moved to go inside to pay. Daddy laid one palm against my chest as he fished his wallet out with the other hand. "Why don't you just wait out here, son?"

"But . . . I wanted a soda," I said, hating the whining tone of my voice.

He shook his head firmly but dropped his staying hand. "I'll get you one. Grape, right?"

"And a chocolate candy bar too," I ordered, slamming myself into the truck's passenger seat. I looked away pointedly so he could see how irked I was feeling.

After about ten seconds, though, I turned to study his retreating back, puzzled by his curious behavior. As he approached the store, a tall, thick-boned man, head the size of a good fall pumpkin, rose and shook Daddy's hand. I saw Daddy's eyes dart my way once, but he carried on a conversation for several minutes before going inside to pay.

"Who was that big-headed fellow?" I asked him later on the drive home, my mouth full of chocolate. "The one who talked to you outside the store."

"Fellow named Carstairs," Daddy answered before falling back into a heavy silence.

Daddy labored on that road every day after work for the next week. I'd come home from school and no sooner would get my homework done than Daddy would be in the door, changing clothes with one hand and eating supper with the other before rushing out to "burn daylight" on his tractor. And I have to admit, the road was shaping up. Wide enough now for two cars to pass abreast, the drive was faster, smoother than before.

The spring rains depressed Daddy, because it was too wet for him to get on the tractor. He stayed inside in the evenings, staring forlornly out the living room windows. The damp must have gotten to him, because he caught a bad cold and had this hacking cough that got on my nerves.

But the rains passed, and as soon as the wind and sun worked their magic, he and I were out there every day. It was during this time, while the ground was still moist and soft, that we decided to tackle the rock.

The rock, a huge gray boulder, lent a bothersome curve to the drive where it jutted out with majestic rudeness. Daddy was determined to get this boulder out and straighten the drive. He'd already tried pushing it with the tractor and had worked most of the rock loose. It clung tenaciously to the surrounding sod, however, as if reluctant to be awakened from an eon of slumber.

We started early the next Saturday, just as the sun was climbing over Preacher Mountain, both of us working on the stone with digging tools. The gray density seemed to go on forever, and before too long, we were layered with sweat and rich, old dirt.

I glanced over at Daddy one time and sudden fear hit me. I didn't like the look on his face, no sir. It was a mean, do-or-die face that daddies just ain't supposed to have. The rock came free, though. Just about the time I was going to pipe up and beg him to leave off, that old rock tumbled with one great heave out of the bank and came to a halt right in the center of the road. The sound was ugly; in my mind, surely resembling the pulling of a dinosaur tooth.

Daddy bent over, gasping for air and staring up at the belligerent half ton of stone. He kicked it once, with clumsy grace, and swabbed at the sweat on his forehead with the back of one hand.

"It's granite, Stu. Ain't that somethin'? Don't see much granite in this part of the state."

I studied a noisy tractor trailer passing by on the highway and pondered how states were defined by their stone. I thought about coal in West Virginia and iron in Pennsylvania.

"Yep, granite." Daddy mused, roughly caressing the surface with callused, gnarled hands. Dropping the long digging bar, he stood back to critically gauge the rock's merit. "I bet your Ma would like this rock in her garden."

I turned to squint up at him, the heat from the summer sun hot on my forearms. "Can't carry no rock that big," I told him. "Best just break it up here."

"Break it up? Hell, I'll just drag it."

And don't you know that's what he did. It took him two full days but somehow he wrapped his logging chain around that stone every which way and dragged it by tractor that eighth of a mile until it rested with heavy kingship in the back of the garden where Mama's cooking and medicinal yarbs were planted. It looked good there too, just as Daddy had seen it in his mind's eye.

A few days later, the straightened road finally met Daddy's strict criteria, and the men came in big trucks to pour out the expensive gravel that gave our drive a new, rustic sort of elegance. Even Aunt Kim called it a work of art. She made Uncle Cockeye pay Daddy too—all the money he'd asked for.

Then Daddy died. One morning Mama woke up cold and went to bump the furnace. When she came back to bed, she missed the rhythmic rasp of his breath.

I thought we'd all die from the missing of him and from the sudden way he was taken from us. People always talk and smile at funerals, but no one carried on that way at Daddy's final service. It was too sad a parting to share glad greetings.

The tall, big-boned man was there, and the story he told Mama and Aunt Esther hurt even more. It seems this Dr. Minton Carstairs was from Trenton, the next town over. Daddy had gone on the sly to see Carstairs eight months ago, when he'd had trouble swallowing. The diagnosis had been terminal cancer; the prognosis death rushing in on winged feet.

After the funeral, I stripped off my suit jacket and fled the press of people to go outside and ponder this bitter pill. I meandered for some time, finally ending up in Mama's yarbs, trampling verbena and mugwort underfoot. The pungent odors lifted to me, bringing tears. Then I was lying across granite, my nose inhaling the sun and chalk smell of bare stone. I stayed there for some time, probably hours, before I felt the indentations beneath my cold fingers.

Roused by curiosity, I pulled myself from the stone and crept around the convex curve to see what was there. Seven sets of characters, so simple, so basic. I suddenly remembered the muffled tapping sound that had pulled me into wakefulness many mornings and realized the effort the message had taken.

I did it.
Sheldon Simmons 1954–1994.

And I wondered. What is it that makes a man remembered when he's gone. A road? A stone? Perhaps it's the secrets and the reasoning behind those secrets. Then again, perhaps it's the fierce determination with which a man toils, carving out a life.

"Angel, or the Mystery in St. Paul's Chapel on 9/11"

by Liz Kollar

The fear was so great that it seemed palpable. Incredibly, the Twin Towers of the Trade Center in New York had become a hundred-and-ten-floor pile of smoking, flaming, twisted steel, destroyed in seconds by two hellish hijacked planes filled with unwary travelers now cremated in the inferno. All around him were nightmarish pieces of steel girders, shards of glass, human parts, debris, so gross, so horrifying that Glenn stood staring at the changed skyline of the big city with an overwhelmingly, tortured spot where his heart was beating.

His face was bathed in sweat, even though the day had darkened and grown cold. His eyes were gritty orbs, red rimmed from the dust and tears and from the long day's labor, searching, ever searching for a piece of someone or something once human, once living and breathing, once strong or beautiful, once man or woman.

This morning he'd found several strands of long black hair, torn like threads from its human spool. Thank God he hadn't seen more. After he'd found a spot to rest his weary body, he'd scraped the dust and ashes from his clothes and his boots into a box along with the hair. Somewhere a family existed that would cherish these human remains. He hoped the coroner could put a name to them, find a bit of DNA, could bring closure to a family, to a life.

He headed now for St. Paul's church, close to ground zero. He knew he'd find some rest on one of the pews in the back of the sanctuary. Other firemen, police, and rescue people, exhausted from the long hours, sat talking softly; some were already sleeping, fully clothed, jackets bunched up into soot-covered pillows under their heads.

A young woman carrying ointments, salves, and bandages touched his arm gently as he attempted to lie down and rest.

"Let me see your hand," she said, eyes dark with compassion and darkly enormous at the sight of so much human suffering around her.

He sat down on the edge of the pew and let her touch the wound on the palm of his hand. He'd cut it earlier on a jagged metal girder but hadn't taken the time to clean it. Now it looked angry and red, a suppurating wound, throbbing insistently, a constant reminder of the evil around him. Her hands were gentle yet determined to cleanse away the grit and the infection that had developed.

"Thanks," he whispered. Somehow he couldn't speak louder in this church, but she understood his hesitancy and smiled as she bandaged the wound.

"You'll need an antibiotic," she whispered back and placed a pill in his hand along with bottled water to wash it down.

Glenn watched the girl's face, saw the beauty behind the white cheeks and tired eyes. Her hair, covered with dust, could have been any color here in the darkness of the church, but since her eyes glowed with a blue intensity, he decided it had to be black, because blue eyes often matched tumbling black hair. She was too young to have such deep lines along her mouth, but her smile was soft, tentative, almost the smile of an angel.

Did angels smile? He thought about it for a moment, but not seeing a halo or wings, decided she was a human, a compassionate human, with the hurt eyes of a young child.

"Go lay down!" she said softly, displaying even, white teeth. "I'll check on your hand later. Don't forget to take the pill and drink all the water," she ordered, looking stern.

He touched her cheek lightly, and as he did so, his heart seemed to leap in his chest. Since God worked in mysterious ways, he thought again that maybe this lovely girl was, indeed, an angel. He believed in spiritual beings just as much as he believed in God. For now, he would listen to her and lie down, because he was so tired he could barely stand. Later, he'd wake up and ask her name, and he'd thank her properly for taking care of his hand.

Asleep, he wrestled with the girders and the jagged shards of glass protruding everywhere like evil monsters. He found bloodied stumps of arms and legs, more hair, stiffened fingers, but after a cool hand stroked his brow, he finally stopped dreaming and settled into the oblivion of complete rest.

The noise of the next shift of firefighters coming into the church awakened him, and he sat up stiffly, painfully. He looked at his hand, expecting to see still-swollen tissue and a bloody bandage. It looked as if nothing had happened to it, no scar, no bleeding, nothing at all. He shook his head to clear it, and then, staggering to his feet, went in search of the first aid station. He looked for the girl with the blue eyes, but there was only an elderly woman bandaging an ankle and a young doctor dispensing medicine.

Where was the girl? Had she been part of his dream? Glenn went out into the night. He had to get back to work. As he passed one of the ambulances that had been crushed by the crumbling tower, he saw people had pasted pictures of loved ones over the hood and the sides of the vehicle, hoping they would be found and identified. For a moment he stopped to stare, and one particular picture caught his eye. It was of a blue-eyed girl with raven hair. Suddenly, he was sure it was the girl who had helped him in the church. Glenn's heart beat erratically as he realized what had happened. God must have provided him with an angel after all, and he knew that some day, perhaps in heaven, he'd meet her again.

Do we have all of life's answers? Only God truly knows. But Glenn went back to the rubble and the smoke, lighter of heart and sure of God's love and mercy.

"Heart Strings"

by Heather Hummel

Had Samantha Sunday not been in the front hallway, the gentle knock on her door may have gone unnoticed. Latching her sinewy fingers around the handle, she tugged at the door, which caught on the Polynesian area rug beneath it. She would have moved the rug a long time ago, if not for the fragile and heavy monk's chair that anchored it in place. She despised the chair. It was the one piece of furniture she wished Richard had taken with him. But its high value kept her from moving it, which risked breaking an arm or a leg. No, that would be blamed on the movers when she would eventually sell it. And so the rug remained at the mercy of the chair.

"Good evening. Are you Samantha?" asked the slight man on the other side of the door; his voice emerged from deep within his throat, thick and determined.

"Yes. You must be Paul. Please come in." Samantha stepped aside while Paul reached down with his right hand, picked up his guitar case, and maneuvered his way through the door.

"Lovely home you have, Ms. Sunday." Paul tipped his head toward Samantha, who watched with intrigue as dark curls tumbled to his forehead when he removed his black wool beret.

"Thank you, and please call me Samantha. We'll use the study. It's this way." Samantha turned and led him through the living room, pacing herself to not appear too anxious.

The bookshelves along the wall displayed several classics by Faulkner, Hemingway, and Browning on the top shelves. A number of Frank Lloyd Wright-style architecture books that Richard had left behind remained on the bottom shelves. Next month the librarian at the university was to sort through them; they were taking up valuable shelf space. The rest of the shelves were lined with Samantha's collection of romance novels. She hadn't displayed them while married, and they were now meant as an inspiration for her to return to writing after a fifteen-year hiatus. Several of her manuscripts, dating back to the seventies, rested in a box in the attic. At the time, she was living in Southern California and publishers were showing interest, but Richard showed more interest, and she was swept away to Arizona by the illusion of the perfect life he presented. The manuscripts, along with her guitar, blue jean cutoffs, and tapestries, had been boxed up and stored in the attic of their new house when they moved to Arizona. The tide of the Pacific coastline had ripped her abandoned dreams out to sea when she married Richard and left California, leaving Samantha as a housewife dressed in Chanel and entertaining Richard's business associates with delightful hors d'oeuvres and saucy baked salmon dishes that he never knew were prepared by the local market.

When they first moved in and Richard was away on business, Samantha would sneak up into the attic and pour through the boxes to reconnect with the girl who had retreated deep inside her. On the rare occasion that she talked to Richard about revisiting the manuscripts, her words were met with chuckles and reminders that she wasn't a gypsy dream chaser anymore. And, oh, don't forget Mr. McCormick and the missus were coming to dinner on Friday. As the years became decades, she visited the memories less often and eventually forgot that they sat in a box ten feet above her head.

After reaching the end of the narrow hallway, she turned into the second door on the left, the study. The other doors were closed, had been for several years. Some of the rooms had been empty and dark since the day they moved in, while others had contained hobby items of Richard's. The movers loaded those items in their truck, closing the doors behind them when they left. But the study door was left ajar on most days.

"You can put your case down anywhere you'd like," Samantha instructed as she turned on a Tiffany lamp that was given as an anniversary gift. Their fifth, she thought. The lamp sat on an end table by the lightly worn brown leather couch. The drawn curtains filtered in an adequate amount of sunlight. Opening and closing blinds each morning and evening became a tiresome effort that she had given up on long ago.

"This will do," Paul gestured toward the couch. There was only one chair, which sat in a tight corner, a wooden desk chair that rocked back and forth as effortlessly as it swiveled.

"Fine. Can I get you something to drink?"

"Water would be good. Wet my whistle, so to speak," Paul said as he made himself comfortable on the couch.

Samantha watched his hands deftly open the guitar case and retrieve his Taylor 712 six-string guitar. She admired its Indian rosewood back and sides before leaving the room to fetch her own guitar, a classic 1965 Martin 21 acoustic, and his glass of water.

Reentering the study and anxious to begin, Samantha said, "I heard you playing while I was in the kitchen. Pleasant sound." She smiled at him as she placed his glass of water on a ceramic coaster next to the Tiffany lamp.

"Don't worry. We'll have you playing your favorite songs in no time." Paul eased over, making room for her on the couch. "I usually make my students sit in straight-backed chairs, but this will work."

Samantha looked at the printed sheet of note and chord samples on the music stand in front of her. "Is that what I'm learning today?" she asked. The note and chord dots on the grid resembled a partially played game of checkers.

"Yes, some of it. How much do you remember from when you used to play?"

"That was so long ago. Another lifetime, really. I don't remember much of the chords and notes, but I guess they'll come back to me as we go."

Paul reached across and placed his finger on the bars that lay across the neck of her guitar. "As a reminder, these are the frets. They're numbered one, two, three, four, and so on," he explained as he ran his fingers along the neck and downward, slipping over each fret as he counted. "And this is the soundhole." His finger had made its way down the neck to the opening of the body.

"Yes, I remember," Samantha said, eyeing his hands. They weren't just strong; they seemed to create pleasure in what they touched, each movement made with intention.

Paul swept his hand back up to the top of her guitar and took one of the six pegs between his fingers, "These are the tuning pegs. They're for adjusting the strings, which tune the guitar."

"Okay," Samantha said, refocusing on the guitar. "Frets, soundhole, and tuning pegs. Yup, it's all coming back to me now. Well, the parts anyway," Samantha said, impatient for the awkward reacquaintance of her favorite instrument to pass.

Paul gripped his guitar and began strumming. His pick sat loosely between his fingers, flowing across the strings with purpose. "Each string plays an integral part of creating a song," he began to explain, breathing his words with the same fluid motion. "We'll go over notes and chords later. Right now I just want you to strum your guitar. Don't worry about how it sounds. Just play so you can get used to the feel of the strings, the weight in your hands, and the pick. Like this." Soft sounds emanated from his guitar. One, two, three, four. One, two, three, four. Samantha followed suit.

"You're getting it," he smiled warmly. "Are you sure you haven't played more recently?"

"Yes, I'm quite sure," Samantha laughed. "Haven't played since the days of my blue jean cutoffs."

"Ah, that long ago? I used to love my old jean cutoffs. Levi's, of course."

"Mine were so worn out. I'd pull each frayed string one by one around the edge until it caught on the seam and I'd have to yank it off."

"Where'd you play?"

"Mostly with friends on the beaches in Southern California." Samantha ran her hands along the body of her guitar, remembering a time when a day didn't go by that she didn't hold it. "We thought we were so good, but it didn't really matter if we were or not. We were having fun."

The next hour of listening to Paul play and talk consumed her attention like a child at a puppet show. Absorbed with creating music, she fell into his rhythm and relearned the simple notes and chords she hadn't experienced in a long while. Her house had been so empty, so quiet, for so long. She was taken aback by the blatant change and by the kindness of the wholesome man who sat on her couch, drawing her in like fall's equatorial undercurrent.

"I'd forgotten how much this means to me," she told him when the hour was up. She looked at his eyes, his face, his hands—her own hands wrapped tenderly around the peak of the neck and the body of the instrument embraced between her long legs.

"You did great. Next time it'll be even easier. You'll see." Paul leaned over and collapsed his music stand. His hands trembled as he placed it on the floor next to the guitar case. The curls atop his forehead flopped to the other side, blocking his eyes from Samantha's view until the backside of his hand brushed them away. "By then your calluses will have developed too," he added before taking a final sip of water.

"Oh, great," she said, looking down at her soft fingers. She somehow knew it'd be worth it though.

Paul packed his Taylor 712 away in its case and clutched the music stand in his hand. "Practice, practice, practice," he said.

"Fifty dollars for today, right?" Samantha removed her wallet from her purse.

"Yes, that'll do." Paul took the cash from her hand and placed it in his shirt's left pocket. He stopped at the front door to retrieve his beret, under which he tucked his curls, and walked out of the door without looking back. Samantha watched as he walked down the driveway, wondering if he'd turn. When all he did was pause for a brief moment before continuing, she stepped inside and contemplated moving the area rug once again.

Simple tunes devoured Samantha's practice time over the next several days. Her days filled with volunteering at the library, another avenue to reinvigorate her writing. Except for a few telemarketers, she didn't receive phone calls. Nor did she spend much time on her computer, a laptop her sister, Amanda, had given her as a birthday present years ago. An occasional e-mail from Amanda was all that filled her inbox. Samantha's so-called friends while she was married kept their allegiances to Richard after the divorce, given that their husbands were friends and business associates of his. Most of the wives couldn't pick their own brand of mouthwash, let alone their own friends. Samantha was different though. Always had been, and when Richard left her, not one of the wives called. They'd signed on for their perfect life and were determined to keep it so. Occasionally, she'd see one of them in the grocery store with their kids hanging onto the cart, begging for candy or Lucky Charms. The wife of the day would act distracted when Samantha passed by. Kids were terrific camouflage.

Three years after the divorce, Samantha remained in the house they'd bought when they had wed. She'd thought about selling it, but she didn't know where else to live. Thanks to her attorney, the settlement she received from the divorce allotted her the freedom of not having to work. Other than her sister, she had no family left, and she sure as hell didn't want to move to Wyoming. No, Arizona worked just fine.

During each evening leading up to her next lesson, Samantha strummed the steel strings of her Martin, thinking about Paul's hands, the way he balanced his leg on the ball of his foot while he played, and the way his fingers stroked the strings, creating music that left her wanting to hear more.

"Good evening," Samantha said as Paul made his way through her front door once again. He removed his beret, unveiling the glossy locks that made Samantha's knees turn to milk. This time she thought she spotted a twinkle in the green eyes beneath them.

The couch in the study felt smaller than it had the week before. Her Martin lay on the floor, strings exposed as it sat in its open case the same way the frayed strings of her jean cutoffs exposed her California tanned legs, luring men on the beach to sit on her tapestry decades ago.

"Let's spend the first few minutes tuning your guitar. I'm assuming you practiced quite a bit," Paul said. He fished out a small battery-operated tuning device and turned it on. Green and yellow lights lit up like an airport's landing strip. "Okay, strum your sixth string," he said, holding the gauge close to her strings. Samantha gripped her pick and stroked it across the bottom string. The lights all turned green.

"Perfect. Next string." And so on up, each string created a flash of green lights. "Are you sure you practiced?" he asked. "Each string is still in tune." Now the twinkle amongst the green backdrop of his eye was evident.

Samantha grinned. "Yes, I'm sure. It must be my touch," she replied. "Maybe I'm not doing it right."

"No, I doubt that's the problem. Let's get to work then." Paul placed the sheet of notes and chords on the music stand and pointed to the G note. "We're going to start with this one today," he said. Samantha emulated Paul's positioning on his guitar and stroked the string that created the G note.

"Perfect," Paul said. "Let's go on to some of the other notes so you can start putting them together into a song." He turned the page on the music stand. "Sorry I don't have a beach for you."

Samantha started to speak, but Paul winked at her, leaving her words on her lips. Her worries of fumbling along were assuaged by Paul's presence. He masterfully generated harmony from his instrument that wrapped the room like a warm blanket. Years of accumulated loneliness dissipated with each strike of a chord, each glance at his hands, each tune created.

"How 'bout 'Anticipation,' and 'Brown-Eyed Girl'?" Samantha begged when Paul asked her what songs she wanted to learn.

"That's certainly enthusiastic!" was all he said, but the next week he brought songbooks from the seventies. They sang along, laughing when out of tune, smiling when they'd hit a note correctly. The finger positioning grew complicated, yet Paul consistently managed to teach her to adapt by showing her tricks of the trade. A lightening of her spirit radiated; the sensation was surreal and engulfed her body inside out. An inner knowing of peace had arrived, but she was not ready to share it with anyone—as though doing so would risk losing it. She went to bed that night knowing she had been transformed, and for the first time since she left California, she felt excitement toward the days that lay ahead.

The only recent drop of the attic's ladder was when Samantha retrieved her guitar. The box she climbed the ladder to recover on Thursday morning sat in the far corner, where it had been placed over twenty years ago and was simply marked, "Manuscripts. 1972–1974." Next to it, a smaller box was marked, "Tapestries." Both boxes were brought down to the study.

Clearing the antique secretary next to the window, Samantha piled the manuscripts in order by date. The first one, "Heart Strings," spanned over two hundred pages. Much of that manuscript was penned late at night in her studio apartment. Built over a garage near Venice Beach, the apartment was her first place as an adult. Slanted ceilings created ambiance, she convinced herself when she moved in after her parents' death, never returning to the home she had grown up in. That house was later sold and the funds were split between the sisters. Samantha paid her way through UCLA, while Amanda moved to Wyoming and never looked back.

Yellow-stained paper didn't deter Samantha as she began typing the text before her onto her laptop, starting with the cover page: "Heart Strings, by Samantha Sunday." There were five manuscripts in all, each originally typed on a manual typewriter. She'd start with the top one and see where it led her. Without a thought, Samantha leaned over and drew the curtains open, allowing a thick ray of sun to stream across the tattered papers.

The following Monday, a warm spring day for early May, Paul's beret came off as it had every other week. The same dark curls relaxed against the forehead beneath them. And the same couch welcomed the musicians.

"Is there anything in particular you'd like to work on today?" Paul asked her as he sat in his spot on the couch.

"Yeah, will you teach me a love song?" Samantha asked as she tugged at the strings of her faded cutoff jeans.

"Restaurante Mismísimo"

by Enrique Herrera

Dining Secrets

Many restaurants in Buenos Aires are very good; some are excellent. And the more they excel, the more difficult it is to find them. Usually restaurants strive to advertise their excellence, their distinctiveness, but this is not so in Buenos Aires, where it is not about how much the food deserves the client but how much the client deserves the food.

In consequence, if you percolate inside one, irrespective of its rank, you will be closely monitored to see if you order the right wine with the right food and all the rest of the details that separate the connoisseur from the mere client. And you will be treated accordingly. In general, you will sense that you are not so much served, as provisionally admitted.

This strange behavior results, in part, from the exceedingly loud praises foreigners pour abundantly on the chefs without any consideration of the dire consequence of doing so.

One extreme case of complete disdain for the life and fortunes of the client is Signor Mismo, who named his restaurant Mismísimo. Up to now people have only rarely been able to find it. It is supposed to be located approximately eight or ten kilometers south of Plaza Congreso in Buenos Aires, on an inconspicuous street, in the underground. The streetlights in those lost neighborhoods are unusually poor, as is the illumination that escapes through the restaurant windows. Therefore, even though there are cases where some have the good luck to find the place, most of the time you can only get there in the company of an established client.

The Invitation

Mr. Lafayette, the owner of an accounting firm with headquarters in Buenos Aires and branches all across South America, said to his chief officer, Mr. Constanzo. "Have you found a good restaurant lately?"

"Not lately."

"Choosing a distinctive restaurant among so many is a daunting task," Mr. Lafayette said, "a task comparable perhaps to a predator following its prey on the Serengeti plains." Mr. Lafayette continued raising the tone of his voice. There is not one prey but many, a sea of moving prey. There is such an abundance (his index finger went up) that the predator would end up spending most of the time in the elusive catch, not on the dinner.

Constanzo, surprised at the enthusiasm of his boss, said, "Hum . . . Isn't that an exaggeration? You said predator and prey? It's only food, after all."

Mr. Lafayette, condescending, smiled. "Good food, and good food is everything, my friend. And that is a fact. I'll show it to you this same evening."

The very slim, bony face of Constanzo grinned. He seemed hungry. "Oh yes, how?"

"I'll take you to the most hidden and unknown of all."

Constanzo acceded.

After a long ride; Mr. Lafayette said with pride, "Here is Mismísimo."

Constanzo saw the building. It was old, big, and not very different from the ones around it. It was covered with large, gray, square tiles. The street was cold, deserted.

"My God," Constanzo said, "such an awful depressing hole."

"You have to understand that Signor Mismo despises ostentation," Mr. Lafayette replied wryly.

"Signor Mismo?"

"He owns the last completely uncorrupted restaurant in town."

"Uncorrupted?"

"Here you will find the silverware, china, furniture, and decorum clients used to expect for ages."

"Is it hygienic?"

"When you cross its threshold, you leave behind all the insanity, all the rush, all the anxiety of the city and find yourself in a spiritual setting, not because of its opulence, but for the dignity and the quality modern times have completely lost."

Constanzo showed a frown. "Are we talking about a restaurant or a chapel?"

Mr. Lafayette threw up his hands as if temporarily lost for words. "I don't know what to think, Constanzo. Perhaps I shouldn't have invited you here."

"I have no problem changing the dining place this evening. It's up to you," Constanzo said.

The weak streetlight showed uneasiness in the bovine eyes of Mr. Lafayette.

"Not at all," he said, "I want you to eat with me in Mismísimo. Look," he put his arm on Constanzo's shoulders; "you are the only one in the office who has some understanding of good cuisine."

"Thank you. I love good food."

"Well, I had to share this secret with you."

"Thank you."

"Frankly, it's a relief. To keep this secret about Mismísimo had become almost unbearable to me."

Already in front of Mismísimo, Mr. Lafayette ran his fingers along the door in the penumbra, looking for a handle. An eye appeared in the peephole, and a moment later the door opened with a grunt. Constanzo saw white teeth smiling from a dark face.

"Yes?" The Indian face asked.

"Mr. Lafayette and a guest."

They entered. The door groaned behind them. In the lobby a big candelabra reflected their figures. Their shadows were magnified on the mirror that covered the wall.

"It has its style," Constanzo murmured, repressing laughter.

They sat at a table for two. Constanzo inspected the place. It seemed quite small, although the walls appeared to be in the remote distance under the elusive light of the candles. Ten, perhaps fifteen tables seemed to be scattered at random. All of them were occupied and were being served by silent and efficient waiters.

Constanzo heard a suave tinkling and scraping of the silverware and the tranquil murmur of a conversation. He nodded approvingly. Mr. Lafayette sighed, relieved.

A circumspect waiter appeared and extended a stiffly starched tablecloth on the table, poured water in the cups from an enormous carved crystal pitcher, and put the appropriate silverware in the right places.

"Tell me," Mr. Lafayette asked the waiter anxiously, "is the house special being served today?"

"I'm sorry, Sir, not today."

"After waiting for so long, more than a month. . . . I wanted to show it to this friend," Mr. Lafayette said.

"You know how difficult it is . . ."

"Of course, I understand, I understand," a saddened Mr. Lafayette said. He then turned to Constanzo and said, "I wished you to know the best dish in Mismísimo. Unfortunately, it's not on the menu tonight."

"Would you like to be served now, Sir?"

"Yes."

To Constanzo's astonishment, the waiter didn't wait for the order and went away.

"Had you ordered already?" Constanzo asked.

"Ah, I should have explained this before," Mr. Lafayette said. "In Mismísimo we eat what everybody eats. Always the same for every person."

"This is unusual," said Constanzo. "Don't they satisfy the client's wishes?"

"Don't worry about it. You have my word. No matter how demanding your taste is, you will relish every morsel you take in Mismísimo."

Constanzo was doubtful.

"You shouldn't dismiss all the side benefits of the system either," Mr. Lafayette explained. "When one reads the menu in a restaurant, it's difficult to know even how to begin. One has to compare, to weigh every decision, and perhaps, to repent. All this raises your adrenaline level. That's not very conducive to a good evening meal."

"I've never thought of that."

"And think of the kitchen, too. Many sweating cooks rushing frantically across the kitchen. They need to prepare hundreds of different dishes at different times for different people. Instead, in Mismísimo we have only one serene chef employing all his talent in an exclusive task. The success is obviously assured."

"Have you seen the kitchen?"

"Unfortunately no," Mr. Lafayette said. "I described a hypothetical scene, based on conjectures made from conversations with Signor Mismo throughout all these years. I must confess the desire to really see the kitchen has become an obsession for me."

"Have you asked Signor Mismo?"

"Oh, many times. He eludes me, changes the subject. I'm a discreet man. I admire him, and . . . wait to ask again another day," Lafayette said. He looked pensively up the ceiling.

"Wouldn't be better if everyone admired the kitchen? Don't you think that is a weakness?" Constanzo asked.

"I don't. Signor Mismo is a real master of his art. He never makes concessions of any kind. I haven't lost my hope to see the kitchen, though."

The waiter returned with two cups of *consommé,* which he set in the right place with impeccable precision. From a small bowl, he slowly served a pale and watered-down bouillon.

Constanzo carefully introduced the spoon in the liquid and tried it. It had a very light flavor, almost tasteless. He frowned and looked for salt and pepper. He found none. Constanzo hesitated. Finally he said, "Excellent."

Mr. Lafayette gave him a long, expressionless look.

"I'm sure you don't find it excellent," he said. "You find it tasteless and without any condiment. I know it because it happened to me the first time too. I looked for salt and pepper also. And I discovered, as you did, that there are no condiments in Mismísimo."

Constanzo was shocked. "Not even salt?" he exclaimed.

"Not even salt. The mere fact you want to pour salt in the soup means that your taste is wrecked. Wait, when you are about to finish the soup, you won't feel the need for salt anymore."

Mr. Lafayette was right; before Constanzo finished the soup, he tasted all the subtle flavors of the soup with delight.

"Now, do you agree with me?" Mr. Lafayette asked after finishing his own soup.

"Surprisingly, I do," Constanzo said.

While the waiter took the empty dishes, Mr. Lafayette said intently, "The lack of condiments is one of the most noted characteristics in Mismísimo. You'll find out the others very soon. No alcoholic beverages at all—in fact, only fresh water. It's the only liquid a human being needs."

"Besides mother's milk," Constanzo said with a smirk.

"I could answer that the normal client in Mismísimo has long passed those early stages."

"Touché," Constanzo said, and then he gave a little laugh.

"Of course, there is also a ban on any form of tobacco."

"By heavens! What is Mismísimo? A retreat for the abstemious? I thought it was a refuge for gourmets."

"A gourmet is not a gourmand. The gourmand, even when he eats to satiety, needs increasing experiences to stimulate his senses. Not a gourmet, who is sober; simple in his taste. Take the ancient Greeks in their tunics, finding pleasure in a simple ripe olive. Or the Japanese in their small paper rooms, contemplating the stem of only one rose. They are the true gourmets."

Constanzo replied, "Just a sip of cognac in a warm cup, every now and then, or a pipe of good tobacco. You couldn't possibly call it breaking loose!"

"If we mix stimulants with narcotics (Mr. Lafayette's index finger went up) the violent upsetting of the sense of taste is such that it loses its most valued property, the fine appreciation for a good meal. During the years I have dined in Mismísimo, I have learned this to my greatest delight." The rounded face of Mr. Lafayette was more satisfied than ever.

"Perhaps there are simple earthly reasons, such as the high cost of the license to sell alcohol, or even the possibility the clients protested the smell of tobacco in such a closed local."

Lafayette was silent for some time and then answered, "Well, remember what Greek philosophers said: What exists is good, and beautiful too. They were right. The genius of Signor Mismo is the addition of one more aspect to the equation."

"And what is that?"

"What it is, is good, and is beautiful, but it is also tasty. Think of that."

"What? No way. That is too far."

"When you meet Signor Mismo, you will understand he is a man of deep convictions. He always goes beyond the limits. Nothing is too far for him."

"A puzzling man," Constanzo said as the waiter served the entrée.

Only after tasting a good portion of meat, Mr. Lafayette added, "I don't like to use grand words, but to me, Signor Mismo is a man who symbolizes the apex of civilization!"

Constanzo raised one eyebrow and devoted himself to eating the roasted meat, which was in the middle of a pool of thick juice without any vegetable or legumes garnish. The thin hale of vapor from the bowl brought to his nose such a tempting smell that his mouth watered. He chewed his portion slowly, analytically, as if he was detecting the subtle tones of a Mozart symphony. The rich scale of flavors was astounding. From the stimulating morsel of the crust to the ooze extracted from inside the meat in the first bite, everything was apparently tasteless, but it fulfilled the soul with immense satisfaction.

When he swallowed, he felt the urgent need to get another piece, and another. When the dish was finished, he realized that neither he, nor Mr. Lafayette had exchanged any words during the serving of this course. When he mentioned it, Mr. Lafayette answered, "Such a meal doesn't need any words, don't you think?"

Constanzo gave a fresh look around the room, finding it barely illuminated, with inconspicuous, clean, white tablecloths and genteel customers.

"Well, I offer my apologies for my doubts," he said. "You have not exaggerated in the least in your praises for Signor Mismo and his Restaurant Mismísimo."

The House Special

Delighted, Mr. Lafayette said, "Oh, it was nothing. Wait until you learn more. You heard me asking for the house special. Unfortunately it's not on today's menu. What you have just had doesn't compare with the delights of this special dish."

"By heavens! What is it? Nightingale tongues? Unicorn filets? Angel's wings?"

"None of that; it has not been revealed by Signor Mismo. Nobody knows. I suspect it is lamb." Mr. Lafayette became quiet, lost in his thoughts. Eventually, he said, "If I gave you my completely, frank, and honest opinion about this dish, you'd think I was absolutely crazy. In fact, just remembering the dish affects me in that way. What portion of the animal it is, I cannot tell. Certainly not cutlet, neither ham, perhaps a portion exquisitely selected from some extraordinary animals that exist only in very special places in the planet. I don't know."

"Where?"

"From Signor Mismo's scattered phrases now and then I concluded, it must be in some remote place in the borders of Russia, on a plateau, where peacefully graze the last herd of these magnificent animals."

"Where exactly?"

"All I can tell is that only Signor Mismo can get the rights to import it. He is the only *restauranteur*, if you allow me the use of this word, in the globe able to do that."

"So, when are we going to get it?"

Mr. Lafayette sighed. "It is a rare event and it depends entirely on good luck."

"Obviously, Signor Mismo could announce it to attract more clients."

"I told you, Signor Mismo renounces any type of concessions. In this case, it's easy to see why. This city is populated with a growing number of professional gluttons. If they were able to anticipate when it would be served, they would become addicted to the dish and would replace the regular clients. This is precisely what Signor Mismo tries to avoid at all cost."

"I just can't believe that we and these few people are the only ones in this city and, for that matter, in the whole world who know of the existence of Mismísimo."

"Well, that is probably true, save a few regular clients, who for some good reason, are not here today."

"Unbelievable."

"Each client has accepted the solemn obligation of keeping the secret." Mr. Lafayette's voice betrayed a vague threat. "It is implicit that by accepting my invitation you have accepted that obligation."

"My situation as your employee is enough guarantee. I only asked how sensible this practice is."

"Do you know what the consequence would be of what you advocate? It would result in a crowd of idiots complaining about the lack of chocolate sauce in the meat, night after night. Could you accept that?"

"No, I couldn't."

Calmed, Mr. Lafayette reclined back in his chair and pressed his hands together, bringing them to his lips as in prayer.

"I am a solitary man," he said. "It'd seem eccentric to you, but I feel this restaurant so deeply that to me it is a balmy refuge in this insane world. Mismísimo is friend and family to me."

And Constanzo, who always considered Mr. Lafayette a tyrant as a boss, felt overwhelmed by a pang of pity in his stomach.

In the next months, the invitations to eat at Mismísimo became a ritual. In the mind of Constanzo, the best way to protect himself in those risky times was cultivating the boss's friendship. Besides, he overheard commentaries in the secretary's kitchen about the good opinion Mr. Lafayette had of him. He was the second in command and could replace Mr. Lafayette at any time.

One day after he had taken a shower and was looking at his figure in the mirror, it occurred to him that perhaps Mr. Lafayette could once have been lean and bony too.

And the food! That incomparable food in Mismísimo! Impossible to refuse Mr. Lafayette's invitations; perhaps after tasting the acclaimed delights of the house special and meeting Signor Mismo, but never before.

After many visits, his wishes were satisfied; the house special was served, and he met Signor Mismo. Both exceeded his expectations.

When the waiter announced in a solemn voice, "Today the house special," Constanzo felt alarmed, because his heart pounded violently in his breast. And the hands of Mr. Lafayette trembled brutally.

This is not normal, he thought; two grown-up rational men as agitated as a pair of dogs waiting to be fed.

"This is what Mismísimo is all about." The voice of Mr. Lafayette surprised Constanzo. "This is the culinary triumph of all times! And we feel uneasy to experience the emotional shock that exults us."

"How did you guess my thoughts?" Constanzo asked in embarrassment.

"Your reaction at the announcement reminded me of what happened to me years ago; first anxiety, then astonishment, and finally shame and rejection for such an animal reaction. You think it diminishes us, humans drooling for food, but it is the most natural thing in the world."

"And the others, do they feel the same?"

"You be the judge."

"Right, let's take comfort the others are doing exactly the same."

"Look at that one there. He is lonely and sad."

Constanzo stared. A man with gray hair was sitting alone. The chair in front of him was empty.

"Oh, I remember," he said. "The empty chair used to be occupied by a chubby bald man, right? What bad luck. The first time he doesn't come and the house special is served."

"Tragic. Shine or rain, he has never failed to come. Imagine his face when he hears the news," Mr. Lafayette said.

Uneasy, Constanzo looked again at the empty chair.

Suddenly, the sound of a new voice.

"Mr. Lafayette! And his friend! What a pleasure! What an honor! Please, stay seated. I will ask for another chair."

Immediately a chair appeared and Signor Mismo sat.

"Our house special is about to be a sensational success, don't you think? I myself was in the kitchen the whole day, pushing the chef to do things in proper form. Oh, I realized your friend doesn't know me. Would you introduce us?"

Like a whirlwind, the words flowed from Signor Mismo's mouth, sweet, gentle, honeyed. They ran in little waves, purring, mesmerizing. Constanzo was subjugated, possessed by them.

The mouth providing the monologue was alarmingly big. The lips were thin and restless, twisted by each sound. The flat nose, the very thin moustache below; and the eyes, spaced too far apart, gave him an almost Oriental look under the yellow-pinkish light of the room. The hair was long and bright, combed straight from brow to neck. It was so pale that it seemed colorless.

"Signor Mismo, this is Mr. Constanzo, my good friend and associate."

Constanzo got up and shook Signor Mismo's hand. A warm and dry hand that felt rough to the touch.

"Such a pleasure, Mr. Constanzo, such a pleasure," the voice purred. "How do you like my restaurant? A great feast is waiting for you, hee, hee."

Mr. Lafayette repressed his own laughter. "Well, Constanzo has been eating here regularly," he said, "and he is about to become a great admirer of yours, Signor Mismo."

"It's a great compliment. I am honored; I am honored, and I turn the compliment back to you with today's house special. This extraordinary meat is far superior to everything you have tried before, I am completely sure. It's worthy of all the secret travails we endure to get it, and to prepare it too."

"I marveled more than once," Constanzo said, "why, Signor Mismo, you undertake the task of offering the special to the public if you have so many problems finding it. You have so many astounding dishes to hold up your reputation."

The smile grew so wide that Signor Mismo's face became perfectly round.

"It is a human reaction; my friend. True, the meat is very difficult to find, but when you finally get what you have been chasing, so to speak, you find great pleasure in sharing it with others. It is an enormous satisfaction seeing the obvious gratification of those who explore these things with you. Don't discount that it's a good business also."

"Considering all of the restrictions imposed on the clients, why not keep the restaurant as a private club, not as a public establishment opened to everybody?"

Signor Mismo's eyes sharpened and immediately turned in another direction.

"Good question! Well, I'll tell you why. A private club revives common suspicions. But there are so many public establishments that just one other establishment ends up being lost in the multitude. It's like a predator before a sea of prey running together on the Serengeti plains. It gets confused and lost."

"I've heard that analogy before," said Constanzo.

Mr. Lafayette blushed.

Signor Mismo continued. "Here it is all about food. We don't care about the names or the lives or our clients. We welcome them when they come. We lament their absence, and of course, we replace them."

The intense tone of the answer stunned Constanzo.

"I didn't intend to interfere," he stammered.

Signor Mismo's tongue wetted his thin lips.

"Not at all, not at all. You don't intrude. I would hate to give you that impression. On the contrary, please, ask me whatever questions you have."

"Come on, Constanzo," Mr. Lafayette said. "Don't let Signor Mismo intimidate you. I know him well. Before you realize it, he will overwhelm you with all the privileges of the house, save, of course, inviting you to visit his precious kitchen."

"This gentleman has to wait some more time for that," Signor Mismo said, caressing Lafayette's arm. "For everything else I am at your service."

"Remarkable. Tell me, Signor Mismo, besides your employees, is there anyone who enters your *sanctum santorum?*"

Signor Mismo turned his eyes toward a portrait on the wall.

"Look at the picture of the gentlemen to whom I conferred the honor," he said. "He was a noble client for many years, and he is a testimony that my kitchen is not inaccessible."

Constanzo looked at the picture. It seemed familiar. "Isn't he the famous writer who, it is said, disappeared in Europe and who used to write those magnificent short stories full of irony and dark humor?"

"Of course, I recognize him now," Mr. Lafayette said. "I remember him. Some years ago he was lean and bony. Look at that portrait now." He then said to Signor Mismo, "You told me he was a fine person. His disappearance must have hit you hard."

"Right, of course, but think of it this way. He was probably greater in his death than during his life. He was a deeply tragic man. He used to tell me that the only happy times in his life were when he sat in this chair. Impressive! Because the only favor he received from me, if you can call it favor, was to allow him in my kitchen, which is only a simple and humble kitchen."

"You assume his death," Constanzo said. "There is no proof of that, his body has never been found."

Signor Mismo contemplated the picture. "No proof whatsoever," he said softly.

The main dish arrived, taking Signor Mismo out of his reverie. He jumped to his feet and started serving it himself. When he raised the lid of the casserole, his eyes beamed through the vapors, which gave a sensual pleasure to everybody at the table. Then, slowly, with extreme care not to lose a drop of juice, he filled two plates with pieces of a dripping meat.

After finishing, as if tired by the task, he sat breathing heavily. "Gentlemen," he said, "to your good appetite."

Constanzo chewed the first morsel slowly for some time. And he swallowed. Then he looked at his fork with glassy eyes. "By heavens!" He said with a gasp.

"You like it, eh? Even better than you had imagined?"

Constanzo, bewildered, nodded. He said. "For those not initiated, it would be difficult to conceive the delights of this dish—as it is difficult perhaps to be able to see his own soul."

"What you just said shows you had a glimpse of your own soul," said Signor Mismo, bringing his head so near Constanzo's, who felt the warm and fetid breath.

Constanzo retreated slightly as not to offend him.

"If I see my soul," Constanzo laughed, "what can I see? Millions of years domesticating plants and animals. For what? Just to eat them. In the end, I can see only claws and teeth and the sacrifice of the living."

"To eat or not to eat," Signor Mismo sighed, "that is the question."

He stood up and rested his hand on Constanzo's shoulder, a suave, almost compassionate touch.

"When you sit alone in your room," he said, "turn off the lights and think on the significance the word 'sacrifice' gives to any religion. Death is inevitable and for some even desirable. Well, I am distracting you from your food."

He bowed deeply. "It was an immense pleasure. I hope I'll see you both again." His teeth flashed, his eyes beamed, and Signor Mismo walked out. Constanzo's eyes followed him as he disappeared through the tables.

"Did I offend him?"

"Offend? Him?" Mr. Lafayette said. "He loves this type of conversation. The house special is a rite for him, I assure you. You raise the subject and he never stops, like a priest trying to convert people."

Constanzo returned to his food.

"A very interesting man," he said, "very interesting."

The routine of dining at Mismísimo continued, only interrupted for few days.

When Constanzo appeared again and sat at the table, Mr. Lafayette asked, "Are you feeling better? You shouldn't be here if you are still fighting your cold."

"I'm okay."

"How did you spend those days in bed? Have you turned off the lights and seen your soul? Hee, hee . . ."

"Mine is the soul of an ordinary man. Instead . . . Signor Mismo . . . he is an extraordinary character."

The waiter came, put all the necessary utensils at Constanzo's place, and left. Some minutes later they were both eating.

". . . absolutely. But you shouldn't miss the opportunity to know him better. Talk to him. You must understand his philosophy. You can find him here before and after dinner hours."

"No, I don't think I would dare to talk to Signor Mismo."

"Do you know what happens to you, Constanzo?" Mr. Lafayette said, his finger pointing to him, "You are not only shy. You lack ambition."

On another day Mr. Lafayette said, "I fear I could be absent the next time they serve the house special."

"You, absent? I don't believe it," Constanzo said. "If that happens, you'll be missed," he added with an imperceptible smile.

"Signor Mismo convinced me to do that. Tomorrow I'll travel around all the subsidiaries in South America. Of course, the inspections are unannounced. I'll stay away for at least one month, perhaps more," Mr. Lafayette said.

"Any problems? Things are not going well over there?"

"It could be better. Things degrade without supervision, you know."

"I didn't hear anything about this in the office."

"I want to discover what tricks they've invented. It's kind of a secret. For some people here, it's my way of acting the tourist. Others think I will be recovering from extreme exhaustion in a clinic. Nevertheless, I leave the business in good hands, in yours, of course."

"In my hands?"

"When you get to the office tomorrow, you'll get a promotion; in fact, you'll be in charge of the firm. It has nothing to do with our little secret. It's obvious that you are the only person who can replace me in my absence."

"So, are you leaving tonight?"

"Yes. To tell you the truth, I kept postponing this trip, hoping to be here for the lucky evening, but I can't put it off anymore. I hope that when you have the dish in front of you, you remember this friend."

Constanzo laughed. "I will, of course," he said, starting to chew.

Signor Mismo appeared suddenly. He sat at the table.

"Gentlemen, it's always a pleasure to see you. About the kitchen, Mr. Lafayette, the invitation comes just in time before your trip. You'll be missed."

"Are you serious?" Mr. Lafayette stammered. "Are we going to witness the works of the chef this evening?"

Reticent, Signor Mismo drew a long line with his nail on the tablecloth.

"I face a dilemma of big proportions," he said, as he fixed his eyes on the line. "You, Mr. Lafayette, have been my guest for many years. On the other hand, our good friend here . . ."

Constanzo said, "I understand perfectly well. This invitation is for Mr. Lafayette only, and obviously my presence is inopportune. In fact, I have an appointment this evening. So there isn't any problem, really."

"No," Mr. Lafayette said, "absolutely not. It's not fair. We shared every meal together, and if you don't come with me, Constanzo, this experience will be less satisfying. I'm sure Signor Mismo can make an exception."

Signor Mismo glanced away from them and looked at the ceiling.

Constanzo stood up.

"I won't be an obstacle for your great adventure, Mr. Lafayette. Besides," he said, "I leave you with Signor Mismo, who will offer you a prime-time show." He extended his hand, which Mr. Lafayette shook enthusiastically.

"You have behaved like a gentleman. I hope you keep coming until I return. It won't be long."

Signor Mismo stepped aside to allow Constanzo to walk away.

While Constanzo was strolling slowly toward the door, he heard them still conversing.

"I'm afraid you'll see this kitchen for the first and the last time," Signor Mismo said.

"But, why?" Mr. Lafayette asked astonished.

"Because we have to move. This place has become too conspicuous."

"And you like a quiet place."

"That's right. As soon as I get the necessary investment, we'll move."

"Can I help in any way?"

"Oh no, Mr. Lafayette. We don't crave your help, we crave you."

Constanzo had reached the outside door. And as he stopped to get his scarf, the mirror reflected the figures of the other two men vanishing through the vapor that escaped the kitchen's doors.

Constanzo opened the drawer beneath the mirror, left an envelope with three hundred thousand pesos, and walked away.

"Jezebel's Letters"

(Originally published in *(Re)Tell Me the Stories,* 2006; based on 1 Kings 21:1–21)

by Gary D. Kessler

Andy Carmichael was the king of the hill in Racine County. His was the largest spread at the expensive end of the county, and the head of his family had been the best friend of every banker within a hundred miles back seven generations. He was ground zero at the local political party picnic, the one who was the center of guffaws, the boisterous jokes, and the lifting of the beer cans—and the one they always called on to start the trip down the fried chicken line. At the county fair, he was always the one asked to pin the blue ribbon on the prize bull amid good-natured jabs and jibes. For all of this, all he had to do was show up and be Andy Carmichael of the Racine County Carmichaels. God surely counted him among his chosen.

Andy's porcelain-blonde third wife, Carrie, twenty years his junior, was someone you could call "studiously showy." She was the sort of woman who would have been breezily termed a trophy wife in one of those big cities up north, or would even evoke knowing looks in the genteel university town just over the mountain and up the road a bit. But you could see that Andy was her whole world by the way she lit up and hung on his every word and movement. Just seeing that was enough to dispel those misty rumors floating among the young toughs down at the Pit Stop Bar.

Andy and Carrie's upslope neighbor, Ned Hollings, was anything but like Andy. His family had been in the county as long as Andy's had, but for most of the generations the two had shared the community, Ned's family had been owned by Andy's. It was only after the failed rebellion that the Hollingses had been given the plot of land farthest up the side of the mountain in exchange for working on the Carmichaels' place for another generation. Ned was not invited to the political party picnics and was not, for that matter, exactly welcome at the county fairs. He wasn't disliked in the community as much as he was discounted and just blended into the scenery. He didn't work any part of Andy's land now. But Andy still kept in touch with Ned, because Ned had the one thing that Andy didn't have and that Andy wanted.

Mother Nature is certainly capricious. Ned had a couple of acres of land on his slope that raised the sweetest and plumpest of grapes, of the prime varieties that were coveted by all of the fancy vineyards popping up all over the county to attract the wine-loving tourists. Andy wanted to grow such luscious grapes himself. But even though he put in vines that extended right up to his boundary with Ned's abundant vineyard, each year Ned's plump grapes were contrasted by Andy's shriveled raisins.

At least once a month Andy got into his Jaguar and raised dust all the way up to Ned's shack to offer him a yet-sweeter deal for his vineyard. And every time he did so, his Jaguar came skittering back down the dirt road with its dejected tailpipe between its wheels. Andy was almost beside himself with frustration. He knew Ned was getting too crippled with rheumatism to be raising grapes, and he also knew that Ned desperately needed money. His own chats with his banker friends had made sure Ned was under that short of pressure. Andy and Ned were from two totally different worlds. The only one who was even speaking to both of them was Everett Slokum down at the county seat, whose family had been lawyers and advisers to both the Carmichaels and Hollingses for generations. Andy had even tried to get Everett to talk Ned into parting with his vineyard, but Everett had just smiled his fatherly smile and said he thought Andy had enough toys already and that Ned probably deserved the comfort of a good grape harvest in the life he endured.

The last time Andy slid down the hillside and stormed into the house, Carrie thought he might do harm to himself in frustration with Ned's continued refusal to sell the vineyard. After he cooled down enough for her to approach him, Carrie took Ned's hand, led him out to the screened porch, pushed him into a wicker chair beside a frosted beer, and began to massage his temples.

"There, there, hon," she said. "You'll get your vineyard. You know it will all work out. It always works out for you."

Andy opened his eyes, and the adoration and calm trust that were reflected in Carrie's face nearly took his breath away. Ah, the simple confidence of the young and beautiful, he thought. But there was something in Carrie's eyes that did indeed bolster his own confidence. Then he focused beyond Carrie's face, out beyond the screened porch and up the hillside, where he could clearly tell where his puny, withering vines left off and the gigantic leaves of Ned's vines started, winding boisterously along their wires and reaching across the rows in splendid profusion. And he jumped out of his chair, turned over the table under his beer glass, and slammed out of the house.

It was shortly after that that people began to notice Ned. This wasn't because of anything Ned was doing—that they could see—but because of the letters. At first people just laughed the letters off, not being able to imagine that Ned was capable, let alone prone, to be doing what the letters said about him. But then the stories began to circulate down at the Pit Stop Bar, where they acquired depth and dimension. After they had floated through Reid's Grocery and the Baptist Women's Reading Club, at least bits and pieces of what was being said began to sink in and to be given some credence.

By the evening that Carrie Carmichael stumbled, disheveled, into the Pit Stop Bar and mumbled through swollen lips to the regulars Frank Tingle and Wayne Bancroft that she had been assaulted by Ned Hollings out in the parking lot, the stories about Ned were no longer being discounted as ridiculous in the community. Frank and Wayne strode out of the bar and up the hillside to where Ned was standing by his vineyard and sluicing the sweat of a day's work off himself as best he could with his crippled hands—and they beat him senseless. Three days later, the *Racine County Register* reported, a remorseful Ned swallowed the barrel of a hunting rifle and pulled the trigger.

Half the county attended the auction of the Hollings land, although no one other than Andy would have even thought about bidding for the vineyard parcel. Andy was there, of course, a fact that an enraged Everett Slokum was quick to throw back into his face.

"How could you be any part of this, Andy?" Everett asked, his face as sorrowful as anyone had ever seen.

"Excuse me?" Andy responded in confusion with an edge of hurt. "I did nothing. I did nothing at all. I'm not guilty of anything."

"Of course you did nothing, Andy. You've done nothing all of your life. You've never had to do anything. But you know what was done. And you are here getting the land you wanted—and that everyone knew you wanted—aren't you?"

Andy just stood and stared at Everett. It wasn't a mean stare; it was a bewildered stare, a stare that was totally devoid of any flicker of understanding. Carrie, clinging to Andy's side, was the one showing the mean stare—and the understanding.

And as the other members of the community became aware of Andy and Everett facing off at each other, they wavered only momentarily before almost imperceptibly shrinking away from Everett and into a protective circle around Andy and Carrie.

Everett learned of the new set of letters circulating two weeks later, letters that told lies about *him.* A week after that he moved to that genteel university town just over the mountain and up the road a bit. But he continued subscribing to the *Racine County Register* and couldn't help but give a small smile the day not too many months later when he opened the paper and saw the report that a sudden blight had destroyed all of the grapevines on Racine County's mountain slopes.

"The Nude Maja"

by Jack Trammell

She wore black because she was expected to be in mourning. It was by no means a fashion statement. White was really the only color that fully befit her temperament and taste. There was not a single stray, honey-colored hair on her black sweater; not a single wrinkle on her scandalously tight black dress; not a single, tiny blemish anywhere on her porcelain ankles, arms, or face. She was here, and that was all that *should* have mattered to the people around her.

But it wasn't all that mattered, and she knew it. Therefore, black.

They were all aware of her. Some of them, no doubt, found her a little bit improper—either she wasn't crying enough, or, for others, not being social enough. Some probably mistakenly considered her a tragic figure. Some were probably secretly attracted to her.

One woman approached her, tilting a glass of wine forward in a cautious toast.

"Cheers, Marie. You're looking good tonight."

Marie hesitated, then smiled politely, and there was a mild crease on either side of her mouth that distracted from the makeup on her face. She was beautiful, though she also had subtle scars that she worked very diligently to conceal. Most people wouldn't have guessed that she had just turned forty.

"I feel good," she said slowly, smoothly. She lifted her own glass to her lips. "I'm trying to miss him."

The other woman, Mish—which was short for her given Slavic name, Michalena—stared at her carefully, seeming for all the world about to say something else. But then she bit her lip, turning her head so that her shiny black bangs bounced on her forehead. Mish was not exactly the master of disengagement.

No one seemed to know what to say to her. Why not? Seven good years were seven good years. Besides, she had once been passionately in love with him.

Marie thought that there was nothing that felt as grand as falling in love again, and nothing equally as tragic, as well. She looked out the apartment window at the city skyline and wondered how many people in the glittering towers were staring into their own glass of wine, lost in the warm thoughts about another person who was just out of reach. How many of them were daydreaming about the touch of someone's hand, or the electricity of perfumed hair brushing against a cheek? Oh, she was certain there were plenty of people out there actually in the midst of the act of love, but it was the passion of distance that really stayed with you like a permanent hunger. It was knowing that you were connected with a person even when you couldn't see them, and could feel the invisible fiber stretching out and around and through every physical obstacle.

There were also plenty of cynics out there in the glittering towers, too, those who had grown so tired of the world that they were relegated to punching time clocks even with relationships and dreams. She wanted to pity those people, but instead she was jealous and possessive. It was too fucking bad for them if they couldn't rediscover any passion.

But it wouldn't stop her. Far, far better, she thought, to be alive, and to feel those emotions that were predestined to rule us, for better or worse. Far better, to feed the growing appetite of love.

"Marie?"

She was jolted from her thoughts by another voice. She turned and found her sister-in-law, a big-boned woman in a red sequin dress she had no business wearing, but whom everyone liked so much that they wouldn't dare say anything about it.

"What are you staring at out there?" her sister-in-law asked.

"Glass towers . . ."

"What?" Her sister-in-law grinned, stretching lipstick and lips simultaneously. "Oh, dear, you just need to give it a little more time. It always takes time. And look, your glass is empty . . ."

Before Marie could protest, her sister-in-law had snatched the glass and flown to the bar to refill it.

"There now, just relax. Go ahead. God knows it won't hurt your figure."

"Thank you," Marie said politely. Then she turned abruptly in her own attempt at nonverbal disengagement, though she hoped she could master the technique better than Mish had.

This time she faced inward, rather than outward, looking at the two pictures on the far wall of the colonnaded, marbled living room. All the other areas of the apartment emanated from the magnificent living room, and the paintings were the focus of the entire flat. They were de Goyas, copies, of course, but the most expensive reproductions available, actually painted by a computer that knew all of de Goya's paintings, and using stored graphical data from the originals, created unique but similar versions. One was the *Clothed Maja,* and the other the *Nude Maja.* Appropriately, an inviting blue ottoman like the one in the paintings was positioned right below them.

Marie knew the history behind them. No one could decide whether they were the same woman or not. Marie thought, though, that it didn't really matter. The beauty was partly in not knowing for certain. The importance was the connection between myth and reality.

Love is like those paintings, Marie had decided. Two individuals get so close that from a distance people have a hard time distinguishing one from the other. They become one like the sun and the summer breeze—and which of those could really feel so good without the other? The duality went even further than that: the nude represented sensuality, the clothed figure, modesty; one reason, and the other irrationality. They were the perfect match.

That was love, that crazy, braided invisible thread that occasionally got too tight and pulled so hard that it hurt. Or even strangled or simply called for change.

"Marie?"

Another voice, only this one had a nasal whine, and was male. It was her husband's boss, tall, gawky, and promoted to his level of incompetence, where, miraculously, he was mostly harmless.

"Yes, Mr. Hampton?"

"Call me Phil, Marie, please. And I'm so sorry about Vincent. There's someone at the door to see you."

She found her plastic smile. "Thank you, Phil. Please invite them in for me."

"Actually, they want to see you at the door," he said, in a bosslike voice.

Marie was annoyed. She immediately looked for Mish, who was so good at the role of bouncer—rude but effective disengagement—and had mastered the art of humiliating salesmen and all other forms of door-to-door missionaries. Mish was supposed to be taking care of things like that, dammit.

Mish was nowhere in sight.

She tried not to lose her cool. She handed her glass to her husband's boss, who looked at it like it was a snake.

"Fill it up for me," she said. "I'll be right back."

How could she "mourn" if people wouldn't leave her alone for a minute or two?

"Marie Sabin?"

He was in a suit, young, crew cut, and holding some kind of badge out at her like you hold a cross out to stop a vampire.

"Yes, officer?"

"I need to talk to you about your husband," young officer said.

Marie searched her head for a different type of smile and pulled one out that was pleasant, sad, and apologetic.

"Officer, we are in the midst of a memorial gathering. Isn't there a better time to do this?"

Mish appeared beside her, and Marie felt instant relief. Mish could handle this, and she would send the young officer back to his precinct office to have one more cup of coffee and another donut or two, and probably with his tail between his legs.

"Ah," young officer said suddenly. "You must be Michalena Virtustov." He botched the pronunciation terribly. "I need to see you, too."

"Mish . . ." Marie said slowly. "This is not a good time. Tell him we'll see him later. Mish?"

Michalena said nothing. She had a puzzled look on her face.

"I know this is difficult to talk about," young officer said, "but the life insurance firm required an autopsy. The coroner found some problems, and I really need to ask you a couple of basic questions. It will only take a moment or two. It's necessary to bring some closure."

"That's what I'm trying to do in there," Marie said, pointing.

He reached behind them and pulled the apartment door closed so that the three of them were alone in the gray, hollow corridor.

"What kind of problems?" Marie said.

"First of all, there were some unusual lesions on his liver. His blood alcohol count was not that high, but I need to know about his drinking habits. Did he drink very much?"

"My husband was an alcoholic," Marie said, deadpan. "Everyone knew that."

The young officer nodded. "Okay. Then about the body . . ." He looked at Mish. "You found him, right?"

Mish nodded sharply.

"There were hair samples under his fingernails that don't match his." He looked at her patiently.

Mish made an oval with her mouth, and then bobbed her head, then pursed her lips.

Marie blurted out, "I'm sure they're my hairs, officer. He liked to pull my hair when we made love."

The young officer seemed embarrassed. Marie noticed that he was very young, and very handsome. His embarrassment was attractive.

Mish jumped in before he could reply. "Now, I must say, officer, that this is extremely stressful for both of us! Is that all of your questions?"

Marie tried to call up tears and instead remained curious. Mish stepped in front of her, taller than Marie, almost as tall as the officer.

"Why is this necessary?" Mish continued. "Go inside and ruin the gathering, if you must; take some samples of hair. But please leave us alone!"

The officer nodded grimly. "I'm sorry, ladies. I will leave you alone. And it's not necessary for me to go inside—I think I can finish my report now." Mish seemed to visibly relax. "However, I do want to ask one last thing, just for my own curiosity."

Marie took a step closer to him, as if magnetized. "What is it?"

"When you opened the door, I saw the paintings. Those are beautiful paintings, by the way—originals?"

"Of course not!" Marie said, barely catching her disdain before it would have bowled him over. She quickly recovered. "What about them?"

"My question is this—did you buy them, or did your husband?"

"I did. Why is that important? Do you like them?"

The young officer shrugged. "I just wondered. They're very nice." He nodded and walked away to the end of the corridor, where the elevator swallowed him.

"Why does he care?" Marie whispered. "Do you think he understands?"

Mish grabbed Marie by the hands and carefully took her back inside. "Maybe he's gay," she said. "Forget about him."

The guests, of course, were very concerned about Marie. Mish sat down with her on the ottoman, beneath the de Goyas, and held her hands while the sister-in-law in the red dress, her husband's boss, and others hovered over her and fed her more wine. Marie felt as if a thousand clammy hands were resting on her bare shoulder. It was disgusting. It made her want to scream.

This time, her gaze went out the window and up into the sky, which was a mixture of clouds and vivid blue space. How beautiful the sky was, she thought, on those clear sunny days when there was not a trace of a cloud from one horizon to the other, and the view was as perfect as a new color discovered for very the first time. That was what love was like. Love was a sky without any clouds in it. . . . Though clouds could be beautiful, too, and had their own kind of shifting, white perfection. Being in love, she thought, is like flying in that perfect sky, and knowing that someone is waiting for you no matter which direction you chose to go. It sometimes meant ignoring the distant clouds, even when you knew a storm was coming.

A voice interrupted her once more—this time a soft, baroque, concerned voice. Marie looked at Mish, who beneath the two paintings appeared to almost be a third frozen portrait. She leaned over and kissed Mish lightly on the forehead.

"Оно сверх теперь," Mish whispered. "Please, just relax."

Marie nodded slowly, still thinking of the young policeman. He liked the paintings . . .

The woman in the paintings was a mystery, her identity, her intentions, her sexuality unknown. In the same way, she wondered about the policeman; the look he had given her when she had mentioned her hair. It made her truly sorry that she hadn't worn white.

POETRY

"Nigger Song: An Odyssey"

(From *The Yellow House on the Corner,* 1980)

By Rita Dove

We six pile in, the engine churning ink:
We ride into the night.
Past factories, past graveyards
And the broken eyes of windows, we ride
Into the gray-green nigger night.

We sweep past excavation sites; the pits
Of gravel gleam like mounds of ice.
Weeds clutch at the wheels;
We laugh and swerve away, veering
Into the black entrails of the earth,
The green smoke sizzling on our tongues . . .

In the nigger night, thick with the smell of cabbages,
Nothing can catch us.
Laughter spills like gin from glasses,
And "yeah" we whisper, "yeah"
We croon, "yeah."

"Geometry"

(From *The Yellow House on the Corner,* 1980)

by Rita Dove

I prove a theorem and the house expands:
the windows jerk free to hover near the ceiling,
the ceiling floats away with a sigh.

As the walls clear themselves of everything
but transparency, the scent of carnations
leaves with them. I am out in the open

and above the windows have hinged into butterflies,
sunlight glinting where they've intersected.
They are going to some point true and unproven.

"Sunday Night at Grandfather's"

(From *Museum,* 1983)

by Rita Dove

He liked to joke and all of his jokes were practical.
The bent thumb jiggling between two ribs, his
Faked and drunken swoon. We tipped by and
He caught us, grandfather's right, right
Up to the cliff of his pure white
Shirt, real Fruit-of-the-
Loom. We shrieked and
He cackled like
A living
Ghost.

He hated Billy the parakeet, mean as half-baked sin.
He hated church-going women and the radio turned
Up loud. His favorite son, called Billy
Too, had flown the coop although
Each year he visited, each
Time from a different
City, gold
Tooth and
Drunk.

Then out came the cherry soda and potato chips and pretzels.
Grandma humming hymns and rocking in the back bedroom.
Dad holding Billy out on a thick and bitten finger,
Saying *Here: Come on Joe—touch him.*
Every Sunday night the same.
Dad's quiet urging and
That laugh: *You've*
Got to be
Kidding,
Son.

"The Stroke"

(From *Thomas and Beulah,* 1986)

by Rita Dove

Later he'll say Death stepped right up
to shake his hand, then squeezed
until he sank to his knees. *(Get up,*
nigger. Get up and try again.)

Much later he'll admit he'd been afraid,
curled tight in the center of the rug, sunlight
striking one cheek and plaited raffia
scratching the other. He'll leave out

the part about daydream's aromatic fields
and the strap-worn flanks of the mule
he followed through them. When his wife asks
how did it feel, he won't mention

that the sun shone like the summer
she was pregnant with their first, and
that she craved watermelon which he smuggled
home wrapped in a newspaper, and how

the bus driver smirked as his nickel
clicked through—no, he'll say
it was like being kicked by a mule.
Right now, though, pinned to the bull's-eye,

he knows it was Lem all along:
Lem's knuckles tapping his chest in passing.
Lem's heart, for safekeeping,
he shores up in his arms.

"Monday Morning"

(Originally published in *Oasis,* 2002)

by Sharon Leiter

Step aside, clear the aisles,
while my wits reassemble
from every far point
of the globe. Must I say
what you know? The hostess
of dreaming would not let me go.

Though we ate your fine dog
several nights in a row,
we had quite enough left
for a pet, and he slept
on the porch, blending
in with the walls.

I bought and I bought,
though the check that I signed
wasn't mine. It was my turn to hire
and I told you the winner was you,
should the money come through.

Once I swear I could hear
the first ting of a ring
from the world at the top
of the stairs. But the straw of
that ladder of sound shredded thin,
left me no way back in.

Now I pray for the power
to open one eye, late for a life
I know nothing about.
Drugged by the heat
of a beating heart,
on the pure white beach of time.

"A Child's Tale"

(Originally published in *Tough Times Companion,* Fall 2005)

by Sharon Leiter

The children did nothing wrong.
They were playing at the shore
when the sea went away
with a bow and a wave,

and there on the ocean floor
lay a thousand fish or more,
thrashing silver and gold and green,
more than the children had ever seen.

So the little ones laughed and laughed.
Oh they never would have stopped.
But the sea came stealing back,
jumped up like a jack-in-the-box.

Though the children did nothing wrong,
now all of them are gone.

"Fame"

(Originally published in the *Virginia Quarterly Review*)

by Sharon Leiter

for Darryl

Let the big waters wash over us.
No one will know we were here
in the small offices of our souls,
gathering the light that floats
on motes of dust.

Others were quoted,
placed in the stone pantheon.

Yet we, too, ran our fingers
through glittering strands
of star hair,
tippled on mysteries,
murmured beloved theories.

Oh, yes, we were there with them,
sporting in the same
celestial playroom.
And if the world took little notice,
how should we complain?
Busy as we were
in the only universe we knew,
through the briefest of eternities,
celebrating our fame.

"Katrina: Ancestral Call"

by H. E. R. Ward

("Created through tears while watching TV and receiving e-mails from Katrina survivors")

Louie Armstrong, your trumpet must be blowing
For the anguish of your people
Sarah Vaughn, please moan for those who can't seem
To utter a sound
Duke Ellington, let your hands run across the keys
To tinkle the sound of tears from those lost in starvation
Lady Day, cry out in soft tones
As you did when you sang "Bitter Fruit"
There was bitter fruit in New Orleans
As folks begged for food and hung in lines for hours
Count Basie, play those chords and hum along
To soothe the anguish of Motherless children

Saints of New Orleans, march down those muddy streets
Playing your instruments to cleanse the toxicity
Of racism and neglect
Play hard and loud in your funeral march
To comfort those bodies who lay on the streets for days
All musicians who have gone from the French Quarters
To a better place Beyond
Spread a blanket of comfort for those who still remain
Like Fats Domino who had to be carried out to safety

Martin and Malcolm, lead us out to find a better life
And remind us when we become complacent
Medgar Evers and Fannie Lou Hamer, give us the Word
To stand before the delegates and say, "We must be heard!"

W. B. Dubois and Frederick Douglas, remind us to stand up
And orate and record our history
So this will not be forgot!
Sojourner and Phyllis Wheatley, lead us to freedom
And help us create the poems that say,
"We can't be turned around!"
Help us to bring forth those who will stand tall

We need warriors to come forth and say,
    "We will not allow our bodies to be stacked up again
    like our ancestors were in ships."
We need children and young people to walk forward and say,
    "We want the best education and we need nurturing so
    we can grow to be strong adults to fight the system bravely!"
We need allies: Black and White, Native and Latino, Asian and East Indian, Gay and Straight, Rich and Poor to stand together and say,
    "We see the Racism and we will not allow it to happen
    anymore"
    "We see it and our eyes can't be closed any longer!"
    "We see the poor and disenfranchised and we will not allow
    that anymore!"
    "We will pull together so that All people will be free!"
    "All men and women will have quality of life and
    will not be ignored and treated with disrespect!"

We need to stand together and march forth
To show the strength of our convictions and shout,
No more! No more! You will not do this to us no more!
This time it's out there and you can't sweep it under the rug
Of power and greed
It won't stay under there anymore!
This must NEVER happen again!
No more! No more!

"No One Can Wear a Hat Like a Black Woman"

by H. E. R. Ward

("Inspired by the Holsinger exhibit at QCC and thoughts of my mom and nana while I was growing up")

No one can wear a hat like a Black woman
As she prepares for church, finding her gloves and
Straightening her stockings
Greasing the children's elbows and knees
The last thing she must do
Is place that hat on her head
Tipped a bit to the side

As she pushes the children out the door
She takes that last look in the mirror
She may have made breakfast, started dinner and
Pressed a few heads but
When she walks out the door
She has a walk that shows pride
With her gloves in her hand and
Her bag tucked under her arm
She walks tall as a beautiful Queen
No one can wear a hat like a Black woman

She may have been on her knees
Scrubbing floors or
Cooking in a white woman's kitchen
She may have scrubbed clothes on a washboard
And set loaves of bread for the week
And she may have made a few sweet potato pies for church

But when she dons that Sunday hat
She walks with an elegance that is regal
And her head is held high with that wide brim

So, no one can wear a hat like a Black woman
Because it covers hard work and a life of struggle
But it adds a sense of pride that can't be removed

Today, she may not be greasing
children's elbows and knees
Because they are grown and on their own
She may not have to press heads
and fix dinner
Because she now lives alone

She may not be on her knees scrubbing floors
Because she is now a supervising scrub nurse
She may not be cooking in someone's kitchen
Because today, she owns her own restaurant

She does not scrub cloths anymore
and set any bread
Because she now sets policies and laws
She may not make pies for church anymore
Because she is now the pastor

But she still wears that hat with much pride
And no matter what she does in her life today
No one can wear a hat like a Black woman

So think about her when you enter church
Look around and admire that woman in the hat
And know that's a special woman
who needs recognition
Because she makes changes in the world
Each and every day!

"La Lectura"

(1st place poetry, Charlottesville VWC, 2006
1st place poetry, State VWC, 2006)

by Jack Trammell

A congregation of ears
Bowed reverently,
Hang on every syllable.
El Lector pauses,
Black eyes squinting over
Gold wire glasses.
"It was the best of times . . ."
He slowly states,
Rolling his tongue
Over every precious word.
The Tabaquero
Roll their fragrant cigars,
Tapping chavetas!!!
Speechless, silent, yet
Filled with words that
Spill like fluttering birds
Out the windows
Into the countryside.
Calloused hands dancing
In rhythm as
El Lector conducts.

(The cigar factory readers, or lectura, became local legends in Cuba and other Central American countries around the turn of the century. They read to cigar rollers, or tabaquero, to keep them entertained while they toiled. The readers played an important role in the Cuban Revolution.)

"The Suicide Jumper (for Kafka)"

by Jack Trammell

The weightlessness of the
Suicide jumper
Dies on the rocks or
Pavement below.
How long does that—freedom—
Persist in its existence?
Forever flavored with
Sins and regrets?
Persist in the hair's
Breadth tenth of a moment,
Before impact?
Persist in the mind . . .
Linger, languish before moving on?
The suicide jumper knows, only,
We stare,
Wondering.

"Mom"

(2nd place poetry, Charlotesville VWC, 2006)

by Marian Styles

I didn't understand until much later
that you married him because a seed was growing
and single motherhood was scandalous
in those days.

Who were you?
You played the organ at church.
Up in the choir loft above the congregation
I could stand with you,
safe and removed from the sinners below,
though all of us were seeking absolution.

You had a piano once . . .
I didn't understand until much later
that you sold it for the money.
How it must have hurt
to lose your one passion.

There was no passion in the note you wrote me
in blue ink on a three-by-five index card.
You drew a funny stick girl
and asked me to make the kids a cake.
It didn't sound like a last letter.

I didn't understand until much later
that you knew you were dying.

Maybe it was the only way
you could break free from a stifling marriage.

I didn't know that years later
I would miss you even more
than I did then.
Yet I never really knew you.

Mothers . . . daughters . . . granddaughters . . .
Your death broke the chain
and I am adrift.

"Nordic Nights"

(3rd place poetry, Charlottesville VWC, 2006)

by Inger Kretsinger

Hovering on the horizon
the sun dispensed with time.
Shadows grew
long and grotesque.

Thereafter,
a mere orange crust
devoured in imperceptible morsels
by silhouetted pine.

The evening sky transformed
yields to a milky white dress
translucent, it penetrates my eyes,
darkness never comes.

The pebbles by the fjord
bleached like ancient bones
beacon half submerged
with tales to tell.

Southern sultry nights
I have known you
so moist to the touch,
dark oblivion.

Am I weaned from you now, and safe.
Can I keep my cool detachment
all through the blond and chilly night.

"Theory and Practice"

by Inger Kretsinger

In theory we love each other
immensely,
and in practice too
sometimes
But it is early Monday morning
and I cannot recall
my lines

We really enjoy to linger
over a meal with a glass of wine
But the Redskins are playing the Cowboys
and we simply haven't the time

We used to hike
for hours
through meadows
and fields and stream
But the windows are getting grimy
and the basement
is nobody's dream

"Womanwalk"

(1st place poetry, Charlottesville VWC, 2005;
3rd place poetry, State VWC, 2005)

by Valarie Massie Watersun

I've heard tell
you were young once

That you gave birth at home in bed
sometimes alone
your screams muffled by a rag

That you grew some of the
best vegetables in the county
That you cooked and mended and tended
men and children and other women

You told me yourself once
about how your baby died
Pneumonia, you said
lips tense with old grief

I see you now
and I love you but
I have to look hard to see
rich auburn hair beneath
white and pink angel fluff;
to see plump, dimpled smiles beneath
thin lips that so often frown in pain;
and nurturing, tender hands beneath
the fragile, nervous, impatience of age

Skin the canvas
under a dripping brown paintbrush gone wild

The leather chair in which you sit,
is worn shiny, a patina of comfort
but never used so much as now
A dizzy head, you say
I fall backward, you say

You've been
in these years gone,
child, girl, woman,
wife, mother, widow,
now grandmother for me

So tell me
What's next, Grandma?
What do you await as you gaze
with such expectation
into the sunny courtyard?

"Very Old Cat in a Spring Garden"

(Previously published in *Pegasus,*
Boulder City, Nevada, 2006)

by Elizabeth Doyle Solomon

Purdy cat does not know her perfect spot
In the sun where she curls to sleep
Is the place where a tulip bulb woke
From its winter sleep a week ago.
I do not move her. She will know,
Soon enough, when the green spears rise.
She'll choose a softer spot that
Does not poke her. When its stalk
Births a single bud, she will not
Praise its coming, nor wait eagerly
Like I for the bloom. Better for
The very old cat to sleep, her white fur
A blossom in my garden.

"Road Food"

(Previously published in *Pegasus,*
Boulder City, Nevada, 2006)

by Elizabeth Doyle Solomon

Road traces the ridge's spine,
Etches a line along fences
Past poison ivy posts,
Dirt lanes to rusted gates,
Ponds of snappers, suckers, snails.
Tree-dappled, sky-covered,
Road leads, feeds spirit starved
For onion-air, hay scent, cow smell,
Food as fine as figs or wine.

"Dried-Fried Lady"

(Previously published in *Pegasus,*
Boulder City, Nevada, 2006)

by Elizabeth Doyle Solomon

Sun-worshiper ahead of me
In the grocery line, baked brown,
Extra well-done, rotisserie skin
Wrinkled, crinkled, mummified.
I wonder if, Egyptian-style,
Brain was plucked through her nose.
Why else would she deep-fry,
Hamburger body in skillet sand,
Or one of those total-tan cocoons?
Leathery hands hissed as her bills
Kissed the cashier's withery white ones;
And when she smiled, I heard cracking,
Chips from her lips, chin skin
Crumbling, exterior flesh falling.
She left a trail, dried-fried lady crackers,
Only bone parts pushing shopping cart.

"Intimate Touches"

(Previously published in *Pegasus,*
Boulder City, Nevada, 2006)

by Elizabeth Doyle Solomon

Intimate touches translate
Emotions into motions,
Words dark as blackbirds
Fly across the page
Out of this writer's cage,
Smith-Corona typewriter.

"Streetlight: A New Orleans Memory"

(Previously published in *Nomad's Choir,*
Queens, New York, 2006)

by Elizabeth Doyle Solomon

Streetlight, city light, siren and horn
Set the city stage where I was born—
Steam boats, tug boats, ocean-going ships
Rode the river. I rode Mama's hips.

Humid and hot, sticky Delta heat
On the buses where whites got front seat—
Streetcars hummed past each house with a maid
While I sucked ice, read books in the shade.

Night jasmine bloomed a scent like perfume
When death took Mama with him too soon—
Streetlight, city light, siren and horn
All muffled my sobs that August morn.

Katrina destroyed without pity
My New Orleans, my native city—
Mama gone, Daddy gone, streetlights too,
Lakefront a sad, devastated view.

Duct-taped freezers, antiques on the street
In the humid-hot sweet-sticky heat—
Red paint marks each house, smeared on the door,
Where nothing but mold lives anymore.

Streetlights, fog horns, hurricane lamps,
Tramps find homes under overpass ramps—
Humid and hot in New Orleans heat,
Where my memories live, sad and sweet.

"Emily Cat's Purring"

(Previously published in *Mid-America Poetry Review,* Warrensburg, Missouri, 2006)

by Elizabeth Doyle Solomon

Emily cat, twenty-year-old brown tabby,
Stretches out in the gravel beside me,
Both of us soaking up thin sunlight.
I stroke her softness,
Feel the ragged rumble of her purring.
It is as old as Emily, new as spring.
She cannot hear her purr. Those deaf ears
Rely on hand-stroke, sun-warmth, spring-light.

"Work Boots"

by Sheila Moore

Walking back from the garden
I stumble over your work boots
left to dry on the porch
after yesterday's rain.
Anger leaps from me, but then,
remembering your hands among
the lilies and against my thighs,
I chase annoyance with
a half-caught breath,
holding out yesterday and
the cool scratch of pillowed daisy
you slipped behind my ear.
I decide to bake an apple pie,
forbidden fruit these days, but
it says love and I need to say it.
And the making—the salutary peeling,
slicing, cutting-in and crimping—
will surely put to flight, for now,
the heart-scalding fancy
of empty porch.

"Thirty-Three, With Brie"

(First published in the *Plains Poetry Journal,* 1990)

by Sheila Moore

Atop a country quilt she sits at dusk,
appropriately clad in something soft
and loose-fitting from Bean or Carroll Reed,
a touch of twisted gold against her skin.

Is this Saratoga? Aspen? Wolf Trap?
Tanglewood? No matter. She is the same
everywhere, smartly poised on her bright stage
waiting for the conductor to begin.

Her wicker basket holds chilled Chardonnay.
There's a good bread, salad with vinaigrette,
ripe yellow pears and a tangy, soft brie.
She does not forget the slender dark mints.

With help from Martha Stewart she has baked
a delicate tart, buttery and crisp.
It sits inside its own cunning holder,
covered over with a linen napkin.

Her husband, lean, fit and tanned—a lawyer
perhaps, or possibly an accountant—
reclines at her side discussing the Dow
with their concert guests, doubles of themselves.

All are thirty-three or -four, thereabouts.
The well-groomed husbands are junior partners,
moving upward along their career ladders.
They are quick, energetic, self-propelled.

Their stylish wives have challenging careers,
as well. Live-in nannies care for children
who are called Justin, Caitlin, or Heather—
bright angels who are verbal and love tests.

She passes out the goblets, cuts the bread.
They sip the wine, enjoying Beethoven
with the succulent pears and nutty brie.
The salad adds a complementary zest.

They wave to fellow members of their club
during intermission, exchange tidbits
about the book fair, the new headmaster,
the dreadful rents they're charging at the beach.

"Ode to Joy" completes the pleasant evening.
Contentment fills her up with gratitude
for lovely music, friends, her golden life,
her joy in being thirty-three, with brie.

"Five Elements Poem"

by Romney Brand

Appearing separate
We are burning
In the same fire
Surrounded by water
Bathed in air
Resting on earth
With space between us
Just enough
To keep our
Conversations
About ideas
Appearing separate

"Special Blessings"

by Romney Brand

On my right is perched
The bird of my desire
Singing of life's colors
Gold, brown, and sky blue
The pure white of lacy clouds
The beige of bleaching bones
To my left side
A more constant companion
A wise raven
He croaks of beginnings and endings,
Of the free void,
Of peace through victory
Only in death
This strange fellow speaks of things I
May never truly know, yet
I have touched them
I hear him always, he
Drowns out his comrade at times
His reason is unknown
He grows so heavy
They grow so heavy

"Wind Blows"

by Romney Brand

Wind blows
Supple branches sigh
Leaves fallen
Whisper their reply
Birds are gone
Nest is alone
Until winter's wane
Flying or blown
Birds return
Each to its own
Nature scorns
Seeds poorly sown

"Common Sense"

by James Culmer

Prescription for the sickness of our nation
Common Sense

Make good sense to the common problems we face
Side effects to what we see are
Hallucination
Hell loose in this nation
But we only see what we want
When we want
But why we want it is a mystery
We lack the sense of a common goal
Pacified to see what they want us to see
But don't hear what we need to hear
If hell affects our nation, when does heaven step in?
It has but diminished by
No prayer in schools
Putting the right hand on the Bible in court
But lying for the sake of self justice
Currency states, "in God we trust"
But trusting in what that bill stands for
"Greed"
Who plays the devil's advocate?
Whoever runs the show?
Whoever holds diplomatic power
Whoever holds the capitalist cane and wears the robe that covers lies
Inches towards lies
Miles away from truth
But smiles come a dime a dozen

Common sense to us is
"Complicating systematic ingeniously collaboration of states democratic policies"
See what I mean?
Makes no sense but
No sense is our common sense
So we sense that
Since the government put
Cents into their
Sense of urgency for the country
Common sense minus nonsense is the common denominator of
No sense for our democratic process
Which in turn makes
No sense

"Straight to Hell"

by James Culmer

Eat, drink, and be merry, disregarding life
    I was on a heated silver hollow tip bullet straight to Hell
All laughs and smiles, boastful and proud
    Yet soul and spirit hurt, no one knew, who could I tell

Took life for granted, I laughed at death
    Matter of fact, I smiled in his face
The green canopy covering mourning family with flowers
    He wanted me to fill that empty space

When death became a reality, two inches from my presence
    No more smiles, no more games, fear had filled my heart
One death demon, another death angel
    Both pulling at my soul, how could I tell them apart

All of a sudden I now feared death
    There was nothing else that could be worse
All through life disregarding the signs, now
    Cold, dark, eyes sealed shut, family scratching at a brand new hearse

It is when death had me cornered up against the wall
    That I hoped the bullet would stop
It slowed down but death pulled harder
    Hoping that six feet into earth's core is where I'll rot

How can I, me, go through this eternal battle
    How can I, me struggle from within
Death trying to kill me, life trying to save me
    My mind trying to convince me who would win

One simple phone call in the midst of the struggle
    Death's grip had no choice but to release
The bullet stop moving and life gave me a second chance
    To do right and try to find peace

"Bare Huntin'"

by Herbert F. Frisbie

My Dad is goin' huntin' and it gives me such a scare.
He said when he goes, this time, he's goin' huntin' bare.

I don't understand at all, and I sure can't see why,
He'd go without his clothes and things that keep him warm and dry.

He's sure to take his gun and knife; and I know he is tough.
But I can't see how those few things could ever be enough.

I'll talk to Mom; and maybe she can show him there's a reason,
So he'll go huntin' in his clothes, and go bare in fishin' season.

"For Sale—Cheap!"

by Herbert F. Frisbie

Being the mother of three small kids,
Most days it's really just fine.
Other days, each of them tries, it seems,
To drive me out of my mind.
I love them all; they are priceless.
Yet, some days I'm tempted to say,
"You can have the whole bunch for nothing;
And I'll pay you to haul 'em away."

"To Me"

by Herbert F. Frisbie

To me a woman's many things;
Perfumes, dresses, hair and rings,
Lipstick, laughter, smiles or frowns,
Corsages, furs and evening gowns.

Long limbs, curves and jewel-like eyes,
Tender touches, soft lips, sighs,
Scathing looks or puzzled frowns,
Bubbly, purring, teasing sounds.

Prideful, patient, some demands,
Warm, vibrant, soft beneath my hands.
A comfort, near me, in the dark,
A treasure chest to hold life's spark.

Someone who'll talk to me, or listen,
And nod or smile or let tears glisten,
She'll try her best and do her part,
To sooth or heal an aching heart.

Lover, friend and confidant;
More than I could ever want.
One to give that needed shove,
Yet be admired, respected, loved.

"Moma's Cookin'"

by Herbert F. Frisbie

I hunger for them good ol' days, when I still lived at home.
Things my moma did for was honey from the comb.
Moma reared me up to be a fairly able gent.
She showed me how to shop and buy so money was best spent.
She showed me how to mend my duds; and I heed her advice.
I wash 'em all, right regular, so's to look and smell real nice.
Mom's done a passin' job on things what she has taught me.
But, I've been havin' trouble with the recipes she brought me.
I try to fix meals just like her; I stew or fry and turn 'em.
But what I fix don't taste like hers. I ain't learned how to burn 'em.

"I'm Always Getting Letters"

by Herbert F. Frisbie

I'm always getting letters, in my mail, that clearly say,
Their pills will make me young again, although I'm old and gray.

My sex life isn't gone, they say; and they can now revive it.
Their magic mixture cannot fail; 89% survive it.

They claim my sex drive will return (this fills me with dismay.
I've waited years for it to die or wander far away.)
They have exactly what I need, so order some today!

There is no risk, for after I have taken 10 or so,
And things don't happen as they said, simply let them know.

Pack up what's left and send it back. (Right here's where it gets funny.)
When they learn what the problem is, they'll send back all my money,
Less P&H, insurance fees for refunds out of state.
When added up I find that I still owe $10.98.

"A Spark of Rain"

by Seth F. Hartman

Dew's fingers fall heavy
Petting wetly as they seep
From blankets of clouds
Lulling sleep, to sleep

And Dream's rain dries
One last droplet of dark
Wets the yawned eye
With night's lingering spark

Then nails claw the rooftops
To seek night's wet cool
And into this storm
Storms the stirred soul—

Journey's gray seas
Of metal steeds flowing
Amidst prows of light
Dream's dark droplet glowing

Sky's nails turn to talons
That rape naked eyes
With splinters of ice
Split from split skies

And the waked tempest snarls
Its fangs white and flashing
Unsheathes pouring claws
Ten thousand all slashing

Yet the remnant of soft rain
Still in lid's corner
That refuge beyond thought
Grows brighter and warmer

And the Pause Between Nothings
Its drizzle receding
Whimpers and dims
Its gray flanks new bleeding

So sleep—if not knowing,
If light in dusk's deep,
Then a candle, now glowing
Lulls sleep, to sleep

"Rights of Spring"

by Margaret Edwards

I'm sitting on my balcony
accosted by a buzzing bee
who doesn't seem to know, today,
that spring is still a month away.
How can I tell you, wretched bee,
you are anathema to me . . .
that now, this early in the year,
I cannot bear to have you here?
Go find yourself an early flower,
and get away from this, *my* bower.
Remove your buzzing from my face
or I may swat you to a place
that's nowhere near a state of grace.

"My *Cat* Visits the Vet"

(A short dialogue)

by Margaret Edwards

You embarrassed me so!
Well, who took me there?
I warned you we'd go . . .
They messed up my hair.

I did this for you.
Tell me another!
And you raised such a stew . . .
I want my real mother.

I'm caring for you . . .
fine way to show it.
and it cost a sweet sou.
So . . . I threw a sweet fit.

You acted the fool!
Let's not go into that.
You need reform school.
Hell no. I'm a CAT.

"Free Dinner"

by Margaret Edwards

The floodlight drew night insects
by the score—
wings gleaming bright—
outside the kitchen door,
while ponderous toad below,
in jovial mood,
cast lightning tongue—
and quickly gulped his food.

"Slow Trip"

by Margaret Edwards

The rain came, and the rain came . . .
the damned stinkin' rain came.
It pelted the car hood
like BBs on brick;
the windshield looked
like a big oil slick;
the wipers kept saying
"squeek-thop. squeek-thop."
I'd like to get home,
so I wish it would STOP.

"Sweet Briar"

by Sigrid Mirabella

Prick my hand, sweet briar.
Sharp, your nettles pierce my heart.
Your breath so pink to bruise my soul. Rose,
You who suck my breath away with your small petals,
Pause me to moon for green rapture:
My breathless days.

O dewy mimosa, excite my nights.
Fitful fragrance, find me again,
That I might dance dressed only in honeysuckle
Braids, dappled beneath pure starlight.
There have me hunt hidden daylilies,
Touch their pure buds before
Day coaxes from them their fleshy blooms.

Embrace me in my impatient hours, mother lilac.
Soft your scent to still my eagerness.
Restore me to wonder the worth of ants, spider philosophies.
Help me, please, to recall the stinging courtship
Of spring-drunken bees. Violets call for them yet
With spicy pollen, pray they will love them forever.
Shall I weave a daisy crown for my head and sit
Amid them in purple fields?

Prick my hands, sweet briar, that my bloody fingers carry you.
Sit you pink upon my wooden windowsill. Shame
Me with your fading face that I dare
To think your wildness set in glass and water.
Forgive me my sins to steal you from thorns,
To believe your pink revives my own.
Precious petals pale and wilt
The scent lingers
Nevertheless.

"Signed"

by Sigrid Mirabella

Eleven years old:
My name carefully carved,
S and G the hardest letters. Youthful,
My sure hand. Unskilled and raw
My truth. Small feet precarious,
Standing upon freckled stone. Huge
And mica mined by me already
Five times over. Did I trust
A wizened beech tree then,
Would stand up to time now,
Repeat my name to them born soon
When I have gone, passed to earth
And rich for trees: saplings
Nourished by breezes and me.

Should I dare dream now?
My forest razed, my beech bark tablet crooked
Between a house and cedar fences, holding
Wood no longer readable.

"Winter View"

by Sigrid Mirabella

Two white lawn chairs
In the snow
One with a red bow

Their view—leafless
Trees, struggling
Red leaves sacrificed to a merciless winter

"You"

by Sigrid Mirabella

The brilliant air cannot compete with you
The intensity of you
The importance of you
Nothing can compete with . . . .

The shining sea-foam birth of you
The heat of you
The cold of you
Nothing can compete with . . . .

The raw power you possess to turn upside down
Into right side up, even
When you don't believe in you
The salt is self-healing
It is not transferable to others

Not me
Not perfect in my answers for riddles without answers
Not wise in my responses to questions asked in haste
Not reflected upon by you
Me

Watching wary waves cast
Sea-stones to a vanishing shoreline
As if to toss away connections
Me

Watching froth pull back
As if to dissolve away into sand
Desert only with no rain to complicate
Stars and sun and the moon traitorous that

The night cannot compete with you
The daylight cannot compete with you
The force of you
The influence of you
Nothing can compete with . . . .

You

"Morning"

by Linda Levokove

Sleepy whispers
tickle my ear
practiced touches
play on my skin,
and your lips
soft as eiderdown
blow butterfly kisses,
nectar sweet.

Promise of love
tenderly orchestrate
the fragile unfolding
of each precious day.

"Sunset"

by Linda Levokove

Sunset is the saddest light,
Heralding the death of day.
The sun yields to night's embrace
As evening's curtain descends

One bright and shining star appears,
Heavens promise of a golden moon.
While cricket orchestras rub legs in unison
And dancing fireflies welcome the evening.

"Singles Party"

by Linda Levokove

Rainbows of garden party dresses . . . .
Softened by moon-glow

Shimmering stars in summer skies . . . .
Promise romance.

Whispers of barely concealed excitement . . . .
Rouge powdered cheeks

And mounds of soft creamy flesh . . . .
Peep from daring decollate

As night dark shadowed eyes . . . .
Sparkle seductively

While red lips, wet with anticipation . . . .
Taste the maleness in the air.

"Scattered"

by Stephen Mirabella

I have little bits of poetry
lost all over the place
scraps of half-remembered
half-devoured
reliquaries of grace

See this napkin stained with
spittle, ink, and smearing words
cranky bits of crappy
Sweep them up with the crusts and crumbs of breakfast
the paid bills and past-due notices

The best lines of this poem
are lost
between the pages
of some book
put back upon the shelf

"Solitude"

by Stephen Mirabella

I live in a good room,
Overlooking the plaza,
Airy but small,
Across from the stars

The moon is my neighbor
And for many years now
It has been our habit
To sip wine and sing
On Friday nights
After work
If she is in town
Howling at the earth

In the room beyond
Lives the Darkness
And no one knows
We are lovers

It is no secret
But our ferocious feral love
—hot, moist, and desperate
In wet sheets—
Feels wilder

When the moon and the stars
Are not at home
To overhear our bestial gruntings

So we strain in the hot night air
Under the muffling sky
Violent in our passion
We climax with the lark

And when the morning comes I cry myself to sleep

"A Recurring Dream"

by Stephen Mirabella

First Night

I saw a fallen branch
Lying broken in the shade—
An accusing finger
Pointing at the traitorous sun

Second Night

I saw a broken branch
Lying fallen in the shade—
A mournful finger
Reproaching the sun

Third Night

I saw
A fallen branch
Lying broken in the shade
Barely visible amid long shadows
And light patches glimpsed through the car window

I thought
The shadow of a bird
Followed us all the way down the gravel drive
As the wheels rolled slowly past the cemetery gate

Someone broke the churning sound of stones
That clogged my ears.
"That branch is pointing at me,"
A voice without passion remarked.
I couldn't see who was speaking.
"Don't be ridiculous," I answered,
And traced the outline of the limb into
The rear window glass, frosted with our breath,
"That branch belongs to me."

A drop of water ran from my fingertip as I spoke
And disappeared down the crack of the car door.

(Untitled)

by Julie Chan

"Now I see the secret of the making of the best persons.
It is to grow in the open air, and to eat and sleep with the earth."

— Walt Whitman

My son, two and a half, careens down
The garden path with child-sized rake
In hand like an untamed piglet,
Gates raised, he bolts from the confines
Of his pen, banshee squeals cut loose,
Could care less who sees and hears him.
Up and down he runs not minding rocks and ruts,
Not minding the small piles of creeping Charlie
And chickweed chump change.
He communes with the earth's grubs,
The cabbage butterfly's gauzy beauty
Hovering around the brassicas,
Seeking indistinguishable places
To lay its eggs, no distinction made
From the lacewings, delicately feeding
On the insect eggs, sweet and crisp peas.

Bite down rabbit deer chicken insect
    human animal.
The garden attracts us all, nourished and
    healthy.
Grow in the open air
Eat and sleep with the earth.

"My Ole Style"

by Lucille Grimm

My hands grip and hold,
The cold brew, it fizzes,
As I twist off the lid,
My warm lips touch,
Lightly the rim,
I consume the darkness,
It fills my mind,
A shadow passes before my eyes,
I search empty spaces,
To find, vague memories tease,
And taunt, did I know you,
Once upon a time?
The darkness, a void,
Collects blurred faces,
I stand on the brink,
A glimmer slips in,
Who Am I?
But, cold is the night,
That torments my mind,
Death, will release this,
Demon of mine,
This demon, I could not,
Confine.

"Dream Dragons"

(Song lyrics)

by Lucille Grimm

Verse One:

Dreams . . . Can be magic,
Dreams, I imagine,
Suddenly I'm flyin,
On wings of a dragon,
Higher I soar,
On a dragon, I roar.

Verse Two:

Stars wink by me,
The moon is a sliver,
Cool, the wind feels,
I start to shiver,
I'm all aglow,
Through dreams, I quiver.

Verse Three:

Yes, I can dream,
If I desire,
Dragons that live,
And breathe fire,
Magic on wings,
Is all I require,

Chorus

Dreams . . . Can be magic,
If you imagine,
How can this be?
Just look at me,
Flyin, free,
Yes, I will be flyin free.

"US"

by Catherine Wolniewicz

Imbued
in an
orange sherbet mist
sent by a fleeting
embrace of
sun
as it slipped behind
our tangled silhouette

we listened
as dusk formed
a tender blanket
of silence
upon us

intoxicated
in
each other
still

"Sneaky Spring"

by Brenda Morris

Spring softly slithers in under
the belly of Mad March,
and then bursts forth
bearing buds, blooms, bouquets.
Colors explode in exaltation
of her petulance presence.
Spring titillates and teases,
promising eternal youth,
then suddenly disappears
in the flaming heat of June.

"Visit at Dad's Grave"

by Lauvonda Lynn Meade Young

A whorled oak flings a spidery shadow
Across iridescent squares of green
Edged orderly side-by-side
In this hapless place
Where old bones lie eternally
Summer gulps its last breaths
Leaves unhurriedly prepare for their
Fall cavalcade—while all of nature
Begins promenading into another season
If only my faith was as strong as yours
I could believe that just as the seasons
Resurrect perpetually, you
Metamorphosed out of your moldy coat
Put on a newbodyandface
Dressed again in spring raiments and
Traveled to Heaven on ethereal wings
If only I could believe
I would no longer be shackled to reality

"Waiting"

by Laurie M Lawson

Tumultuous morning blends into horrific afternoon.
I have to leave my toys behind and my pets!
"When will we go back home?" I ask.
Mom just cries as Dad is pulled away.
So many questions, questions, questions.
And Mom just cries.
Vacant eyes, scared eyes look down at me.

We are poked and prodded by doctors
And some are taken away.
Their families scream as if in great pain.
"Why Momma, why?" I cry as I cling to her tired arms.
"Shush, just be quiet," she shouts.
I am cold and bored and anxious.
I think we will come to great harm.
And Mom just cries.

The line stretches forever in the cold.
Now we must take off our clothes.
"No!" I shout but Momma says that I must.
I am forced to take off my new dress
By a soldier whose eyes are filled with lust.
Soldiers, who hours before played silly games
And sang songs with us kids.
And Mom just cries.

Into the showers we go.
Old women, young women, children.
Droopy, sagging boobies, small ones, and ones
Not even developed.
“Why Momma do we have to wash?” I ask.
“Shush, be quiet.” Says Mom as we stand under the stream.
I do not feel so well. Hot, dizzy, crowded, choking
Choking, choking, choking, choking, choking, choking.
And I die as Mom cries.

Our story does not end here.
Our bodies are placed none too gently into great ovens.
No apple strudels or fresh bread for us anymore.
No more happiness, friends, love, or cheer.
We rise, light as air up to heaven.
We will never cry or be cold anymore.
And the world cries.

"On the Edge of a Great Precipice"

by Laurie M. Lawson

On the edge of a great precipice
Sadness can not even describe the cold
Rocky bottom to which I have fallen.

Compare a child's first sip of Daddy's beer
And the self-rage of an alcoholic.
A tiny tongue sticks out or a whole body
Is wracked with vomiting and illness.

Novel and exciting to constant bombardment
Of the body and mind.
Lazy, tired minds must die or haul themselves up
This craggy, sharp, and steep climb.

Sunlight and happiness are not signposts
On this journey.
Wrong route, keep walking and searching.

No person can help, no money can buy,
No physical attributes can sway,
No personality can dazzle, no sharp whip can stump,
No thing will aid your journey.

Dogged perseverance and shadowed faith
Provide minimal comfort and support.
Some will choose the "easy way out."
Do not pity them nor judge.

Peace pervades their ashen faces.
Anxieties, tension, guilt, anger, and sadness will follow them.
Parasitic cycles will not end.

Those who choose to climb, will do so
While wasps lay eggs under your skin
Attempting to steal your will to live and strive.
Feet will bleed, sweat will slicken tricky steps.
Your very own gasps of breath will blow dust and grit
Into your eyes and blind you momentarily.
Those few seconds with eyes closed are your only respite
From this torture.
Pray for distractions.
Climb!

PROSE NONFICTION

"The Final Challenge"

(Excerpt from *Thomas Jefferson on Leadership*, 2002)

by Coy Barefoot

The boisterous sea of liberty is never without a wave.
— Thomas Jefferson

In his award-winning study of the character of Thomas Jefferson, *American Sphinx,* historian Joseph Ellis writes that "different versions of him as both hero and villain are loose among us, and different claims on the Jefferson legacy have become a permanent feature of contemporary American culture." Jefferson can be "all things to all people."

The nature of his legacy will long continue to be a source of debate and discussion, as well it should be. For when we contemplate the influence, character, and philosophy of Thomas Jefferson, we come face to face with the paradox at the heart of the American experience—how do we reconcile the ideals of individual freedom, human quality, justice, and the pursuit of happiness? They are not always and in every circumstance mutually compatible.

For many people Jefferson is the apostle of democratic liberty—his inspiring prose and extraordinary life offer illumination at every turn. For others he is the ultimate symbol of America's ability to screen injustice and inequality behind a veil of eloquent rhetoric that sings the promises of progress. Either way, we can agree that Jefferson provides us ample fodder to consider improvements in our own lives.

Key themes have emerged as we have considered his life from the perspective of leadership—an emphasis on self-improvement, education, and responsibility; an enduring faith that human beings have the capacity to do great things with their lives if they are given the motivation, opportunity, and freedom to succeed; a belief in character, merit, and talent over wealth and privilege; an unwavering optimism for the prospect of a democratic society; an understanding that effective leadership means empowering others; and a decidedly practical approach to opportunities and challenges.

Jefferson's pragmatism teaches us to remain absolutely fixed on the goals we have set before us as a free people. But we should remember that those goals are not good government or even less government; compassionate conservatism or enlightened liberalism; bipartisanship, profitable industries, peace in the streets, or democracy itself. No, those are not the goals.

Our goal as a free people is the preservation and strengthening of individual human liberties—protecting everyone's inalienable rights to life, liberty, and the pursuit of happiness. All else—government, business, or the law—is just a collection of tools we have developed to help us achieve those ends. And as Jefferson so wisely cautioned us, we must not confuse the two or sacrifice the end to the means.

Perhaps the most important thing we can learn by considering the life and leadership of Thomas Jefferson is that the battle against tyranny, corruption, and injustice is never finished. Jefferson was an ardent student of history, and he had a firm grasp on the realities of power in society. He understood that "the natural progress of things is for liberty to yield and government to gain ground"—and not just government, but any human institution that profits from the suppression of self-rule and civil liberties.

Circumstances of history present every generation with new challenges that demand a reinvigorated commitment to the preservation of liberty and the cultivation of inspired individuals to lead the fight. Leadership is no academic enterprise. Freedom is never a guarantee.

At the start of the American Revolution, wealthy men could avoid the military draft by putting up money for substitutes to take their place. The poor, on the other hand, had no choice but to enlist and risk their lives. Historian Howard Zinn has written that this situation led to rioting in the streets of colonial America, where people were heard to shout, "Tyranny is tyranny, let it come from whom it may!"

Thomas Jefferson swore "upon the altar of God eternal hostility against every form of tyranny over the mind of man." In his own lifetime, that meant risking everything to take on a government of aristocrats often guided by self-interest and not by the best interest of the majority of people. It meant going up against the Anglican Church, which was intent on using the powers of state to extend its authority.

What about today? Where does tyranny take shape in our own time? There are some people who identify it precisely where Jefferson did two hundred years ago—in an indulgent government dominated by the interests of the rich and powerful, or among religious institutions that seek to exert undue political influence.

Others find tyranny in an activist judiciary, in the commercial media, or in the militarization of law enforcement. Still others see it in the globalization of mammoth corporations that wield unprecedented power throughout the world, putting private profits ahead of democracy in the name of "free trade." Tyranny has the potential to exist wherever the door to democracy is slammed shut, where the fundamentals of liberty are subjugated to concerns of profit and power, and whenever consumerism becomes more important than citizenship.

No matter where people take their stand against the autocratic tendencies of any institution, Thomas Jefferson is there to inspire their mission. The positive aspects of the legacy of his leadership teach us never to be complacent when the principles of democracy are at stake. A global justice activist Sarah Blackstock has written:

> The struggle is about insisting that democracy is more than regular, well-managed elections where citizens choose representatives from among a narrow group of like-minded elites. Democracy is about self-rule. It's about people participating in the political activity and decisions that affect our lives. It's recognizing that

> neither politicians nor a faceless market drive society. It is people—our work and ideas—who create the kinds of worlds we live in.

Inspired by Jefferson's leadership, courageous men and women will always stand at the ready, prepared to fight tyranny of any form, no matter from where or whom it may come. Acclaimed historian Rhys Issac has commented that

> Jeffersonian principles stand as a perduring expression of the highest collective aspirations of the nation, while the confounding inequalities of his own and our present times remain a constant admonition that the revolutionary struggle is always to be kept up. It must be avowed that his predicament is still the nation's: the predicament of being enmeshed in forms of systemic injustice that seem forever to require radical redress.

You have heard the call to leadership. Your final challenge is to accept that call, to make the decision to be a leader, and to join the fight against every form of tyranny over the mind of humanity.

Some men look at constitutions with sanctimonious reverence and deem them like the arc of the covenant, too sacred to be touched. They ascribe to the men of the preceding age a wisdom more than human, and suppose what they did to be beyond amendment. I knew that age well; I belonged to it, and labored with it . . . Laws and institutions must go hand in hand with the progress of the human mind. As that becomes more developed, more enlightened, as new discoveries are made, new truths disclosed, and manners and opinions change with the change of circumstances, institutions must advance also, and keep pace with the times.

— *Thomas Jefferson*

"James Monroe: Bona Fide Hero of the American Revolution"

by Rick Britton

It may be doubted whether so small a number of men ever employed so short a space of time with greater and more lasting effects upon the history of the world.
— British Historian George Otto Trevelyan

After firing-off a few ineffectual shots, the Hessian pickets turned tail and bolted south into the small town of Trenton, New Jersey, loudly spreading the alarm. Immediately on their heels, at the "long trot"—despite driving sleet that cut like a knife—stormed the ragged American advance party. The fast-moving Virginians—a company of the Third Regiment under Capt. William Washington and his young lieutenant—quickly took up a position on a small hillock at the "V" intersection of King and Queen Streets. They sent a shower of lead whistling after their enemies.

Trenton—that early morning of December 26, 1776—was little more than several dozen houses lining the two main parallel streets, King and Queen, which ran south from their intersection for a few hundred yards until reaching Assapink Creek. It was Gen. George Washington's determination to destroy the village's Hessian garrison. To do so, he needed to eject the enemy force from it.

Responding to the picket firing, half-awake German grenadiers of the Rahl Regiment stumbled out of their quarters in the town and attempted to form ranks on King Street. Officers shouted at them to ignore the abysmal weather and get into position. Well-trained in traditional European warfare, the mercenaries were startled by the rapid approach of the American rabble, and their wild appearance. Their assailants were filthy, barely covered in tattered uniforms, and amazingly—in defiance of the season—some were barefoot. Reddened snow marked their aggressive steps.

The Virginians surged forward, firing as they came. Crouching behind the cover of a tanyard fence, Washington and his youthful lieutenant directed their riflemen to volley into the despised Hessians. Several dark blue-coated Germans, fumbling with their dampened firelocks, screamed, and tumbled into the snow. In return, the scattered enemy musketry flew high, whizzing over the Virginians.

Behind them, the intersection of King and Queen was choked with rebel soldiers. Additional Third Virginia men pushed their way into the town. Manhandled American cannon were sighted down King Street and began belching grapeshot, the blasts echoing along the narrow roadway between Trenton's homes. Shutters, windows, and dooryard fences shattered under the force of the iron hail. More Hessians fell.

Moments later, however, their defense was bolstered. Days earlier the German commander, Col. Johann Rahl, had placed two of his cannon—brass three-pounders—in front of his headquarters on King Street. Now their Hessian crews came running, carrying the rammers and ammunition. With a fury, the cannoneers began loading the fieldpieces, the grenadiers on the street forming to either side. Those guns, once they opened fire, would add new weight to the German side of the argument.

The critical moment had arrived. Both sides understood the situation. For General Washington's plan to succeed, the German force on King Street had to be broken up: the three-pounders must not be allowed to fire. Without hesitation Captain Washington and his lieutenant decided on a bold plan. Instantly, they ordered their Virginians to rise and rush the enemy artillery. "The American riflemen paused only once in their charge," wrote historian Richard Hanser. "At a command from their leaders, they halted, sank down on one knee, took careful aim, and sent a withering volley at the Hessians."

When they continued forward, reaching for their hatchets and long knives, Captain Washington fell wounded—hit in both hands—and command of the company devolved on his young lieutenant, eighteen-year-old James Monroe, future president of the United States. He shouted for his men to take the cannon, reminding them of General Washington's countersign for the engagement—"Victory or Death."

James Monroe, sometime resident of Albemarle County, is well remembered as our nation's fifth chief executive, author of the Monroe Doctrine. His eight years in office—1817 to 1825—are today recalled as "the era of good feelings." Few Americans, however, remember his service in the army during our war for independence. At the Battle of Trenton, New Jersey—which many consider one of the war's pivotal actions—James Monroe was in the thick of the fighting. On King Street, with a courage that foretold of his later self-assurance, the young lieutenant helped lead his company into the very jaws of death. For the balance of his days, Monroe looked back on the engagement as one of his proudest moments.

James Monroe was born in Westmoreland County, Virginia, on the Northern Neck, on April 28, 1758. (Interestingly, Westmoreland—one of the Old Dominion's oldest counties—was also the birthplace of two other presidents: George Washington and James Madison.) In an autobiographical sketch, Monroe later described his father, Spence Monroe, as a "worthy and respectable citizen possessed of good landed and other property." His mother he portrayed as "a very amiable and respectful woman, possessing the best domestic qualities of a good wife, and a good parent."

Monroe's schooling began at age eleven, when he was enrolled at Campbelltown, a local boy's academy run by the Rev. Archibald Campbell. "Campbelltown, considered the best school in the colony," wrote biographer Harry Ammon, "was limited to twenty-five pupils. Here Monroe was so thoroughly drilled in Latin and mathematics that when he entered William and Mary in 1774, he was at once admitted into the upper, or college, division."

The choice of William and Mary—in Williamsburg, the colonial capital—was made with the help of an uncle, Judge Joseph Jones, of Fredericksburg. An influential man, Jones had served variously as deputy king's attorney for Virginia and, beginning in 1772, as a King George County representative to the House of Burgesses. Later, during the Revolution, Jones joined the Committee of Public Safety, a state executive body, and the Virginia delegation to the Continental Congress. Extremely well-connected, Jones's acquaintances included George Washington, Thomas Jefferson, and James Madison. Encouraged by Judge Jones, Monroe set his sights on a political career.

In 1774 Williamsburg was simply abuzz with politics. In fact, politics critical to all thirteen American colonies had begun dominating the town even before the future president stepped into a college classroom. A mere two weeks before his arrival, the House of Burgesses—in response to England's "Intolerable Acts"—ordered, wrote historian Emily Salmon, "a day of fasting, humiliation, and prayer and adopted resolutions denouncing the coercive acts of Parliament." When the royal governor—John Murray, the earl of Dunmore—dissolved the assembly, the Virginians met in Williamsburg's Raleigh Tavern and called upon the other colonies to send representatives to a congress in Philadelphia. Judge Jones was an active participant in all these early rumblings.

Naturally, serious study was extremely difficult for Monroe in the midst of this world-shattering turmoil. Nonetheless, he applied himself as best he could. The opening actions of the Revolution were fought at Lexington and Concord, in Massachusetts, on April 19, 1775. The following day in Virginia, Governor Dunmore attempted to reassert his authority by ordering Royal Marines to seize a store of gunpowder belonging to the city of Williamsburg. Virginians from all across the Old Dominion, in response to this outrage, rose up in armed, organized bodies and marched against the royal capital. Rattled by this show of force, Dunmore, wrote Ammon, "respectfully offered to pay for the powder" and "sent his wife to the safety of a British frigate."

"The [William and Mary] students, accustomed to taking a serious interest in politics," penned Ammon, "now became directly involved in the everyday turbulence convulsing the capital." When one of the student leaders organized a military unit, James Monroe purchased a weapon and joined up. Doubtless the institution's professors fretted over their young charges drilling so enthusiastically on college grounds. In June of 1775, the ties to the mother country were permanently severed when the Virginia Burgesses rejected England's conciliatory resolves and established a Committee of Public Safety to run the colony. Dunmore retreated to the security of a heavily armed English warship.

The war in Virginia was on. On June 24, Monroe participated in a surprise attack on the governor's palace led by Theodorick Bland Jr. Finding no opposition, the small force of twenty-five men captured two hundred muskets and three hundred swords. These much-needed arms were handed over to the local militia.

In September of 1775, fighting erupted in the Norfolk area, where loyalist sentiment was still strong. After losing the Battle of Great Bridge on December 9, British forces abandoned Norfolk in favor of their powerful fleet stationed in Hampton Roads. On New Year's Day, 1776, that fleet bombarded Norfolk, and Redcoats came ashore to capture military supplies and burn buildings. The fighting raged through the night. The fires blazed unchecked. "[T]he burning of Norfolk convinced many in the colonies, not just Virginians," wrote Salmon, "that the war for independence must proceed."

James Monroe officially joined the revolutionary effort in the spring of 1776. Unable to stay out of the stirring events whirling around Williamsburg, the future president and his roommate, John F. Mercer, enlisted as cadets in the Third Virginia Infantry commanded by Col. Hugh Mercer (who was no relation to the young student). War fever was at high pitch, and the ranks of the unit filled quickly. Perhaps because of their status as college attendees, Monroe and Mercer were soon made lieutenants.

Throughout the spring and into summer, the Third Virginia trained in the farm fields outside of Williamsburg. Noted Indian fighter Gen. Andrew Lewis, in charge of the local brigade, supervised the regiment's instruction, emphasizing strict discipline and daily drill. "On Lewis's orders," wrote Ammon, "all officers were required to wear short-fringed hunting shirts." Rugged and enthusiastic, eighteen-year-old Lt. James Monroe adapted well to the rigors of military life. "Slightly over six feet tall, broad-shouldered, with a massive if somewhat rawboned frame," noted Ammon, "he was an impressive figure."

The war began in earnest for the Third Virginia in August of 1776. That month the regiment received orders to reinforce Gen. George Washington's beleaguered army in New York. Outnumbered by a British force of thirty-two thousand that had recently landed on Staten Island, the American general, with only twenty thousand fit for duty, was desperate for more men. His position seemed untenable.

The British were quick to take advantage of the situation. Washington was defeated at the Battle of Long Island on August 27. Two nights later, under cover of heavy fog, he retreated to the island of Manhattan. On Sunday, September 15, Washington's inexperienced troops were routed as he attempted to withdraw them north out of New York City. Once halted, the dispirited American army took up a strong defensive position on Harlem Heights.

Seven hundred strong, the Third Virginia joined General Washington's battered forces at Harlem Heights that same day. They had trudged north from Virginia in the summer heat. During the march, command of the regiment had been turned over to a new leader—Col. George Weedon of Fredericksburg. Lieutenant Monroe was made second in command of the seventh company under Capt. William Washington, a distant relative of the general's. The men composing the regiment were from hardy stock. Many were backwoodsmen, expert marksmen. Some had already faced the British as militiamen or Virginia minute men.

It's possible that James Monroe first saw action the very next morning. As the sun rose on September 16, 1776, the quiet between the opposing forces was broken by British buglers insolently sounding the fox-hunters' call: "Fox in sight, and on the run!" The Third Virginia men, many of them hunters themselves, felt the insult's sting and longed for an opportunity at revenge. In that morning's Battle of Harlem Heights—a small affair, but a morale-raising American victory—a detachment of Monroe's regiment, including perhaps the young lieutenant himself, was sent in as reinforcements. The unit acquitted itself well in this, its first fight, standing firm and trading volleys with the heretofore invincible Hessians.

Within a few days, two dramatic events further angered Lieutenant Monroe, as well as his brothers in arms. On September 21 a large fire broke out in New York City's downtown section, eventually claiming between four and five hundred buildings. The British blamed the Americans for starting the conflagration. That same day one of Washington's men, Nathan Hale, was captured on Long Island in the guise of a Dutch schoolteacher. He was hanged as a spy the following day, but not before uttering the galvanizing: "I regret that I have but one life to lose for my country."

In early October the British juggernaut was again set in motion, and Washington's men began suffering a long series of reverses and retreats. The Americans were forced from Harlem Heights to New Rochelle—from New Rochelle to White Plains. When British general Sir William Howe attacked on October 25, James Monroe participated in the brief, but bloody, encounter. From White Plains, General Washington withdrew most of his army across the Hudson, to Hackensack, in New Jersey. From there, beginning in mid-November, he began his disastrous winter retreat southwestward across that state.

Through the bitter cold, Monroe and the Third Virginia Infantry tramped across the Garden State. Enlistments in the American army were expiring, and the desertion rate was high. The situation was extremely grim. Colonel Weedon of the Third Virginia wrote that "General Howe had a mortgage on the rebel army . . . but had not yet foreclosed it." Washington retreated to Newark, and from there, on November 22, to Brunswick. Thinking ahead, the general ordered that all boats on the Delaware River—especially the forty- to sixty-foot-long Durham freight boats—be collected at Trenton. When the last of Washington's ragged little band, fewer than three thousand men, was finally ferried over the river the morning of December 8, pursuing Hessian grenadiers entered Trenton with great pomp and circumstance—their flags flying and music playing. It had been a narrow escape.

Once safely across, Washington began making plans and marshaling his forces. His patrols kept him aware of British movements. Within two weeks, reinforcements built his army back up to nine thousand effectives, but most of these would soon simply melt away. "Washington found himself forced to do something before December 31," wrote historian Lt. Col. Joseph Mitchell, "or his troops would go home, their enlistments expired."

With the British forces in possession of New Jersey, Philadelphia threatened, the winter fast advancing, and his outnumbered army shivering around its campfires, General Washington had but few options. "Some enterprise must be undertaken in our present circumstances," Col. Joseph Reed wrote Washington on December 22, "or we must give up the cause. . . . Our affairs are hastening fast to ruin if we do not retrieve them by some happy event."

The "happy event" that George Washington conceived was a surprise attack on the fifteen hundred-man Hessian force stationed at Trenton. He determined to hit them in the early hours of December 26, the day after Christmas. The Germans, Washington understood, were very fond of celebrating the season with too much food and drink. Also, the American general knew—thanks to his spies—that the commander at Trenton, Col. Johann Rahl, was averse to winter fighting and overconfident. He had referred to the rebels as "a miserable lot" and "country clowns." Washington planned to catch Rahl with his guard down.

James Monroe, along with the men of the Third Virginia—half-clothed and hungry—stood in ranks at attention on the cold, wind-swept afternoon of Christmas Day, 1776. Colonel Weedon stepped in front of them to deliver a short appeal. It had been written just recently by an aide to Gen. Nathanael Greene, and had appeared in a Philadelphia newspaper.

"These are the times that try men's souls," began Weedon loudly, reading the words of Thomas Paine. "The summer soldier and the sunshine patriot will, in this crisis, shrink from the service of his country, but he that stands it now—'We will stand!' shouted the thin ranks of the Third Virginia—deserves the love and thanks of man and woman," continued the colonel, proudly scanning his infantrymen. "Tyranny, like hell, is not easily conquered; yet we have this consolation with us, that the harder the conflict, the more glorious the triumph." Amid thundering cheers, the regiment faced to the right and marched toward the ice-clogged Delaware River.

Capt. William Washington's company of the Third Virginia, including Lieutenant Monroe, was one of the first units to cross. It's interesting to note that in Emmanuel Leutze's world-famous painting, *Washington Crossing the Delaware,* the German artist placed James Monroe, contrary to the facts, in the same boat as the general, standing immediately behind him. Despite the stirring nature of the illustration, it is chock-full of other mistakes. Monroe, for example, is holding an American flag that had yet to be designed and the boat is too small. The movement was undertaken at night, not in broad daylight. "Both Washington and Monroe had grown up on rivers and knew about boats," wrote Richard Hanser humorously. "Neither would have been so foolish as to stand up during a stormy crossing."

"After crossing the river," Monroe later remembered, "I was sent with my command to the intersection of the Pennytown and Maiden Head roads, with strict orders to let no one pass until I was ordered forward. Whilst occupying the position, the resident of the dwelling [hearing a commotion] came out in the dark to learn the cause, and encountered my command. . . . He was violent . . . and very profane, and wanted to know what we were doing there [on] such a stormy night. . . . When he discovered that we were American soldiers, he insisted that we should go to his house . . . and he would give us something to eat. I told him my orders were strict and we could not leave, when he returned to the house and brought us some victuals. He said to me, 'I know something is to be done, and I am going with you. I am a doctor, and I may help some poor fellow.'" When Monroe and Captain Washington received word to "hasten to Trenton," the good doctor—whose last name was Riker—went with them. His later presence, in Monroe's time of need, some would call divine providence.

Weedon's Third Virginia was given the task of spearheading the attack on Trenton from the north. The company under Captain

Washington and Lieutenant Monroe was the vanguard. As they trotted forward, with the frigid sleet in their faces, they could hear firing on the opposite side of the town. General Washington had detached a portion of his twenty-four hundred-man force, under Gen. John Sullivan, to strike the Hessians from the south and cut off their retreat. Sullivan was hitting them right on time.

When Monroe's men shoved back the German pickets, other Hessians began spilling from their barracks. Some managed to pull off a few rounds. As the Virginians came under fire, they wisely took advantage of whatever cover they could find. From upstairs windows, from the corners of buildings, and from behind the tanyard fence, the Old Dominion marksmen picked off many a German. With American reinforcements advancing down King Street to their assistance, they felt confident of victory.

The threat of the Hessian artillery, however, changed all that. To stop the mercenaries from bringing them into play, Monroe's company charged. When Captain Washington was shot, "the command fell on me," Monroe later wrote, "and soon after, I was shot through by a ball which grazed my breast. I was carried . . . to the room where Captain Washington was under the care of two surgeons. . . ." The ball had done much more than "grazed" the young Monroe, however; it had pierced his chest and severed an artery. Blood fountained up through his uniform. "I would have bled to death," he later admitted, "if this doctor [Riker] had not been near and promptly taken up the artery." Indeed, if not for Dr. Riker, wrote Hanser, "the future fifth president of the United States would have perished, at the age of eighteen, in a pool of blood on a slushy street in Trenton, New Jersey." (Monroe, unfortunately, never learned the first name of the man who had saved his life.)

Nonetheless, despite the loss of officers, the attack was a tremendous success. The Virginians, wrote Monroe, "rushed forward . . . and put the troops around the cannon to flight, and took possession of them." From the streets of Trenton, the Hessians fled east into an orchard. There the rattled fugitives were confronted on three sides by advancing Americans. The chilly waters of Assapink Creek sealed their last avenue of withdrawal.

"Our Men pushed on with such Rapidity that they soon carried four pieces of Cannon out of Six," General Washington wrote on December 28, "Surrounded the Enemy and obliged 30 Officers and 886 privates to lay down their Arms without firing a Shot. . . . The Enemy had between 20 and 30 killed." Colonel Rahl had been mortally wounded attempting to lead a bayonet charge back into Trenton. On the rebel side, two officers, Monroe and Washington, and three privates were wounded. Two American soldiers were later found frozen to death along the route of march from the Delaware.

"Washington's victory at Trenton was complete," wrote historian W. P. Cresson. "It turned the trick of revitalizing the cause and rousing the fainting spirits of the patriots." According to a staff officer who witnessed the action, the results "will rejoice the hearts of our friends everywhere and give new life to our hitherto waning fortunes. . . . [General Washington] pounced upon the Hessians like an eagle upon a hen. . . ." The English agreed. "All our hopes were blasted by the unhappy affair at Trenton," commented Lord Germaine. "The Hessians will be no longer terrible," wrote another member of the British government, "and the spirits of the Americans will rise amazingly."

In this pivotal action of the American Revolution, Lt. James Monroe had played an important role. "The capture of the two Hessian cannon was, in fact, a turning point of the Battle of Trenton," penned Hanser. "The clearing of the upper end of King Street permitted George Washington to complete a maneuver" that inevitably led to the German surrender. "These particular acts of gallantry have never been noticed, and yet could not have been too highly appreciated," wrote Gen. James Wilkinson, "for if the enemy had got his artillery into operation in a narrow street, it might have checked our movement and given him time to reflect and reform."

For his conspicuous gallantry, Monroe was rewarded. "I take occasion to express the high opinion I have of his worth," wrote Gen. George Washington of the young officer. "The zeal he discovered by entering the service at an early period, the character he supported in his regiment, and the manner in which he distinguished himself at Trenton . . . induced me to appoint him to a captaincy."

James Monroe's army career would continue—and he would eventually reach the rank of lieutenant colonel—but in his later life nothing shone so brilliantly in his memory as the decisive action on King Street the morning of December 26, 1776. During an 1817 tour of the country, the fifty-eight-year-old Monroe, president of the United States, stopped in Trenton. Although the town had grown quite a bit, the old Revolutionary—"the last of the cocked hats," as he was called—was moved by his recollections to deliver a stirring address. In it, wrote Ammon, Monroe referred to Trenton "as the site where the hopes of the nation had revived at the ebb tide of the Revolution. Of his wound he said nothing, but the local press adequately reminded the citizens of his heroism."

"UVa Women before There Were UVa Women"

(1st place nonfiction, Charlottesville VWC, 2006)

by Gary D. Kessler

It is somewhat ironic that the most memorable people from my graduate studies at the University of Virginia at the close of the 1960s, when that institution was barely hanging on to its final vestiges of an all-men's school, were women. Caroline Dinegar, my international law professor, who was—typically for the time for her gender—denied tenure despite being the most Jeffersonian educator I knew at the University, was one of those. I'll never forget the evening she and a group of my classmates stopped at Alderman Library, where I was the assistant circulation desk librarian, to help me close up the library so that I could accompany them to a Jefferson Society lecture. Like a general, she dispersed my classmates to the far corners of the building to roust out foot draggers as she herself climbed, tight skirt and all, onto the ledges of the giant windows in the Alderman's main entry hall and, teetering on her high heels, closed them shut one by one. She had been a foreign service officer who, incongruously, was afraid of flying. She said, however, that she was more afraid of not having lived an interesting life, so she stuck with a foreign service career and gritted her teeth through many an around-the-world flight.

Caroline Dinegar wasn't my only woman professor at UVa. in those waning years of academic male supremacy. There also was the gentle and demure Alice Leng with the disturbing hacking cough. Alice had the daunting task of establishing a Chinese language program at the University, made all the harder because I initially was the program's only student. In three years of grueling effort with one student and two teachers, I learned quite a bit from Alice Leng. Unfortunately, very little of it related to language, at which I am not the least bit adept. However, I learned much about China from the death throes of an imperial dynasty to communism, with a stopover at nationalism, honing an interest that led me to a career in Asian affairs. Alice's father had been the last minister of personnel at the Chinese imperial court. He also had been China's leading calligrapher, and from him, by way of Alice Leng, I was propelled into a life-long experimentation with minimalist art, using Chinese brush painting techniques.

I also learned much about life, marriage, and perseverance from Alice. Her husband, Tony Leng, was my faculty adviser and Chinese foreign policy professor. Alice was from Beijing and Tony was from Szechwan. Neither could speak to each other in Chinese, as their native dialects were radically different. They only were able to converse in English, which, in Tony's case, was rather faulting. Theirs had been an arranged marriage, in keeping with the customs of the Chinese upper class at the time, and theirs was a devoted marriage undaunted by the lack of easy communication. Alice worked hard at establishing the Chinese program at the University, even though she was deathly ill the entire time. She died of cancer not long after I left the University. I had not done her efforts the least bit of good, but she sent me off with her blessing and a wan smile in her typical generous and gracious fashion.

Another memorable woman was the head of my department at the Alderman Library, Roy Land, who had been the University's circulation librarian back to the days when the book collection was still housed in the Rotunda. Incongruously, although she could, when convenient, be the model southern belle, she had lived a life of a flapper, covering several continents, including China, where she had helped to modernize the systems of National China's central library—and she had the photographs to prove out her adventures. No Marian the Librarian this, but a vital woman with a wonderful, deep-throated laugh and the ability to level the room with a few well-chosen words. By the time I knew her, she was largely possessed by the bottle, but the bourbon hadn't managed to dim one iota of her wit, glittering presence, and ability simultaneously to have a load of fun and appear the most southern of ladies on the verandah. At one point late in her long career with the University, she was evicted from her little house on Dawson's Row, famous for dispensing bourbon, wisdom, and a few risqué jokes in the wee hours of the morning. The pretext for this travesty was that the University was going to level Dawson's Row and build a classroom building there. Forty years later, Dawson's Row and Miss Land's cottage are still here—but I would much prefer that it was Roy Land who was still here.

The most bizarre person in my memory from the University in this period, however, was Anna Anderson, aka the Grand Duchess Anastasia of the Russian Romanoff dynasty.

Anna Anderson, without having the vaguest notion she was doing so, posed what was possibly the biggest challenge Roy Land had ever faced as circulation librarian at Alderman. Anna, who was walking in a fog every time I encountered her, appeared to believe that any book that mentioned the Grand Duchess Anastasia was her personal property, and she systematically and frequently stripped the University library system of all such books. We would—or, more often, wouldn't—catch a brief glimpse of a four-foot-not-much little woman in brown slacks, a tunic top, a short black feathered boa around her neck, a beret perched on choppy-short mousy-brown hair, and a gnarled hand covering her mouth slip around the corner into the library stacks. Thirty minutes later the library would once again be bereft of its early twentieth-century Russia collection. To this day, we have no idea how such a tiny woman could slip a whole bookcase of books out from under our noses, but Anna did it repeatedly.

Our basic problem was that University professors had totally unrestricted borrowing rights to books in Alderman Library. A University Russian history professor, John Manahan, had married Anna Anderson to keep her from being deported back to wherever it was thought she had come from other than the Russian imperial palace, now firmly in the grasp of the communist regime that had executed Anna's claimed immediate family.

Professor Manahan was quite understanding of the library's predicament regarding his delusional new wife, and he dutifully promised to return the books she periodically confiscated. But he was slightly ajar himself and never could seem to remember to carry through on his promises. Until the budget burst, the library just bought replacement books. Then for a while, we moved all of the Anastasia books to one shelf area in the stacks and tried to institute an "Anna patrol." We'd watch the broad walks leading up to the steps of the library for signs of an Anastasia assault and send a team off to clear the shelf and hide the books whenever Anna approached. But, on the whole, she was just too short and too fast and clever for us. In the end, we had to send in master librarian Roy Land with a bottle of bourbon and her gift of persuasion.

For the next year, until I completed my classroom studies at the University and wafted off to Washington, D.C., to try to follow in Caroline Dinegar's footsteps and in the world Alice Leng had opened up for me—and winding up as some aspect of a spy—I was engaged as the library's own special Anna agent. Roy Land's somewhat convoluted solution to the problem of the "grand duchess and the purloined books" was to telephone John Manahan whenever our Anastasia books went missing. Professor Manahan would immediately schedule an outing for Anna, which both came to see as a rare treat. He would leave the back door of their hunkering and disheveled University Circle home unlocked, and I would slip in and go on a book hunt. Anna never let on that she missed the books that had been retrieved—and, indeed, why would she? She knew exactly where she could find them again.

It didn't take long for me to begin to suspect that Anna was on to us and was just enjoying her new routine of outings with her husband. I also remember initially thinking that Roy Land and the University were just being typically medieval and wimpy with their approach to faculty privilege. But near the end of my residence at the University, I overheard Professor Manahan talking with a visiting colleague about his marriage. The visitor made some passing comment that Professor Manahan could possibly be seen as being taken advantage of and as being willing to go to extremes in his own involvement in Russian studies by taking Anna Anderson under his wing and putting up with her strange ways. In response, Professor Manahan openly acknowledged that he was generally seen as a little more than slightly mentally unbalanced himself, but that he was old, rich, and unencumbered and hadn't really felt the need for a spouse in the traditional sense when he had married Anna to permit her to stay in the United States. He said that Anna, in terms of her connection with the Anastasia legend, had been used by people in power or coveting power all of her life and then had been discarded when she was no longer of use to anyone. He, Manahan, felt that she deserved to have someone take care of her in her last years, someone who would watch over her no matter who she was or wasn't. Someone who would accept her for what she wanted to be—and that his experience of the University and the Charlottesville area was that this was a haven of tolerance and retreat for the Annas of the world that would help him in this endeavor.

I rather liked having the University and Charlottesville in my memories after hearing that and couldn't help but think that, once again, Roy Land had come up with the most civilized and elegant of solutions to one of life's not-so-big-really problems.

"Strasshof"

(2nd place nonfiction, Charlottesville VWC, 2006;
Excerpt from a work in progress tentatively titled
"Time Remembered, Grief Forgotten")

by Michael S. Zbailey

"Katya! Katya!"

I heard father calling for me, but I could not see him. Crowds of people and German soldiers were rushing around in all directions. I was lost, at least for a moment. Then I saw Father waving frantically to me. This was a new experience for me. I was eleven years old, but I had never been inside the train station in Belgrade until that day in June of 1944. It was a cavernous building that showed little damage from the German bombing a few years before. I think that the Germans saved it for their own use. Mother and Father held my hands and walked with me to the counter for the final check before we boarded a train for Linz in Austria. Aunt Elizabeth was living there. Mother had spent weeks getting the appropriate papers for all of us. She spoke fluent German, which she learned from her German governess in St. Petersburg. She spoke the language so well that she could pass for a German citizen and used this to get travel permits so we could leave Belgrade. Mother was a nurse. She told the authorities she was going to work in a German army hospital in Linz. It was a slow process, but it had worked so far. Father and I were cautioned not to speak at all, even among ourselves, so that we would not be found out. Father could speak German, but not very well, so Mother did all of the talking.

We were Russians, but my family had lived in Yugoslavia since 1921 after they escaped from Russia and the Red Army. Both of my grandfathers died fighting the Reds in the civil war after the

Revolution. We spoke Russian and lived in a section of Belgrade where everyone was Russian. We had our own Russian Orthodox Church and our own schools. Now my parents were telling me that we were running away from the Russians. They called them Soviets.

I remember what Mother said to Father when the decision to leave was being discussed. It was very emotional. "The Soviets have long memories and they are paranoid. They are suspicious of all Russians living outside of Russia. Our friends have told us what happens to those that the Soviet Army suspects of being anti-Soviet. Siberia is the best that we could expect."

Through rumors and secret sources, Father knew vaguely how the war was going, "The Germans are losing the war, and the Soviets are advancing toward Belgrade. The Americans are in Rome, and we have heard that the British and Americans are in France. We must run toward them and safety."

We had been bombed and then occupied by the Germans, and we had prayed for salvation from them, but apparently salvation at the hands of the Soviet Army wasn't what my parents had prayed for.

The Orient Express had once plied the route between Belgrade and Vienna, but we had none of the luxuries of that train. The passenger car had rows of wooden seats and didn't have any compartments. The seats were scratched and worn from heavy use. The floors and windows were in need of cleaning and maintenance. We took the seats near the front and pretended to sleep or read German books during the trip. Many of the passengers in the car were soldiers on leave from the army. They laughed, smoked cigarettes, and talked loudly among themselves. When some left the train, others came in to fill up the car. After two days in this cramped, smoke-filled car, the train finally crossed the border into Austria.

Several of the soldiers had recently been at the Russian front and were talking about the progress of the war. I watched out of the corner of my eye as Father drew closer to them and listened to their boasting. Ignoring prudence, Father spoke to them in his halting German, saying, "How is the war going on the Russian front?"

Mother let out an audible gasp. She couldn't believe that Father had spoken to the soldiers. She waited. I think that she was hoping they wouldn't notice as she took Father's arm and led him back to our seats.

The soldiers yelled at him: "You are a Russian, aren't you? Why are you asking questions? Why do you want to know? You must be a spy."

Their superior officer was summoned and began to talk to Father, but Mother interjected herself into the conversation; "I am German. We are on the way to Linz. It is silly to think we are spies. Look, we have our child with us." She reached into her bag and withdrew our documents and gave them to the officer. "See, we have papers."

The officer scoffed at her. "Probably forgeries. I must report you to the authorities. Stay where you are."

We were taken off the train at Graz. The guards weren't very gentle as they pushed and shoved us into a small, dirty room at the rear of the train station. I think that the room was a storage closet. It was hardly bigger than a compartment on a train. Mother and Father sat on a box, and I sprawled on the floor and waited. Nobody talked for fear of being overhead, and the silence was broken only by the noise of the activity in the station.

After one hour, a German soldier opened the door and looked in. "Are these the Russian spies?" he asked the stationmaster. We all rose and Mother began to talk to him. " I have papers," she said. "I am a German going to my sister's house in Linz. My husband is Croatian. We are all Catholic. We are not spies."

"We'll decide that later," he said. "Come with me."

Two soldiers stood outside the door and escorted us to a train that was waiting at a siding. It was not like the other trains. These were boxcars with rough wooden sides. I could see people inside standing and looking out through the cracks. One of the doors was opened, and the people inside leaned forward to stare at us. With some effort, we climbed up into the car and the long door was pulled shut behind us. There must have been sixty people—men, women, and children—in this small space. The smell in the car was very foul, and I thought that I might become sick from it. We found a place, but Mother and Father had to stand because there was not enough room for all of us on the floor. Mother began to talk to the people nearest to us. Many were Jews from Austria. Others were Serbs, Russians, and Gypsies. Nobody knew where we were headed, but some guessed it was to Czechoslovakia or Poland to work in the factories making war material. Others said Vienna or possibly Munich.

"I don't know where we are going." said an old Jewish woman who reminded me of my grandmother. "We've been on this train for two days. The Germans call this a forty-by-eight boxcar. It holds forty people or eight horses." She made a sweeping gesture with her arm, "Look around. There must be sixty or seventy people in this box. They feed us once a day. Our toilet is a bucket in the corner. The horses must have been treated better than this." She helped us get comfortable in our space on the floor.

Mother spoke to me in a whisper. "We're not going to be here long. We have done nothing, and besides, we have not had a hearing or a meeting or a discussion of any kind with the authorities. They will probably let us go when we have a chance to talk to them.

The next morning, in the hazy light, as the train began to slow, I could see a sign in the train yard. It said *Strasshof.* It was very active and noisy outside. We had been on the train for twenty-four hours. I was told that we were about thirty kilometers west of Vienna, almost in Bratislava. That's all anyone knew. The doors slid open, the cool air blew into the car, and all of us breathed deeply to gulp in the fresh air.

"Mother, are we going to stay here?" I asked in childhood innocence.

"I don't know. I will talk. I will try to get us out."

There were hundreds of people standing on the platform, waiting for something to happen. Many were stretching and exercising to relieve their cramped muscles. The German guards did not let anyone move from the space near the railcar they had just left. Then a weary-looking man—he seemed like an old man to me—started walking down the line, looking at each person individually for about ten seconds—sometimes a little longer. Then with a wave of his arm, that person would be put into one of two separate lines, one near the train and one on the far side of the platform. We did not know then that this was a doctor, who was examining all of us. In those few seconds, he was selecting those who appeared to be stronger and able to work. As the doctor approached us, Mother looked him in the eyes and in a loud voice that surprised me, said, "I'm German. I'm not a Jew. I'm Roman Catholic. I'm a nurse. This is a mistake." That's all she had time to say.

The doctor hardly looked at us and waved us to the opposite side of the platform. Then he continued to walk in a slow, almost mechanical way, seemingly detached from the duty he was performing. Many mothers and their young children were left in the line near the tracks. Old men and women were also there along with those who looked weak or sick. When he had walked the length of the entire train, the doctor turned and departed. That was it. The people nearest the tracks were told to get back into the boxcars they had just left. The woman who had helped us was one of them. Even as we were being herded away from the tracks, the steam of the train was already making a hissing sound and the train began to move. I could see scrawled in white chalk on the side of the car that we had just left, the word, *Auschwitz.*

We crossed a moat on a wooden bridge and stumbled through a gate into a large open area. High barbed-wire fences surrounded this entire camp. There were low wooden buildings as far as I could see. We were then herded into one of the nearby buildings. I walked into a large, open room with the rest of the people. It was plain, with rough, wooden floors. The men were being separated from the women. Father was sent through a door on the far side of the room with the other men. The women were ordered to take a different door into a larger room, maybe thirty feet square, with windows on two sides. There were about ten or twelve men standing around the outside walls of the room. All of us were carrying our clothes and other belongings in suitcases and in backpacks. An older man in a dirty army uniform ordered us to take off all of our clothes, every bit. He said that the clothes would be disinfected and returned to us. I looked up at Mother to see what she would do. With her arms outstretched, she guided me into a corner, as far as we could be from the soldiers. She began to remove her clothes and I did the same. The stripping of our clothes did not permit modesty or dignity. We began to remove our clothes under the watchful eyes of the men who were guarding us.

I heard a loud scream coming from the middle of the room, where a young woman was crying hysterically. Then she ran for the door, trying to escape from this degrading scene. I thought that they might kill her, but before that happened, her mother grabbed her and dragged her back into the room. The young woman vomited onto the floor, and soon the smell was penetrating my nose, even though I was far away. A guard swaggered across the room and hit her across the face with his hand. She quietly removed her clothes and placed them on the counter with the other bundles. She continued to cry, and I could see blood on her nose and face.

Following instructions, we went into another room, and several of the men followed us. Each had a book and wrote down information as they asked us questions. Mother told them we were from Yugoslavia and that she was German and Catholic and a nurse. She said that I was fifteen years old and a good hard worker—even though I was just eleven, but I was big for my age.

We were ordered to form three separate lines. Several men, officers I think, came into the room and stared at us. Silently, they pointed out three attractive young women and ushered them out the door. Still naked, the rest of us stayed in line, which began to advance toward a bench, where a soldier cut the hair off each woman and a second man shaved off all of the other body hair that was visible—under the arms and between the legs. I watched, as my blond hair fell to the floor, and I thanked God that I was too young to have breasts or hair anywhere but on my head. Numbed and embarrassed by these shocking events, the women avoided any eye contact with each other or with the men in the room.

We'd been standing naked for over an hour when we were ordered to a separate building to take a shower. The door was opened, and we went outside and crossed a patch of dirt and rocks and entered another building. We'd heard the rumors that the Nazis would tell people they were going to take a shower but then murdered them with gas from the showerheads. We were packed so tightly that I could hardly move. Everyone was looking at the twelve showerheads that protruded from the ceiling. I had a plan. I thought that I might escape the gas if I fell to the floor under the other women and then I could crawl out to safety. Mother embraced me, and I could see that she was praying. The showerheads clanked and shook noisily for several seconds. All of the women stood in silence and watched the showerheads. I could see the moving lips of several women who were watching and praying. The clanking continued for several more seconds, but it seemed longer than that. Then water. The water was very cold, but there was a loud sigh and everyone smiled with relief. If a person could be happy under these conditions, I was happy. We were all still alive.

"Golf Course Campsite"

(3rd place nonfiction,
Charlottesville VWC, 2006)

by Leonard Tuchyner

In 1977 I was traveling from the flat, swampy, ocean world of South Florida to the land of the Blue Ridge Mountains. It was quite unfair, because I happened to be traveling at the height of the fall foliage season. Its breathtaking beauty overwhelmed me, and I never left. My two best friends at the time were Carla, my girlfriend, and Aric, a big beautiful Labrador retriever.

One sunny autumn morning, we embarked on a hike along a path we thought to be the Appalachian Trail. The plan was to go as far as we could in one day, camp out and then hike back the following day.

We started our trek near Humpback Rocks, which is a huge outcropping that graces one of the highest points on a prominent ridge in the Blue Ridge mountain range. The access road came right off of route 64 at the top of Afton Mountain. In the seventies, that pinnacle sported a Howard Johnson's hotel and restaurant. The highway continued further west to the town of Waynesboro.

This is the town the author Terry Brooks mentions in his novels, *The Black Unicorn* and *Magic Kingdom for Sale, Sold.* In those stories, it is from Waynesboro that the hero departs to find a magic kingdom in the mists of the Blue Ridge Mountains. The thick fogs of the Blue Ridge are legendary. In fact, the fog is often so thick that tourists have been known to cut pieces of it off of the fog bank, box them, and take them home as souvenirs.

I can imagine wandering around, surrounded by such a mist in the mountains. You could get so lost and disoriented that you really could end up in fairyland.

It was in that very place that we went on our overnighter. Even though there was no fog on this particular day, we did manage to get lost. We did not end up in fairyland, but we did find ourselves in a place just as unbelievable and wonderful.

The three of us climbed up the heavily worn trail in the brisk autumn morning, along with many other early hikers who were anxious to experience the open expanse of the craggy cliffs that compose Humpback Rocks. We hiked past the side path that would take us to the Appalachian Trail to pay our respects to the landmark. This was not a good place for those who are fearful of heights. The view was crisp and clear as we gazed down at the panorama of golds and reds blanketing the slopes below us in cascades of color. As arduous as the climb was, the experience of the rock so filled our senses that we were immediately refreshed.

After our brief visit, we turned back to find the intersecting path. We carried one knapsack packed with food, water, tent, and sleeping bags. When we reached the main trail, we headed south.

Aric knew what a trail was. He knew we were on a hike and that his job was to scout way up ahead. He was also responsible for making periodic visits back to the lagging humans, just to make sure we were not getting into trouble and to hurry us along. He made constant forays into the bush but always returned faithfully. For every mile we two-leggers walked, Aric must have covered at least three.

The way was very narrow and rarely offered the opportunity for two people to walk abreast. There were occasional stretches where the ground was relatively level and smooth as it cut through an open glade. Most of the time, we found ourselves climbing or descending steep rocky grades. Loose or embedded rocks were the usual fare. These rocks were often jagged and ready to turn an ankle or bruise a foot. The loose rocks had a penchant for slipping and rolling under foot. Cara had the ability to see with very sharp eyes and to analyze instantaneously the placement of each step before taking it, so that she did not even have to break stride. I, however, didn't have vision that was quite as sharp. My hiking was an act of faith. Sometimes I could take a step with certainty. On other occasions, the step was only a half guess. But often it was a complete step into the unknown. I found that pretending I was drunk could be helpful. That way I could maintain a loose, lurching kind of balance that could adjust to surprising events. There was one method I devised that was particularly useful for late autumn, when the leaves carpeted the ground. These leaves hid the rocks along the trails and acted like a graphite lubricant, causing one's feet to slide over slanted surfaces. These leaves also hid the cracks between the rocks, in which a foot might be trapped while the body continued to move downhill. These conditions were particularly treacherous on a steep, downhill slope. It was like walking on banana peels. The feet slid forward, while the upper body lurched backward. A rush of adrenaline, caused by the fear of falling, created a compensatory countermovement that was designed to correct the imbalance but usually was an abysmal failure. One ended up on one's backside anyway and hopefully not on a weapon-like rock. Taking normal steps under those conditions was out of the question. I dubbed the procedure I used as the "drunken crab." One proceeds down the trail sideways like a skittering insane crab. Imagining you are a chimpanzee can also be effective if you can make appropriate mimicking sounds.

We trekked all day up and down mountain ridges. The trail was, at times, difficult to follow, because the leaves often obscured it. Nevertheless, with Cara's eyes, Aric's nose, and my dogged determination, we managed to find our way. As dusk approached, the rocks gave way to grasses and the trail vanished. We tried to pick up the trail further ahead, but with the waning light and the overgrowth of grass and brambles, we failed. Instead, we found ourselves in the middle of an in-process housing development. It was quite disconcerting. The workmen had gone for the day, and it was like a ghost town with modern suburban buildings.

In the advancing darkness, we made several forays into the surrounding woods. Eventually, we thought we might be on a trail, sort of. We felt our way along it, trying to find a suitable campsite. But by this time, it was so dark that we could hardly see the ground beneath our feet. Curiously, we found a patch of what seemed like short-cropped grass. It was surprising to find that in the middle of the Blue Ridge Mountains. It was too dark to look around, even for a reasonable place to do our business. So we just accepted fate and pitched our Timberline pup tent by feel, wondering who was to blame for not taking a search light. The only person not perturbed by it all was Aric.

The night noises were a little scary, because we didn't really know what kind of place this was. Thankfully, our trusty guard dog was outside, and I could always tell myself that the different things I heard prowling around out there must be him.

We got up at dawn to break camp. When we crawled outside the tent, we found that we were on a perfect patch of manicured green grass bordered by a half circle of trees. The three of us ventured to the open end of this little alcove where we had landed, to find that we had pitched our camp on a huge golf course cul-de-sac. We ran back to the tent and packed up before anyone caught us camping on their superbly manicured grounds. The golf course was not yet opened for the day, and no one apprehended us.

We eventually found the trail again and hiked back without incident. Actually, it was Aric who found the trail. We knew that he knew it was time to go home, and we two humans just trusted our four-legged friend to get us there. It was a relief when we found ourselves back on a recognizable path heading north.

Later we figured out we had been on the Wintergreen golf course. We were new to the area and did not know such a place existed. To this day, I have not met anyone else who has camped on a golf course.

"Escape Across the Frozen River Don—January 1920"

(1st place nonfiction, Charlottesville VWC, 2005;
1st place nonfiction, State VWC, 2005;
Excerpt from a work in progress tentatively titled
"Time Remembered, Grief Forgotten")

by Michael S. Zbailey

It was dark when Sophia and her two children arrived at the north bank of the frozen River Don. The moon was full, and the trees on the far embankment were clearly visible in the reflection of its light off the snow. Behind her, in the distance, she could see the silhouettes of two horsemen on the ridge. Sophia thought they were forward scouts of the pursuing Red Army. The trail down the embankment to the river's edge was packed hard from the pounding feet of the refugees who had already passed. Sophia held Luba's hand as they scrambled and slid down to the shoreline. Zinaida stumbled closely behind. The retreating White Army had passed this way earlier, and the fires they had used to light their way still burned on the thick ice. At twenty degrees below zero, the fires mocked them by giving no warmth.

As Sophia walked into the open expanse of river, the wind hit her with its full force. She stopped to catch her breath. Luba and Zinaida clung to her and each other as they bent their heads down, braced against the wind, and focused on the heels of the boots of the refugees in front of them. One step, another step. The refugees walked in clusters in a ragged line between the ruts in the ice left by the artillery wagons. The flames of the fires were bent horizontal by the wind that swept the river clean of snow. One step, another step. Keep moving forward. The wool scarf around Sophia's face and ears muffled the sounds of the trudging feet. Only her eyes were exposed to the air. The scarf was stiff and rough with ice that formed with each breath that she took. One step, another step.

Sophia had given some of her clothing to Luba, who had been showing signs of frostbite but who was enduring without complaint. The wind blew through her coat, which was full of holes from standing too close to fires. She regretted bartering away much of her extra clothing for food, but they had to eat and she had had no choice. Starve or freeze—which was better? She knew that they might be carrying lice that sought the warmth of their skin under their clothes. She no longer cared about something that would have appalled her just a short time ago. The lice transmitted typhus, but there was nothing to be done about it, no way to bathe or sanitize or wash clothes. That was just the way it was, and she wouldn't think about things beyond her control. For now, the goal was to reach the shore, climb the embankment, continue on, help her children, get enough to eat, try to stay warm. One step, another step.

Sophia once loved winters in St. Petersburg, especially riding in a sleigh at night with Gregory on the frozen Neva River. With a bearskin robe covering them and hot bricks at their feet, they would watch the brightly lit palaces and stately homes on the riverbank fly by. Sometimes they would even see the tsar's sleigh gliding across the ice with bells jingling and the passengers laughing in the cold crisp night. Then back home to a blazing fire and hot tea from the samovar. So romantic at the time. Life was good before the war. Now she was retreating with the White Army. Paying the price for loyalty to the tsar and Mother Russia. Only Gregory and his rear guard protected them from the advancing Red Army. Here there was no warm place, just the endless expanse of ice, then more snow at the far shore, and more walking. When they reached the shore and climbed the embankment, Sophia looked back at the endless line of humanity moving in clumps slowly and quietly across the ice. With the river behind them, the anticipated safety at their destination, Novorossiysk on the Black Sea, was still two hundred and twenty agonizing miles ahead.

Sophia followed the other refugees through a field and into a village that was now occupied by the Volunteer Army, where they would have to seek whatever shelter or warmth that could be found in the barns and other out buildings. As they staggered down the road, she heard hoofbeats behind her. Sophia had not noticed that the two soldiers on horseback had followed them across the river and onto the road. Turning quickly, she pulled the children close to her as she saw two riders galloping toward them. She covered their faces with her arms and braced for a punishing blow. With snow flying from their sudden stop, the two riders dismounted and slowly approached Sophia.

"Gosposha Belenky?" asked the first horseman, who wore the familiar insignia of an officer in the Volunteer Cavalry.

Sophia nodded but did not say a word.

"My name is Lieutenant Ivan Odinov, and my fellow officer is Ensign Rozansky. We are from Borbovitch's Guard Cavalry Brigade. Our commanding officer, Colonel Belenky, sends his greetings and his regrets that he could not be here to meet you. He is still at the front across the river."

Sophia stood upright. She knew the Odinov family, which was prominent in the society of St. Petersburg before the war, but she did not know this young man, who appeared to be in his early twenties. She looked at the officer and responded, "Thank you, Lieutenant." In a formal style that she had not used in a long time she continued, "Please send my regards to the colonel and tell him we are fine and on the road to safety."

"The colonel has learned of your travels and has sent us to look after you for a few hours. We will take you to an abandoned farmhouse, which is isolated off the road. You will be safe and warm there for a few days. The colonel expects that the Reds will be delayed for a time before they approach the river. One of our ships will break up the ice, and that will delay them longer, but the river will freeze over again very quickly."

The officers helped Sophia onto one horse, and then Zinaida and Luba onto the other, and led them to a farmhouse. A soldier was standing at the front door. The children ran into the warm room, where a burning wick floating in a small bowl of oil cast a dim light. Sophia did not rush to the stove but stopped, bowed, and made the sign of the cross before the icon of the Blessed Virgin Mary that hung on the wall near the door. The two soldiers followed and did the same. Sophia could smell the sweet aroma of the burning wood and indulged herself in the first warmth that she had felt for days as she approached the potbellied stove in the middle of the room.

The young cavalry lieutenant bowed to Sophia. "The colonel has several presents he wants to give to you. Food—bread, sterlet caught in the Don, some army rations and tins of peaches, and asparagus." With a shrug of his shoulders, he commented, "A strange assortment, but that is all we have. I am afraid that everything is frozen, but it will thaw soon."

Sophia nodded approvingly as she sorted the food on the table.

With a wide smile of delight, the lieutenant added, "And some tea! The colonel said that you love tea and this will help you to keep warm on your travels. We have no samovar, but he said he is sure the tea will be good no matter how it is made."

"Yes. Tell him that it has made me very happy, even without the samovar the tea will be very enjoyable."

Reaching into his bag, he withdrew another item, "The colonel also sends you some heavy cloth. I have a needle and thread that you can use to make coats if you like."

Sophia smiled at the young officer. She didn't tell him that she didn't know how to sew because, in her previous life in St. Petersburg, the servants did the sewing for the family.

"Thank you, Lieutenant. Please tell the colonel that we appreciate his gifts and thoughtfulness. Will we be able to see the colonel while we are here?"

"I don't know," the lieutenant responded. "We are acting as a rear guard while our forces regroup, so he may not be able to join you here. We have become specialists in guarding the rear, it seems. We cannot stay, but the guard will remain for two days for your protection. He will sleep inside the door." The lieutenant's tone turned solemn as he continued. "The colonel suggests that you refresh yourselves for only three days and then be on your way again. He is also concerned about typhus, which we call 'war fever.' We lose more men to that disease than to the enemy, so he says to disinfect as often as you can. The cold is the worst time, because the lice want to be near the body for warmth, and they spread the disease."

Sophia thought that they would never have discussed such things in her previous life in St. Petersburg. Changing the subject, the lieutenant continued, "Bataisk is just a few miles ahead. There are still trains leaving, and you might be able to ride from there. The trains only depart in the daytime because of marauders in the area. Your destination is in the mountain region, and it is protected, so, God willing, you will find safety there."

Sophia stood silently in the dim light for a minute as she attempted to mask her true feelings and said, "I will pray for your safety, Lieutenant, and that of my husband and all of his brave comrades. Our cause is noble, and I'm sure that we will prevail."

With some hesitation, the lieutenant again reached into his saddlebag. Pulling out an object wrapped in a dirty piece of cloth, he spoke so that only Sophia could hear. "There are thieves and bandits all over the countryside. Even some of our soldiers behind the lines are robbing refugees and causing them harm." As he removed the cloth, he continued, " This is a seven-shot Nagant revolver. It is good, reliable protection." Holding it up to the dim light, he showed her the marking just above the grooved wooden handle. "See, made in Tula at the Emperor Peter the Great Army Factory—1913."

Silently, the lieutenant demonstrated how to load and shoot the revolver. After several attempts, Sophia felt comfortable with the basics of that maneuver and put the revolver on the table.

The lieutenant bowed to Sophia again and whispered, "The blessing of the Lord be with you and your family on your journey." He turned, and both officers bowed to the icon on the wall and left the farmhouse. The sound of the horses leaving the farmyard faded into the night. Sophia and the children were alone, basking in the warmth. Sophia picked up the blue steel revolver. It was heavy in her hand. She said a quiet prayer that she would never have to use it.

The farmhouse was very comfortable, and the little stove provided the unaccustomed luxury of warmth. Sophia and the children were clean and warm after two days in the farmhouse. With some luck, she had found a seamstress in the village, who, for a few pieces of gold jewelry, made heavy coats for all of them. Sophia gathered up the food from the table and added some hard bread she had purchased from the seamstress. The guard was now gone. By the light of the floating wick, Sophia and the children prepared to depart in the morning.

The light was shielded from the window so that it would not attract attention. Suddenly, Sophia heard voices and two drunken soldiers appeared in the doorway, talking and laughing loudly. Seeing the family, the soldiers looked at each other and laughed knowingly. "Give us some food and money, and we will go." Grabbing Luba, one of the soldiers said, with a sneer, "We will take her."

Luba struggled and scratched the soldier's face before his strong arms wrapped around her. Sophia lunged at them and pulled her out of his arms. The soldier punched Sophia in the face and threw her to the floor. Blood trickled slowly from a cut under her eye. Luba crouched behind her mother for protection.

Sophia screamed, "Deserters! Bastards! You should be at the front with the soldiers. With my husband. Take what you want. Leave her!"

The soldier laughed. "You have nothing here we want, except her. We will take her and go."

Sophia rose slowly from the floor and staggered a few steps toward a table near the wall. She pulled the revolver out from under some blankets. The soldier was not looking at Sophia, but he turned when he recognized the sharp click of a revolver being cocked. With a look of surprise, he stared at the barrel of the Nagant revolver being pointed directly at him.

The drunken soldier, suddenly sober, said " Little lady. Don't shoot. Put down the revolver. We were only making a joke."

"I know how to use this revolver." Sophia responded. "Get out!"

Thinking that he could quickly disarm this woman, the soldier suddenly lunged at Sophia. As he reached for the pistol, Sophia pulled the trigger and the sound of the gunshot echoed loudly throughout the room. The soldier had deflected the weapon but not enough and the bullet passed through his right shoulder and he lay bleeding at Sophia's feet. The pistol had fallen to the floor, and Sophia quickly picked it up and aimed it at the second soldier, who was too startled to react. The blood from the first soldier's wound soaked through his heavy winter coat and he labored to breathe, but he was still alive.

Sophia pointed the pistol and shouted at the second soldier who stood motionless, "I have six more shots. If you want to live, go! Take your friend. If you come back, I will kill you. You are both cowards. I should kill you now for the glory of Russia."

The soldier struggled to put his companion's arm over his own shoulder. He guided him toward the door, and they stumbled outside into the cold. Sophia lowered the pistol to her side.

Her dress was spattered with blood. "Maybe they will come back," she thought. "I should have killed them both. But they are deserters and cowards; they won't come back." Sophia put her arms around her children and assured them that everything would be all right. Then they began to clean the blood from the floor.

"Glory-bound in Search of Greatness"

by Jack Trammell

The descriptors used to evaluate Confederate brigadier general John Hunt Morgan's 1863 raid of Indiana and Ohio range from "spectacular" and "incredible," to "foolish" and "worthless." Morgan biographer James A. Ramage calls it nothing more than a pinprick in a healthy arm.[1] Bruce Catton classified this campaign with all others of Morgan, saying that it undoubtedly made headlines but didn't influence the outcome of the war.[2] Even the fact that the campaign is frequently referred to as "The Great Raid" is potentially contradictory or misleading, because many historians and military analysts would argue that it was anything but "great" in its effect on the Confederate effort to win the war and actually served against it by boosting morale in the Midwest, where Union support had been waning. One biographer even determined that Morgan must have been insane to undertake such a mission.[3]

Historians, however, are obviously not the only people qualified to determine historical significance. To the peoples of southern Indiana and Ohio, the arrival—and rapid departure—of Morgan's command was *the* defining event in the war. It left a mark on the collective population that it is still evident today in popular culture. Nearly every town or village in this region, and even many individual families, have their own anecdotes about the raid.[4] Unlike Shiloh or Gettysburg, Morgan's raid was high drama that stirred up incredible excitement without the long casualty lists both sides had grown weary of.

In the South, too, the impact was significant in terms of emotions and morale. It was on this raid that Morgan sealed his ranking among the immortals and icons of what is often termed the Lost Cause when discussing the Civil War, and if lacking in military significance, the raid was bursting with potent symbolism and propaganda of immense value to a flagging, often unpopular Confederate government. In several ways, Morgan's Great Raid was the Civil War in microcosm, with the South making daring and bold military gestures, but ultimately victimized by superior numbers and a flawed war strategy.

A Short Chronology

In late April of 1863, tiring of picket duty in southern Kentucky and middle Tennessee, Morgan dispatched scouts north to the Ohio River. He had decided to take the war to the people who were behind the invading Union armies and to destroy whatever materials and resources he could at the same time. He even flirted with the idea of linking up with Robert E. Lee, who was headed into Pennsylvania on his last serious invasion of the North. In private, Morgan planned the details of a mission that would take him into Indiana and possibly further.[5]

Whatever his private motives, those around him supported what he publicly proposed to do, which was raid north toward Louisville. Brig. Gen. Joseph "Fightin Joe" Wheeler, Morgan's immediate superior, gave his permission not once, but twice, for Morgan to raid as far as Louisville, but never had an inkling that Morgan would cross the Ohio River and continue northward.[6] Commanding general Braxton Bragg of the Army of Tennessee did not have a clue concerning Morgan's true plan either and never forgave him for the indiscretion. Morgan's closest officer, his brother-in-law, Col. Basil Duke, was one of the few officers he shared his real intentions with, and Duke was seriously concerned about the dim prospects for success.[7] All in all, Morgan's decision to cross the great river can only be termed as rash, stubborn, and reckless, but in some ways it was very much typical of the risk taker he had become.[8]

Leaving his pregnant wife, Mattie, for whom he made careful arrangements, Morgan made his mind up to go and then never looked back. On June 20th Morgan's main force (about twenty-five hundred in number, divided into two brigades under Duke and Col. Adam Johnson, and accompanied by two small batteries of artillery)[9] crossed the Cumberland River in Tennessee and moved slowly in the general direction of Monticello, Kentucky, fighting several small skirmishes along the way.

On July 2nd the command crossed the Cumberland River a second time, this time in Kentucky at Burkesville. On July 4th Morgan foolishly attacked Union forces from Michigan, which were positioned strongly on the opposite side of the Green River at Tebb's Bend, and suffered seventy-five casualties for his troubles. Morgan bypassed this force, although he could have defeated them with time and effort, and instead continued north toward Lebanon. Speed was of the essence.

On July 5th Morgan's forces fought a six hour battle in Lebanon Union forces under Col. C. S. Hanson. Morgan's men burned buildings in the center of town, where the Union soldiers were holding out, and eventually forced their surrender. Tragically, though, Morgan's younger brother, Tom, was killed before the town was brought under control. Morgan remained silent with grief while his men went on a rampage in revenge.[10]

The small army had to continue moving northward. On July 6th, at around four in the morning, Morgan arrived in Bardstown. By ten in the morning, his men reached the tracks of the L & N twenty-five miles south of Louisville, where they burned a trestle, robbed a train, and dispatched a company of 130 men under Captain Davis to threaten Louisville.

On July 7th Morgan camped near Garnettsville, Kentucky. A few miles away, in Brandenburg, his advance detachment captured two steamboats, the *Alice Dean* and the *John. T. McCombs,* both of which were lured into ambush, robbed, and then outfitted to assist an amphibious crossing the next day.[11]

On July 8th, in a tedious operation that dragged on for seventeen hours, the two steamboats ferried Morgan's men across the Ohio River and into Indiana. After the crossing was complete, the *Alice Dean* was burned, but the *J. T. McCombs* was recaptured by Union forces and sent by Union cavalry into Louisville with the news of the invasion of the Hoosier state.[12] The "glory" phase of the Great Raid officially began.

Interestingly, Union forces in the area did attempt to thwart Morgan, without ever really understanding what his intentions were. In one case, General Henry M. Judah had moved to cut off Morgan's retreat to Tennessee, never suspecting that the raider was headed in the opposite direction. In another case, Maj. Gen. Ambrose Burnside, who was busy in Cincinnati organizing his piecemeal army that was spread throughout Kentucky, did send forces under Brig. Gen. Edward Hobson to cut off the Ohio River route from Morgan. Hobson, however, arrived a few hours after Morgan had already crossed the river.[13] The Union missed several opportunities in the early stages to stop Morgan, but the truth is that even men in Morgan's own command didn't always know their real destination until after they arrived.

On the night of July 8th, Morgan and his men camped about five miles north of the river. The citizens of Indiana were already in a state of panic. Governor Oliver P. Morton immediately began preparations for mobilizing every healthy male in the state. The telegraph records for these weeks reveal a massive effort to respond to the danger of invasion.[14]

The next day the only official battle of the Great Raid was fought at Corydon, Indiana. Just outside the town, along a wooded ridge, four hundred and fifty men of the 6th Indiana Legion under Colonel Lewis Jordan formed a line of battle. Morgan's artillery began lobbing shells into the town itself, and the first wave of invaders charged the ridge. Four Indiana soldiers and sixteen of Morgan's command became casualties in the initial charge, which wasn't a serious attack. A few minutes later, Jordan saw that it was hopeless and surrendered. More than three hundred Indiana militiamen were quickly paroled before Morgan moved on. The vanguard passed through New Salisbury and camped near Palmyra.

The next day, three hundred and fifty militiamen near Palmyra retreated before confronting Morgan's main force. All through the raid, Morgan split his force into different groups, confusing every effort to intercept him, and on this day, one column destroyed a railroad bridge, while another captured Salem and paroled another two hundred militia members. In Salem, Morgan forced the town millers to pay a ransom to avoid having their property destroyed.

Morgan encountered stiffer resistance later at Vernon. A large Home Guard force there refused to surrender. He wisely decided to bypass this situation, skirting to the southeast.

That night Morgan slept in Lexington, Indiana. Forces were converging on him from all directions, including a force under Maj. Gen. Lew Wallace (of *Ben Hur* fame) with more than one thousand Indiana soldiers. But no one would be able to catch him in Indiana.

On July 11th Morgan's men entered Dupont, capturing over two thousand Mayfield hams, which resulted in an odd spectacle for any who were brave enough to peek out their windows. Raiders strapped as many as half a dozen hams on each of their mounts.[15] Morgan slept in Dupont that night at the Thomas Stout house.

On July 12 Morgan's main force reached Versailles. Union forces, including those under Hobson, were only hours behind Morgan, so he wasted no time in paroling the three hundred prisoners he had taken. In the looting that occurred before leaving, Morgan's men captured vast stores of whiskey, which they freely consumed. Two of Morgan's men were fatally shot later that day near Sunman. That night, Morgan slept in an old school house known as the Ferris School, only a few miles from the Ohio River.

The next day Morgan's men passed by Klump's Tavern—where patrons of today can still enjoy a drink—and soon reached the Ohio River at Harrison. An exhausted Morgan napped for a few hours before moving into southwestern Ohio. Forces under Hobson were less than two hours behind him.

The Ohio portion of Morgan's raid was a continuation of the same story, perhaps at a slightly more frenetic pace: burning bridges, buildings, canal boats, and depots; ripping up railroad tracks; seizing funds; and forcing civilians to cook and provide food.[16] Like its sister state, southern Ohio found itself in a state of panic. The authorities did not fail to act, however. More than one hundred and fifteen thousand men were placed under arms to counter the Morgan raid in Indiana and Ohio.[17]

The Ohio portion of the raid covered July 13th to the 26th. Morgan skirted north of Cincinnati, again avoiding heavy forces that had been arrayed for his benefit. Federal cavalry that had tracked him through Indiana stayed with him in Buckeye country while he crossed the main part of the state in about six days. On July 18th, Morgan arrived in Portland, Ohio, fully expecting to cross back into Virginia (actually West Virginia) and circle back to Kentucky and Tennessee. The ford on the Ohio River was guarded, but Morgan was not overly concerned. That night he slept imagining that his greatest risks were about to be put behind him. He failed to post pickets, however, and the next day everything was fated to begin unraveling.

On July 19th, as they were beginning the Ohio River crossing, Morgan's men made an unpleasant discovery. Around the corner of Buffington Island loomed the steamship *Moose,* ready to open fire. To make matters worse, the pursuit chose that moment to arrive. Hobson, Col. August Kautz, and Brig. Gen. Henry Judah fell on Morgan's men with numerically superior forces of militia and cavalry.

From this point on, things went from bad to worse. Morgan encouraged those who could make it to complete the crossing. About three hundred men made it back to Bragg's army this way. Another seven hundred or so became trapped with Basil Duke and Colonel Smith, fighting tenaciously until they were overwhelmed and forced to surrender. The rest of the command accompanied Morgan north in an attempt to find another safe place to cross.

Morgan never crossed the river. Arcing further north over the next seven days, the Confederates found themselves pressed harder and harder on all sides. Small pockets of Morgan's remaining forces were picked up daily, and finally Morgan himself and a remnant of about three hundred men were forced to surrender near West Point and New Lisbon, Ohio.

The Great Raid was over, but its footprints were impressed on the landscape of Indiana and Ohio. This path can still be followed today.

The Modern Traveler

The present-day traveler wishing to retrace Morgan's route through Indiana and Ohio faces several obstacles, not the least of which is that Morgan's columns were frequently split, taking several different routes, sometimes in purposefully confusing directions. Also, today some of the places Morgan's men passed through are part of restricted properties, like the Jefferson Proving Grounds in Indiana.

There also is the issue of historical markers, with the consensus among Morgan historical followers being that more are needed in both states, as well as in Kentucky, where the raid really began in earnest. (There are approximately twenty-three in southeastern Indiana, for example.)

Approximately 175 miles of southeastern Indiana roads follow Morgan's trails.[18] Probably double that, or more, miles of roads are in Ohio. There are also a number of houses and business establishments surviving from the time of the raid, including some where modern-day visitors can pause for a refreshing drink, or stay overnight in the same place Morgan or his men stopped.

Where to Find Detailed Information

A group of individuals devoted to preserving the Morgan trail has formed under the name, "The Morgan Raid Project Team." This group, organized by Dick Skidmore of Hanover, Indiana, was formed to "identify, interpret and promote" the Morgan Trail. The group will have guide books, tapes, and free educational materials available. For more information, contact Historic Hoosier Hills at (812) 689-6456. The Kentucky, Ohio, and Indiana Departments of Tourism can also provide tourist information about the famous raid.

Lora Cahill, author of the tour guide book for the Morgan Heritage Trail, bases her maps on historically accurate maps from 1876, juxtaposing them on modern maps for convenience. Current maps can be obtained from the various departments of tourism, as well.

Morgan's raid has become such a part of the local folklore that the modern traveler will not be able to escape its influence. Thanks to the effort of concerned citizens and historians, following Morgan's path to glory should become easier and more informative.

Endnotes

1. Ramage *Rebel Raider* (Lexington: University Press of Kentucky, 1986), 181.
2. Bruce Catton *Short History of the Civil War* (New York: Dell Publishing, 1960), 151.
3. Ramage, *Rebel Raider,* 158.
4. Lora Schmidt Cahill, *The John Hunt Morgan Heritage Trail in Indiana,* 1st draft (Corydon, IN: K-Hill Publications, 1996) introduction. (Cahill is a native of Morgan Raid country.)
5. Ramage, *Rebel Raider,* 159.
6. John P. Dyer, *From Shiloh to San Juan (The Life of "Fightin Joe" Wheeler)* (Baton Rouge, LA: L.S.U. Press, 1989) 82.
7. Ramage, *Rebel Raider,* 159.
8. Ibid., 158–59.
9. Cahill, *John Hunt Morgan Heritage Trail,* 5.
10. Ramage, *Rebel Raider,* 164.
11. Ibid., 168.
12. Cahill, *John Hunt Morgan Heritage Trail,* 9.
13. Ramage, *Rebel Raider,* 168–69.
14. "The Telegraph Dispatch Books of Governor Oliver P. Morton," as reviewed at webmaster@ai.org (actual manuscript resides at Indiana State Archives).
15. Cahill, *John Hunt Morgan Heritage Trail,* 24.
16. Ramage, *Rebel Raider,* 170.
17. Ibid., 172 and 174.
18. Dick Skidmore, "Indiana Group Promotes Morgan 1863 Raid Route," *Civil War News* 22, no. 6 (July 1996).

"The Seven Wonders of the Old South: Natural Bridge"

by Jack Trammell

From the Mississippi River past the dramatic promontories of the Blue Ridge Mountains to the Carolina outer banks, the most famous natural landmarks of the antebellum South all played prominent roles in the Civil War and were physically impacted by the violence of conflict.

Formed millions of years ago by seismic uplift, running water, and the erosion of an underlying carbonate layer, Natural Bridge has been a source of geological wonder dating back to prehistory and the native cultures of the region. The great 215-foot-high arch of Paleolithic limestone is located in a region filled with other karst features (caves, caverns, underground rivers, arches, sinkholes, and so forth) at a mountainous junction between the Southside of Virginia and the upper (southern) end of the Shenandoah Valley. A Monacan Indian legend tells of the miraculous appearance of the bridge as the tribe was fleeing from certain destruction at the hands of enemies, and how they were able to rally by using its advantageous defensive features. In a similar vein, the bridge served as a funnel for Union forces approaching defeat at Lynchburg in 1864.

From the earliest recorded records, visitors have proclaimed awe at the sight of the bridge:

> "The most sublime of Nature's works." (Thomas Jefferson, first private owner of Natural Bridge)
>
> "Natural Bridge is nature like art . . .on the very spot where art would otherwise have been required for the construction of a bridge." (Henry Howe, nineteenth-century Virginia historian)

> "Look at that coloring. Does it not appear like the painter's highest skill, and yet unspeakably transcend it?" (nineteenth-century European traveler)

Herman Melville compared the tail of the great white whale in his novel *Moby Dick* to the widespread opening on the arch.

In addition to its beauty, the bridge has also served as an important transportation feature for hundreds, possibly thousands, of years. Below Natural Bridge runs Cedar Creek, a rushing, tumbling trout-filled waterway that cuts through a sharp gorge, and Natural Bridge provides the only reasonable means of crossing the creek in the area. The Monacans, and other natives before them, referred to the great north-south pathway that ran through the Shenandoah Valley and crossed over Natural Bridge as *the* "Great Path." Before the Civil War, the Great Wagon Road (present-day Route 11, running parallel to Interstate 81) ran over the same path, originating in Philadelphia and carrying settlers west and then south through Maryland and the Shenandoah Valley. During the war, the Great Wagon Road was the single most important means of transportation in the valley, and it figured prominently in all of the campaigns fought there, including the famous 1862 Valley Campaign that made Stonewall Jackson's reputation.

In fact, Jackson's campaign headquarters was only a few miles north of Natural Bridge, at the Inn at Narrow Passage. Jackson undoubtedly visited the site before the war, and he encouraged his wife, Ellie, to take rest there periodically while he finished end-of-the-year duties at Virginia Military Institute in Lexington. During the war, many of Jackson's men passed over the bridge as they moved back and forth in the valley.

One of Stonewall Jackson's personal heroes, George Washington, was the first to formally survey the Natural Bridge in 1750. Washington carved his initials in the bridge, where they can still be seen today. Jackson very likely had seen the famous initials and perhaps even added his own (although those historians who know him well might argue that he was much too serious most of the time to engage in such triviality).

The bridge's strategic importance during the war was not limited to the critical road running over it. Beneath it, and all around it, were caves that were mined for saltpeter, an essential element in the production of gunpowder. Remnants of saltpeter operations are still evident in the rocks and caverns dotting the Cedar Creek canyon. The creation of a domestic gunpowder industry was of such importance to the fledgling Confederate nation that liberal subsidies were offered to any private citizen who could produce any amount. Soldiers badly needed on the most-active military fronts were often siphoned off frontline duty to guard and supervise nitre (saltpeter) production.

The bridge also continued to be a major tourist attraction during the war, comparing favorably to another popular destination, Niagara Falls. Stage coaches traveling the Great Valley Road regularly stopped at Natural Bridge so that passengers could enjoy the views. In many publications of the Civil War era (and still today), Natural Bridge was identified as one of the seven natural wonders of the world. Following in the tradition of Jefferson, who bought Natural Bridge for 20 shillings and set up a cabin for friends and visitors there, many soldiers from both sides couldn't resist the temptation to stray from their march on the Great Valley Road to see the bridge from below. Many attempted to carve their initials into the rock, as Washington had done. Some attempted to climb the bridge, though reportedly only two individuals had done so successfully before the war, and each had nearly lost his life in the attempt.

The bridge saw the most activity in 1864 during Union general David Hunter's valley campaign. As part of a grand Union strategy to attack Confederate forces simultaneously on several fronts in June of 1864, General U. S. Grant ordered Hunter's army to raid down the Shenandoah Valley and seize, if possible, the communication and transportation center of Lynchburg. President Abraham Lincoln and Grant could not have chosen a more unpopular leader to subdue the valley. Hunter was an abolitionist and a Virginia native who had remained loyal to the Union. He had aroused great indignation in Richmond earlier in the war when he conscripted and freed blacks without authorization in South Carolina. There were standing orders that he was a "felon to be executed, if captured." Hunter advanced toward Staunton, incorporating several other Union forces in the area into his army along the way.

Opposing Hunter was Confederate general William E. "Grumble" Jones, renowned for his austere dress (the opposite of his former superior, J. E. B. Stuart) and unpredictable temper. On June 5th, 1864, Jones prepared to make a stand near the village of Piedmont, and Hunter obligingly attacked at the crossroads. An untimely gap along the Confederate right, and the sudden death of Jones as he led a counterattack in the center, turned what had been a stalemate into a Confederate rout. The road to Lynchburg (and over Natural Bridge) was open to Hunter. For General Robert E. Lee fighting Grant in Virginia, it was an unmitigated disaster. The breadbasket for his Army of Northern Virginia—and much of the upper South—was in danger of being lost permanently. To try to stem the bleeding, he rushed a division westward, and then a few days later, an entire corps. Considering the perilous state of affairs around Petersburg, it is amazing that Lee thought to send nearly a third of his army.

In the meantime, Hunter played havoc with the upper valley. On June 11th, his combined army of eighteen thousand men occupied Lexington without firing a shot. The next day, he ordered the Virginia Military Institute (whose cadets had contributed to a dramatic May 15th Confederate victory at New Market) burned to the ground. A famous statue of George Washington was "liberated." Civilian homes in the area were also destroyed, including the private residence of former governor John Letcher. The local citizenry was appalled, but was left defenseless. A few days later, Hunter's army began the arduous journey over the mountains toward the military target of Lynchburg.

On June 15th, Confederate scouts reported Union forces at and around Natural Bridge. Their myriad campfires dotted the landscape that night. The Union soldiers were arrogant and confident and spoke boldly of Lynchburg's coming fate. The local militia in Rockbridge County was called out, but the remnants of Jones's Confederate force remained disorganized in its retreat to the lines around Lynchburg. Very little resistance was offered. The isolated bands of resistance that did crop up were quickly pushed aside, and dozens of Confederate soldiers were captured.

Many Union soldiers reported their visit to the bridge as they moved southwesterly toward Buchanan on the way to Lynchburg. Some tried to pause long enough to carve their initials into the stone.

> "We will pass the Natural Bridge [tomorrow] and that is a sight I should like to see."
>
> "We passed near the Natural Bridge."
>
> Confederates near the bridge, however, had little time or energy for sightseeing.
>
> "In all my experiences of war I have never been so chased, pursued, dogged," Captain A. J. Tynes wrote to his wife on June 13th as he stopped near the bridge.

A young Rutherford B. Hayes and William McKinley passed over or near the bridge with Hunter's army. Years later, as president of the United States, McKinley would return "under so much more agreeable circumstances" and pay his respects to the arch.

On June 14th Hunter's force proceeded to Buchanan, and under circumstances similar to Sherman's in Georgia later in the year, broke all contact with the North as he headed over the mountaintops. Confederates under General Jubal Early scrambled to prepare the defenses at Lynchburg, and the stage was set for a dramatic confrontation. On June 17th–18th Hunter's army was defeated at Lynchburg, and the immediate crisis in Lee's rear was averted.

Events at Natural Bridge returned somewhat to normal. Sometime later in the year two bushwhackers were apprehended by Confederate soldiers in the vicinity. One was shot and the other released when it was determined that *she* was a female in male costume. Some locals returned to the work in the saltpeter caves above Cedar Creek. Traffic, as always, flowed over the bridge along the Great Valley Road.

When the war ended, tourist traffic picked up, and later Virginia Route 11 (the Great Valley Road) became one of modern Virginia's busiest highways. Today, Natural Bridge remains a popular tourist destination, drawing roughly three hundred thousand visitors per year. But the marks of the war remain on Natural Bridge—the initials carved in stone, the saltpeter caves (where in some cases rusting equipment still lies), and the ghosts of thousands who came by and paused to marvel at one of nature's most incredible works.

"Assignment to Porto Alegre, Brazil, 1950–1952"

by Catherine D. Peaslee

The mid-twentieth century opened with my departure with my husband, Sandy, and our two daughters, Sally and Mei-Mei, for Brazil from Joliet on the Elgin, Joliet, and Eastern Railroad by way of Washington, D.C. Our final destination would be Porto Alegre, capital of Rio Grande do Sul, Brazil's southernmost province, where Sandy would be the new vice consul in the American consulate. His new assignment had followed his return home from almost a year's internment in the American consulate general in Shanghai, China, by the victorious Communists.

For our stay in Washington, D.C., I had booked a room with our old friends at the Bouma Guest House, where Sandy and I had often stayed while he visited me in Washington, D.C., on leave from the U.S. Army at Camp Ritchie, Maryland, during the war. From there, we would depart for New York City and board a Moore-McCormick ship for Rio de Janeiro, Brazil's capital. The new capital, Brasília, was still on the architect's drawing board.

Carnaval was just beginning when we arrived in Rio, where the embassy had reserved a hotel room for us. After tucking Sally and Mei-Mei in bed, Sandy and I departed to dine on snails dipped in garlic butter. Noise from the street celebrants filled the night until dawn. Then it was time to pack up and catch the plane for Porto Alegre.

It was evening when we arrived in the Porto Alegre airport and drove into the city. Everywhere graffiti commanded: "*Norteamericanos,* go home!" Had we left one Communist revolution only to arrive amid another? We certainly were not welcome.

Our first home in Porto Alegre was the Preto (Black) Hotel. The name was uninviting, but it was the best hotel in the city. The name of the Teatro Sao Paulo suggested we would see grand opera and concerts with famous European artists. However, after a performance of *Rigoletto*, I was quickly disabused of that hope. Rejects from European stages sang the leading roles, and the chorus was a shabby collection of the city's unemployed. We didn't return to the theater until the next year, when Marian Anderson made a guest appearance.

The best feature in our hotel home, according to Sandy, was a bidet in the bathroom. He pronounced it the "perfect" place to soak Mei-Mei's dirty diapers. Why don't our bathrooms at home have bidets? I never heard a satisfactory reply. Somehow, the word "bidet" might be anathema to Christian morals, free market economics, and Republican politics.

While Sandy went off to his new job as vice consul under Consul General Lansing Collins, the girls and I stayed in the Preto, where I studied Portuguese. Few people in Porto Alegre spoke English, so learning Portuguese was necessary if we were to meet Brazilians. Also, it was much easier to learn than Mandarin Chinese.

The consular staff was small: Marvin Mayeux, Gloria Wasielewski, and the U.S. Information Service officer. Local Brazilians were the other administrative employees. "Dona Barbara," Lansing Collins's wife, a tall, glamorous blonde with three daughters, small replicas of their mother, was the queen bee.

Sandy, the vice consul, helped traveling Americans and reported on the local political scene (Communist activities) and the economy (wheat, soybeans, and cattle).

The Communist Party in Porto Alegre was a combination of intellectuals and workers. Their nonmilitant leader was a medical doctor, prominent socialite, and concert pianist. Our cook, Maria Antonieta, belonged to the local party. "After the revolution," she warned me as she scrubbed the kitchen floor, "you'll be down here and I'll be up there." I wasn't worried. Maria Antonieta's fine cooking was enough for me to tolerate her politics. More difficult was her demand that her two dogs must share our living quarters in a very small house and garden.

Like its neighbors, Uruguay and Argentina, Rio Grande's economy was based on cattle raising and export crops grown on large ranches, or *latifundia* (great landed estates). Its economy and culture reminded me of Texas without oil wells. President Getúlio Dornelles Vargas was a "gaucho" from Porto Alegre's cattle-raising province, Rio Grande do Sul. He was a wily politician who had climbed to supreme power from humble beginnings. In 1930 the military had overthrown the republic and installed Vargas. As *presidente,* he had centralized the federal government's power, reduced states' rights, and declared himself the supreme ruler, imitating the dictators in Portugal, Spain, and Italy at that time. In 1945 the military overthrew Vargas, and he was out of the presidency until 1950, when he returned to office, his "second coming."

Vargas inspired jokes and *Carnaval* lyrics such as the samba title, "Here I Stay, from Here I Do Not Go Out!" If there was a shortage of cooking oil, a power failure, or currency inflation, a *Braseilero* didn't get mad. He just blamed Vargas. Despite Vargas's blatant abuse of power, the Brazilians loved him and tolerated his failures until 1954, when he committed suicide.

How different it all was after living in wartime China. But after we left Brazil for Hong Kong, Brazilians reaped the harvest of tolerating Vargas and neglecting their incipient democracy. The military took over.

Just as I had learned vital lessons in China (Americans are *not* the most civilized race in the world, nor the most democratic, humane, tolerant, and generous), in Brazil I learned that race is subjective and viewed very differently by Brazilians and Americans. Skin color is much less important to Brazilians than to Americans.

Our home, locally known as the "Coca Cola House," a perverted product spelling after its previous owners, the American representatives of the Atlanta soft drink empire, had internationally diverse ethnic neighbors. On one side was a large family of blonde-haired, blue-eyed *Teuto-Braseileros* (German Brazilians). The opposite side housed *Luzo-Braseileros* (Portuguese Brazilians). Daughter Sally's best friend was Marie-Hestaire, a Lebanese *Braseilera,* as was the owner of the corner *armazem* (grocery). His customers bought not only groceries but also shot glasses of the potent local liquor. From morning until nightfall our neighbors visited the *armazem* to buy their shots "to kill the bugs."

Our sixteen-year-old maid of all work, Jessie, lived with her extended, intergenerational black family across the street. By the time I hired Jessie, we Peaslees were all speaking Portuguese, more or less. We only spoke English when we socialized with non-*Braseileros*. Among these were the Collinses, our consular staff members, and the British consul general, Lord Hamilton Gordon, and his Lady. She was reputed to have been a Bulgarian countess. Very conscious of protocol, she expected her butler, when serving dinner, to wear white gloves. The British vice consul's wife, an American, was a total convert to British etiquette. Conversations with our British counterparts were mostly about their system for sharing a single copy of the *London Times*. In true British fashion, the aristocrat outranked the pleb. His Lordship had first dibs on the *Times* copies, which he arranged chronologically. When he finished an edition, he passed it on to his vice consul. Nobody complained. They were possibly more compatible than were the disparate characters in the American consulate.

The few *Norteamericanos* in Porto Alegre in those days were a varied crowd: representatives from American banks, the manager of the American-owned transit utility, American agents for a hush-hush military base in the hinterlands, and assorted expatriate Americans.

In midwinter we all gathered for the Fourth of July celebration hosted by the American consulate. The most exotic guests were the loyal contingent from the interior of our neighboring province, Santa Catarina. Descendants of Southerners who had fled to Brazil during and after our Civil War, they steadfastly resisted integrating with the natives and maintained the standards and culture of the old South. They spoke with a soft Southern drawl, and they always sent homemade fudge to the consulate at Christmastime in midsummer.

When we sailed down to Rio on our Moore-McCormick ship, we had crossed the equator into an upside down world beneath the Southern Cross, where Easter lilies bloomed at Christmastime and poinsettias at Easter. In December we invited friends to the Coca Cola House for a Christmas Eve party. As I awaited our guests in the tiny living room, I heard the strains of a Christmas carol beyond the front door. Rushing to find the music's source, I met our first guests, Necy and Don Bird. Necy was playing her accordion, which she called her "geita," while Don carried an Easter lily.

Necy and Don became our dearest friends. Necy, the daughter of *Luzo-Braseileros* whose family had prospered in the cattle business, practiced dentistry, and was the most fastidiously hygienic person I ever met. To avoid germs she compulsively washed her hands and always wore protective white cotton gloves. Aside from this tic, Necy was beautiful, witty, and generous, like many other *Braseileras*. Don, a *Norteamericano*, had met Necy when he was stationed in Brazil during World War II. After they married, Necy's family included Don in their meat packing business, and he adopted their ways. They all lived outside Porto Alegre on a cattle ranch near Pelotas, a small town at the mouth of the *Lagoa do*s *Patios*. When Necy and Don came to Porto Alegre, we often dined or partied together at the Clube de Commercio or the British Club.

Singer Marian Anderson's brief appearance in Porto Alegre to fill an engagement at the Teatro Sao Pedro was the peak event of our two years in Brazil. The news that she was coming with her accompanist for a Sunday night performance electrified the city. Everyone seemed to know Anderson's story of when the Daughters of the American Revolution in Washington, D.C., had denied her the use of Constitution Hall for a concert, Eleanor Roosevelt had offered her an alternative site: the steps of the Lincoln Memorial.

After the Collinses departed from Porto Alegre, Sandy became the new U.S. consul. He led the small delegation one Saturday that met Miss Anderson and her small, white male accompanist at the Porto Alegre airport. Following the picture taking, we all drove into the city, where Miss Anderson would stay at the Hotel Preto. Elaborate preparations had preceded the great occasion.

The timing was awkward for Miss Anderson's concert on a Sunday evening, because all the businesses would be closed, including the restaurants and social clubs. I had to find an alternative site, because we had invited guests to a reception after the concert. Following the reception, we would serve dinner to the great artist and her accompanist upstairs in our bedroom, the largest room in the oddly arranged house.

Jessie, our young *empregada* (employee), was ecstatic when she learned of the plans for Miss Anderson's visit. She did all she could to help arrange our rooms to accommodate the great event: she moved furniture and helped prepare the food and drink with Marie Antonieta in the tiny kitchen only a few square feet larger than our magnificent wood-burning stove. Also, I trusted her to keep Sally and Mei-Mei happy and to put them to bed before we moved upstairs for dinner in our bedroom.

By Sunday afternoon all was in order for the evening's postconcert festivities. Expectation weighed heavily on us all. How would Miss Anderson respond to so many non-English-speaking admirers? Would she notice the bed in our makeshift dining room?

By eight o'clock on Sunday night we were seated in the Teatro Sao Pedro, eager to enjoy the concert of our lives. Miss Anderson, six feet tall, arrayed in a gorgeous Chinese Mandarin coat, sang her repertoire of German lieder and American folk songs. The spiritual, "Were You There When They Crucified My Lord?" was the final number. It silenced the listeners and brought tears to our eyes. Anderson's rich, deep, contralto tones, as much as her words, reminded us of her people's sorrows, losses, and tragedies in modern times. The Brazilians, as much as others in the audience, understood her message. As many African slaves were imported into Brazil as were imported into North America, and their descendants were still an oppressed minority. But Brazil, following the emancipation of its slaves toward the end of the nineteenth century by Dom Pedro II, never endured the Jim Crow laws and discrimination enforced in the United States until recently.

After the concert ended, we drove back to the Coca Cola House. There, Miss Anderson, like an African empress, presided over the reception. Who remembered her humble origins in Philadelphia, the daughter of a woman janitor?

After the last guest departed, we moved upstairs to our bedroom-dining room, where dinner awaited. I have forgotten what we ate or what we said, but I remember seeing Jessie lying on the floor outside our little girls' bedroom, waiting for another glimpse of Miss Anderson. She had fallen asleep.

After the excitement of Miss Anderson's visit subsided, Sandy returned to his new job as U.S. consul. It meant dealing with recalcitrant individuals with strange problems: the woman, a concert pianist, who begged Sandy's help to protect her from her murderous husband; a young American imprisoned in an unheated cell with open windows, who called one midnight to complain, "I'm freezing. The jailers left me with no blankets"; an umbrella-wielding old lady who forced an unscheduled landing at the airport after she attacked the other passengers; a consulate clerk who drank too much at the British Club and threatened anyone who disagreed with him; and, lastly, a young woman clerk from the State Department whose Bohemian ways scandalized the Brazilians.

At home I adjusted to baking angel food cake in a wood-burning stove; the disappearance of our Sears' milk pasteurizer from the back porch; the electricity shortage, which Maria Antonieta blamed on the mayor (not a Communist); and the death of Jessie's mother followed by a voodoo ceremony. The problems of entertaining guests in a house sufficient for a family of pygmies were chronic.

The view of our neighbors' blank wall from the dining room I disguised with gauze curtains. The space limits I extended by using a large drop leaf table and nested end tables. The cramped space and scanty furnishings ensured that social occasions were intimate.

Sandy and I struggled with our Portuguese, although Sally and Mei-Mei soon became fluent. Sandy hired a student named Horatio Nunes to come and tutor us on a weekly basis. He explained to me why Brazilians had such a penchant for giving their children original names and young Brazilian males' extraordinary machismo.

Gradually, we absorbed the Brazilian ethos. We learned why Brazilians believe God is a Brazilian and the national motto, *Orden y progresso* (Order and Progress).

We began hoping to remain in Porto Alegre longer than the usual tour of two years. Why not? But the Foreign Service's administrators act in strange, unseen ways. I never learned why the State Department notified Sandy that his tour in Porto Alegre would end after two years, but like good civil servants, we obeyed orders to pack up, close out our lives in Brazil, and move to the consulate in Hong Kong. I was pregnant with our third daughter, Peggy, who was due in August 1952. She would be a *Braseilera* only in inception.

In only two years we had learned to love Brazil and its diverse, friendly, and creative people. We especially appreciated their self-deprecating sense of humor. They made jokes of life's vicissitudes and their good humor was infectious.

"My Memoir: On Learning to Drive"

by Liz Kollar

"It's so easy," my husband, Frank, insisted. "There's nothing to it." Anyone with two eyes can drive a car.

"What are you afraid of, Mommy? Boogieman gonna get you?" my children teased, joining their father in his efforts to get me to take driving lessons from him.

"Look at all the idiots on the road," continued my husband, winking at the kids, "If they can drive, so can you."

This was fifty-five years ago, when we had one, very old, second-hand, now extinct car, known as the Nash, no money in the bank, and a big mortgage on a small house. Things in those years were tight and often difficult, and my sense of humor was stretched as dangerously thin as my silk stockings.

There were dozens of reasons why I should learn to drive and not one legitimate reason why I shouldn't, except perhaps cowardice and the three little boys watching me accusingly from the back seat. Unfortunately, my kids were right. I was afraid because six years earlier, when I was nine-months pregnant with my first child, I'd taken the challenge thrown at me by my husband. He would teach me and I would learn. Little did he know what lay ahead of him.

It didn't matter that my pregnant belly barely fit behind the wheel. It also didn't matter that there were no air bags and seat belts hadn't, as yet, been invented or mandated. I didn't need one. I was wedged behind the steering wheel, unable to move except for my eyes staring stonily at the road ahead of me. My nearly new husband seemed to have lost his mind, and I could barely look at him, let alone listen to his loud, demanding voice.

We'd entered a cul-de-sac lined with a dozen cars and filled with houses sitting thirty feet, or so, back from the street. My husband asked me to make a U-turn at the end of the road, where most of the cars were parked bumper to bumper. My palms started to sweat and my heart began to race faster than the motor of my Nash. I had to do this right so that he wouldn't laugh at me or holler. Frank sometimes had a short fuse, and he wasn't long home from WWII sea duty on board his Liberty Ship, the *Henry B. Brown,* where he was used to giving commands like: "Hard a-port," and "Mind your helm," and everyone saluted him and said, "Yes Sir!"

I didn't salute, but I overreacted to his commands and turned the wheel more "hard a-port" than I was supposed to, and I surely didn't "mind my helm." The car rounded the turn . . . fast. With my foot frozen to the accelerator, the car took off sharply to the left and raced between two cars parked by the sidewalk, narrowly missed them, and continued up the front lawn of a house with a big picture window behind which a man stood watching me try to maneuver. With a horrified roar, Frank kicked my foot off the accelerator and braked the car to a stop, inches away from the window from behind which the frightened man had made a hasty retreat.

You guessed it. The car stopped but so did my driving venture for a long time to come. Because of the shock, I began having labor pains. My rattled husband got behind the wheel and rushed me home to grab my suitcase and head for the hospital, where my first-born made an appearance a few hours later.

Seven years after that event, hopefully having become a mature adult, the mother of three youngsters, and pregnant for the fourth time, I found it extremely difficult to find excuses for my lack of knowledge concerning cars and how to make them work. It had progressed to the point where four pairs of accusing eyes would be turned on me every time the subject came up—my husband's and my three son's . . . and come up it did, every day.

"Mommy, why can't you pick me up in a car like other boy's moms do after school?" my five-year-old son, Kevin, wailed in great frustration. He was angry and dirty from the long walks to and from first grade, which I did with him every day, all the while pushing a baby carriage with number three son, Teddy, alternately sleeping or howling under the covers.

"Gee, Mom, my feet hurt from walking so much, and besides, all the other kids get rides," complained my seven-year-old son, Frankie, with an injured look on both feet and face, after playing "kick the can" with his friends all the way home from school. He was also an avid collector of seedpods, stones, frogs, and salamanders, and these all needed transporting along with his school supplies.

I had to admit, my husband worked long hours and was never home on time to take us to dental and doctor appointments, PTA and teacher meetings, plus trips to the store for groceries and other necessities. Not knowing how to drive forced me into either walking with the boys and the baby carriage or begging a ride from one of my neighbors.

Also, when it rained or snowed, pushing a carriage was decidedly difficult, and after awhile, my neighbors hid when they saw me coming.

Came the day that I made my big mistake. I promised the men in my life that I would try to learn if I could have a car of my very own. I hated that old, decrepit Nash.

Here entered the Valiant . . . also old and blue, but mine. All I had to do was keep my promise and learn to drive so that I could perform all the chores my family desired. It didn't matter that I was scared to death of driving or that I was sure I'd hit the nearest telephone pole and kill my poor defenseless children. (Remember! As yet, there were no seat belts or car seats for kids.)

Frank called my bluff, and now there were two cars crowding our driveway, his and mine. I had to keep my promise and I had to save face. Off I went to the motor vehicle agency to get a learner's permit.

Our neighbors laughed at the thought that I could learn from my husband, but, seven years older and wiser, he surprised everyone by acting gentle and considerate. No matter what foolish mistakes I made, he'd kiss me after the ordeal and pat me on the back with icy hands.

The five of us did very well swerving our way through vacant schoolyards and empty country roads. My seven year old hung over the seat and kept insisting I shift to first and hide from the cops. Today, he is a retired Long Island police sergeant, and I often wonder if I was the catalyst that made him become one of our men in blue.

Next to him stood his younger brothers, one drooling, the other dispensing words of wisdom in his childish gibberish. "Zoom faster, Mommy!" "Make the car jerk again!" "A hill, Mommy. Don't look!" This one became a doctor and the drooler became a manager of a big oil company, which figures. I've spent a lot of money on gasoline.

The day came when my husband insisted I stop fooling around and go take my driving test, and I sat behind the wheel nearly incontinent. Next to me sat a hostile stranger with a mad gleam in his eye. "Betty! Start the car!" He yelled hoarsely. Jerked into action, I started the car and we drove in silence, while the boys, lined up along the back seat, making faces at me in the mirror and giggling nervously. Except for an occasional, "Keep to your right!" "Slow down, Barney Oldfield!" or "Can't you see that STOP sign?" from my husband, we finally arrived at the driving area reserved for nervous fools like me. It was expressly designed to cause stomach ulcers and heart palpitations, and I felt sorry for the poor man who climbed into the car with me after Frank and the boys climbed out. He looked as if he already had both medical conditions plus a nasty cold, because he kept wiping his brow with a handkerchief and clearing his throat as we took off on our designated test route.

Amazingly, all went well, and since I'd also previously passed the written and eye tests, I received my license with a measure of pride and a good deal of relief. This was also true for my husband, who now decided to get behind the wheel and take over the driving. I sat next to him, boiling mad, while the boys sat in the back seat planning all their future rides when their daddy wasn't home.

It started early the next morning when I automatically became the family chauffeur. As yet, I hadn't learned to park well between cars, and my husband suggested I go and park in the municipal parking lot, where there was plenty of space. Therefore, after dropping off sons Frankie and Kevin at Catechism lessons and with my two year old hugging my neck to keep from falling through the windshield, I decided to go to the local five and dime to buy the boys a treat. As I drove through the heavy traffic, totally unmindful of my husband's warning, I found and swooped into a large open space right in front of the store. Perfect! It was big enough to park three cars and I just couldn't pass it up. Now, having parked like a pro, I took my youngest boy's hand and marched triumphantly into the Woolworth store.

Yup! You guessed it. When I returned to the car, a huge delivery truck was jammed against my back bumper, while a flaming red sports car was just a hand span in front of me. I glanced woefully at my watch. It was time to pick up my older boys, but now I was stuck, and I could see there was no way out of this predicament. About fifteen minutes passed as I sat dejectedly in the front seat, playing, "Round and Round the Garden Goes the Teddy Bear" with Teddy, when the owner of the sports car returned and pulled out. I took a deep breath and quickly followed him.

The following day, returning home from an early morning doctor's appointment because I was now expecting baby number four, I noticed a police car trailing along in back of me. Worried that I was doing something wrong, I slowed to a snail-like twenty-two miles an hour to let him go by. Unfortunately, he passed me, but immediately pulled over to the curb and parked in front of me. I wasn't quick enough to turn away and scraped my Valiant along the entire length of his patrol car. Luckily, the only damage was to my car and my ego. The Valiant lost the chrome strip under the door, while I lost my self-esteem. I was given a ticket by the surprised cop and soon found myself in court fighting a careless drivers' summons that had actually made the front page of the local paper. The judge was sympathetic; the newspaper had to retract its story about the careless local housewife, and my husband and boys had a good laugh at my expense. I almost wished there had been a big fine and then Frank would have had to pay it. That would have been a lot funnier, at least to me.

The next day it poured all day long. Of course, that meant driving to and from school, which indeed was my purpose in learning how to drive. Half blinded by a wildly weaving windshield wiper and torrential rain, I managed to find a parking spot next to the school, where I turned off the engine to wait for the boys to come out. Suddenly, I was shocked to see what appeared to be smoke rising from the hood of the car. Normally, I am of average intelligence, but here my brain failed me; I thought the car was on fire.

I jumped out into the pouring rain to pry open the hood, but how to do this was now the big question. I hunted everywhere for a button or lever that would magically make it fly open, all the time feeling the hood like an anxious mother taking the temperature of a sick child. My hair was soon plastered to my head and my body soaked, and I stood wailing in frustration, when a lovely man came to my rescue. With a quick flick of his finger, he opened the hood and turned to look at me with a strange expression on his face. The "steam" from the heat of the motor and the cold of the rain on the hood had disappeared. With a shake of his head and a grin, he disappeared as well. I'm sure he thought I was one of those idiots my husband was always talking about.

Five minutes later, the boys came out of school. It was time to head home. Lifting the starter handle situated up by the steering wheel, and pressing firmly on the accelerator, I tried again and again to start the car. Nothing happened. The car just sat there like a stubborn mule. Luckily, a neighbor of mine came over to see if she could help. I pressed my foot on the accelerator as hard as I could to show her that the car wouldn't start.

"Must be the carburetor," I mumbled . . . the same words my husband Frank always seemed to say when he had a problem with his car.

She shook her head much like the lovely man who had opened the hood for me earlier. "Betty," she said, smiling sweetly, "why don't you try turning the key in the ignition first?"

Face flaming and kids giggling, I thanked her, started the car and headed for home. "One word out of any of you . . . gets it," I said, as we drove off in complete silence.

The following day I made four trips, all uneventful. But, of course, there were still fifty years of driving ahead of me and anything could happen.

ON WRITING AND PUBLISHING

"A Life-in-Writing"

by Priscilla Randolph

Writing is to be my legacy. But to whom? I have no children. I have no literary heir.

Writing is my child. Writing is my soul's companion—perhaps to lie alongside me in my grave.

Writing is to be fully engaged in the exploration of self's life and the life outside one's self.

Writing glorifies solitude, the strength of heart and character, the onslaught of pain, the quest for transcendence, the summons to a higher good.

Writing confines me in the blissful strict seclusion of notebooks.

Writing seeks a physical likeness for such words as "radiant," "pure," "ideal." Writing is words' aim to outdo other words. For example, "beauty." The hunt is on for an even more heavenly word than "beauty" to describe beauty.

Writing is escape from what proves too hard to face, withdrawal after dealing poorly with reality.

Writing is one thing I've never run away from.

Writing could impress my views upon people—upon "the world," that is.

Writing is to express indignation and to right wrongs in an often staccato or sputtery voice: the injustice of racial discrimination or the universality of tyranny.

Writing is an organizing force for the need to justify myself—as if my actions, my deeds, indeed my words are suspect and need constant attending to.

Writing is to explain myself to myself—a person who captivates my attention but is demanding to live with. My writing is also to explain myself to others, but then I have not shown my writing to countless others.

Writing is to treat myself meticulously and harshly. Yet, at the deep-deeper-deepest level, I know I am worth fighting for.

Yet, my writing severs me from people. It helps foster my illusion that I am within the mainstream, but often I feel outside of it. I want my writing to be a conduit to others; I am not so sure it is.

Writing is good for tirades, for ripping apart and reassembling self. Writing is good for the climax to anger, and the quieting-down afterward. I am the only person hurt.

Writing calms me for the business of creativity.

Writing is solace.

Writing sprays prayers up to heaven like fireworks. (Pray, God, make my words truly sing!)

Writing is to reveal—or conceal—self.

Words are my desire. I *desire* them—and *passionately.*

Writing encourages ambitions and sublimates unrequited desires.

Writing enables me to see why I am embattled, and why I persist.

Writing preserves me, keeps me alive. Yet, writing strands me at the far reaches of a limb.

Writing assuages a tenacious curiosity. Relatives once counseled me not to ask so many questions; it was too exhausting.

I am aching to be heard.

I ache for people to be around to read to.

"A Myriad of Murgatroyds"

by Sarah C. Honenberger

"Miserly Murgatroyd mated madly. He planned it that way." She scratched through the second sentence and wrote instead, *"It happened accidentally."* She stared at the remaining seven words.

What if Murgatroyd were mysterious instead? His couplings might be cautious, his pickups polite. Did she really want to go on and on about a skinflint, her words selected skillfully to show something rare and insightful that would make a reader gasp? Her stories would be printed and bound with artistic covers and dedications in which she'd be forced to acknowledge parents and writing teachers. If—no, when—the books became internationally renowned, media personalities would insist she appear in designer clothes and make significant conclusions about world peace. Her face flushed, yearning for her former anonymity, she shifted uncomfortably on the wooden chair.

What if Murgatroyd did not attack his carnal conduct with such conviction? If Murgatroyd mated mildly, the story would twist and flail, its spindly lines failing. She imagined the scene at his psychiatrist, where Murgatroyd mewled and blubbered about his ineffectual machinations; the lonely nights of barhopping, the tragic days considering suicide when woman after woman refused his invitations. Polite no-thank-yous would pile up around poor Murgatroyd until he preferred burial to more pointless philandering. Wiping her sweaty palm on her sleeve, she prayed for Murgatroyd to find meaning in his life, to know God, to meet a meek Mary who mated just as mildly as he.

On the other hand, Murgatroyd might scurry between lovers and never arrive at a new understanding. Despite chapter after chapter of obscure orgasms, the protagonist, the author, and the reader might fail to discover redemption worthy of literary merit. Cringing, she twisted her hair around her finger. The pen lay on the page in open accusation.

What if she fell asleep? It happened all the time, starving artist inhales fumes from faulty heater, hospitalized with temporary blindness, or better, permanent brain damage. Murgatroyd would slip back into her mind's recesses. He would shrink from his full-blown procreative state to a vague possibility in an unseen dimension. No, he'd be less than that, an inkling, a mere dot on a hypothetical brain scan before her sobbing family choked the life support and sent her to an early grave.

She closed her eyes and concentrated. Ah, but what if Murgatroyd took over? Now there was an idea. Like a flaccid balloon before hot air transformed it to a Mardi Gras parade celebrity, Murgatroyd might rise from his sexual series and become a whole person, with children begging to ride his shoulders and a wife depending on him for vacations at the shore and flowers on Valentine's Day. Murgatroyd would have to make arrangements for all of them, investing and bargaining and polishing his shoes for the day when his mother contracted Alzheimer's and had to be put down.

She lined through *put down*—that was animals—*put away* was more correct. And Murgatroyd would be correct. He would be reliable, an Eagle Scout, his bow ties never crooked. Of course, before any of that could happen, he had to escape the crazy copulation of the first line.

If, by some miracle, he did expand and fill the pages and then the room, why wouldn't it be her, the writer, who became less than a possibility, lost in an unseen dimension, a mere inkling?

She shook her head. She'd lost her train of thought. Rising, stretching, she poured a glass of water and sipped quietly, searching for a way to start again.

What if the lump under her arm were cancer, gnawing away at the very bones and muscles that controlled her pen? Murgatroyd's life teetered on the probability of a lingering and horrible death. Her head in her hands, she trembled with anticipated sorrow, afraid to look up and see her sunken reflection in the window glass.

What if she simply walked away? She could fling down her pen, push the chair back from the table, and exit behind the curtain to door number three. Murgatroyd would wander, across and back on these three pages, lost and misunderstood. One day he'd soar in sybaritic summits and another wail in wilted woe. Without recognition, he'd pass the faces of his offspring and his former following, guessing at their lives, never knowing what he'd missed.

Eventually, Murgatroyd would die, alone and unfulfilled. An end without an end, she thought it a waste of seven words. With a deep breath, straightening her shoulders, she took up the pen.

"On Being a Writer"

by P. M. H. Atwater

You cannot separate a person's life from the craft of writing. Life is art. Writing is but one way of expressing that art.

We each have our stories about being a writer, what led us to express ourselves in that manner. And our stories, if closely read, actually reveal how our life evolved over time, how we changed, how we faced and handled the challenges life brought. Even so simple as an article submitted to the popular press becomes another "signature we signed" in the ongoing ebb and flow of who we are and what we believe and who we are becoming. What we write is what we live.

That seems like an odd statement to make, considering that my long list of publications is mostly based on original fieldwork, the type of research that becomes papers presented to one's peers that lead to official findings that inspire clinical, prospective studies that become part of the fabric of information that influences our lives. I submit to you that a writer, even such as I, cannot separate heart from hand. After I share with you my story, my evolution in the field of authorship, perhaps you will agree with my view on being a writer. If you do not, then at least you will know where I'm coming from and why.

It was the middle sixties and I was miserable. Being married with three young children and working full speed in an office that never experienced a slowdown, then going home to equal demands on time and energy, overwhelmed me—mostly because I had this gnawing feeling deep inside that I was in the wrong place at the wrong time and I had absolutely no way to change this or turn my life around or to know how. I was stuck. Then a woman in another office down the hall stopped me as I walked by and said: "How would you like to have your handwriting analyzed—for free?" I tilted my head in response.

"There's this sheriff's deputy I know," she continued, "who is studying to become a professional graphoanalyst and work within the court system. He has lots of handwriting from criminals. What he needs now are samples from regular folks. All you have to do is write out a paragraph, doesn't matter the subject, and send it to him. He'll mail you his interpretation of your handwriting and what it reveals about your character. Your job is to write him back and let him know how accurate or inaccurate he was. That's it." My affirmative reply netted me his address.

I chose the front part of the phone book, where it gives usage instructions, wrote a paragraph in longhand, and mailed my offering. Months later, long after I had forgotten about it, the reply came—single spaced, small type, virtually no margins. I couldn't believe what I read. This man was so thorough he could even tell the type of food I preferred, and with precise accuracy. All except one thing. He kept saying over and over again in the analysis, "You are in the wrong job. You should be a writer. Your handwriting shows strong literary ability." When I wrote him back, I noted his one error. I knew nothing about writing, nor did I harbor any notion or desire to write.

Still, I could not forget his analysis, those statements about me being a writer. It haunted me. So, in a style typical of my youth when faced with a puzzle I had no solution for, I morphed into the cop's kid I was and started asking questions (as my dad had once taught me)—what is writing? how does one become a writer? who do I ask? The "who-do-I-ask" part gave me the courage to walk up to perfect strangers, introduce myself, and launch a volley of, "Do you know anything about writing, where I might go to learn, is anyone you know a writer?" One man had a clue: "I know the president of the Boise chapter of the Idaho Writers League. Here's her name and phone number."

Imagine my excitement when I called her and was invited to attend the club's next meeting. The moment I walked in the door of the large room where they met, I swear I left the planet. There arrayed before me were men and women of a broad span of ages and interests who were alive with ideas and happy chatter and nonstop creativity. I had never encountered such people before. They mesmerized me. When I asked how to join, the president told me I had to attend two meetings and submit three works, which would be judged by their membership committee to see if I had any talent. I would then be subject to the group's vote. I did as asked, recalling my high school English teacher's caution: "Always write what you know." Well, I knew about cooking; I knew about childbirth; I knew about what it was like to have a daughter born with a hip deformity. My only times to write were coffee breaks and lunch hours. The result was mailed to the club.

The night of membership consideration I will never forget. A piece of mine was read—"The Beauty of Pain." No one said anything. I covered my face with my hands in a gesture of utter desperation and embarrassment. How stupid I was to think I could write, how very, very stupid. A man who wrote professionally for the *Saturday Evening Post* broke the silence. "Looks like we have a natural-born writer on our hands. I vote her in." I almost fainted. The following week I told my mother I was giving it two years. If I couldn't be a full-time professional writer in two years, I'd admit my folly and give it up. My mother's reply was classic: "Do you have any idea what you need to know to be a writer? Do you have any idea of the training and education you need, the vocabulary? Do you have any idea about how competitive the field is?" And on and on. Finally, I faced her and said: "No, mother, I don't know any of that. That's why I'm going to make it."

I learned technique from the club. My off time at work crammed with paper projects, envelopes, and stamps. Six months later, a feature of mine on tombstone rubbing was published by the *Idaho Statesman,* the largest newspaper in the state, replete with cameraman and photo shoots, me and my kids out in a cemetery, rubbing reliefs from tombstones with heelbar wax on parchment. Six months after that I was elected president of the club. The passage of another six months netted me a full-time position with the Idaho Department of

Commerce and Development . . . as a writer. I made my goal in a year and a half, foregoing the temptation to chide my mother for her negative remarks.

The nearly three years I worked in the Idaho State Capitol building were heaven on earth. There was nothing I couldn't accomplish; always I did the right thing at the right time, met famous authors, stood in for the governor, created the first tour-guide service of Girl Scouts and Boy Scouts coming in from all over the state. Awards. Meritorious pay raises. Widespread recognition. The more well known I became, the more distant and sullen my husband and the more difficult my life. Politics changed as they are wont to do. When I refused to write for the next governor, my job turned into a "deep freeze" and I resigned.

I freelanced for a while and did shopping center promotions as my marriage slipped away and a divorce followed. I turned to technical manuals writing at Idaho First National Bank as a way to earn a paycheck. A promotion to the analytical department opened up another frontier, the prospect of becoming a bank manager. I had begun classes toward that goal when my health failed me. I died. . . not once, but three times during a three-month period in 1977. Each time I had a near-death experience and each one seemed somehow to lead into the next as if progressive. When I had recovered, the nightmare of not being recovered at all hit me hard. I had to relearn how to tell the difference between left and right, how to see and hear properly, how to repair a worn-out body and reroute a confused mind, and how to rebuild all of my belief systems. I was reduced to babyhood during therapy to relearn crawling, standing, walking, running, climbing stairs. I identified more with the "other side of death" than I did with where I was, and in so doing, discovered aspects of myself and a way to heal naturally and fully that exceeded either belief or fact, mine or anyone else's.

What filled me with driving passion, though, were words said to me during my third near-death episode, when a voice spoke, a voice I came to call "The Voice Like None Other." I felt it was of God. The Voice said, "Test revelation. You are to do the research. One book for each death." I was shown what that meant and what was to be in each book. Books two and three were named, not book one. Nothing detailed how to do this or how long it might take me. I accepted the job, a sort of "heavenly assignment." Always I have had the very clear sense that the only reason I survived the health crisis I had was to do this work, the research—about what I had just gone through, experiencing an afterlife and what that might mean, what it implied, and what the larger scope of transformative experiences revealed about humanness and the realms of spirit.

Getting well meant getting busy. So I did. I quit my job on the very day of a major promotion and pay rise, sold a home I had just bought, sent my youngest to live with her father at her request, gave away or stored all that I had, stuffing some things into my little Ford Pinto as I took off—leaving behind everyone and everything I knew and loved. I saw the sun set silver over the Pacific, followed thousands of miles later by a chance to witness the sun rise golden over the Atlantic. I worked as a secretary in Washington, D.C., and as a technical manuals writer in Roanoke, Virginia, all the while doing my research, finding other experiencers as myself who had had a near-death experience. Using police investigative techniques as my protocol, out spewed the questions: "What happened to you? Tell me about it. And? Tell me more." I found that people responded to body language and facial expressions quicker than words, which enabled languaging to remain simple, open, and nonleading.

Three years later, after marriage to the man of my dreams and settling in Harrisonburg, Virginia, Kenneth Ring, a noted researcher of near-death states, discovered I existed. He came calling, and, after an overnight stay, invited me to join with my peers in the field of near-death studies. "You're ahead of the rest of us," he said. Ken told me about Raymond Moody Jr., M.D., and his landmark classic *Life After Life* (Mockingbird Books, 1975), and then he said: "You must write a book, too. The world needs to know what you know."

Within days of having begun my book, I injured myself and dislocated ribs. I remember lying on the floor so that I could breathe without pain, and screaming, "God, this will not stop me. I am writing that book." Encouragement from Mark Mayell, then editor of *East West Journal,* became the spark plug that kept me going, page after page, hour after hour, for years. *Coming Back to Life* saw the light of day in 1988, thanks to Dodd, Mead & Company, in New York City. Attacks against me were immediate: who did I think I was, me an experiencer doing research, and besides I was a woman and I didn't even have a degree; how dare I. Rumors abounded that I was mentally ill or on an ego trip or psychotic. Those I trusted the most turned against me—my publishers "died" soon after, when Dodd, Mead & Company became the first old-line New York publisher to be taken over in a hostile takeover by a corporate raider. Even my editor's husband died. Death everywhere. Hope died, too. What saved my book was the paperback version put out by Ballantine Books. It sold quite well. But I never saw a dime. Because of how my publisher was obliterated, all royalties disappeared. And because the agent I had at the time stole most of my advance money, and we had taken out two loans to help pay for the book's promotion as well as a third to buy back world rights, we wound up staring at payments larger than our income. A nightmare manifest.

I dealt with this by plunging into another book, a continuation of my research, entitled *Beyond the Light* (Birch Lane Press, 1994). Part of the time I journeyed to Montreal, Quebec, to obtain my L.H.D. so at least I would have some sort of degree, a doctorate—not from an accredited college but an earned doctorate, nonetheless, with a thesis to boot—that became *Future Memory* (reprinted through Hampton Roads, 1999). Relearning brain function and languaging since my experiences with death necessitated more than once a redo of writing skills as I honed my observational ability. While I persisted in this, the attacks against me grew until my psyche deafened and I lapsed into a deep depression. I came out of it months later, somewhat numb, yet fixated on research. The opinions of others no longer mattered. I had a job to do and I refused to be deterred. This gave me the energy I needed to outlast my critics.

Today, my research base is one of the largest, covering nearly four thousand adult and child experiencers of the near-death phenomenon. I have written seven books on my findings, some of which are now being verified in clinical studies. One more: *Beyond the Indigo Children: The New Children and the Coming of the Third World* (Inner Traditions/Bear, 2005). It is the first study of today's young that uses objective research combined with mystical tradition and prophecy to explore what may well be a quantum leap the human family is now making in its evolutionary spiral. The addendum to the book, what keeps it updated, is on my Web site at www.pmhatwater.com. Look for "Beyond the Indigo Children EXTRAS."

Yup, it happened again. Hurrying to catch a plane at the Pittsburgh airport, I fell flat on my face, broke my left wrist, my hand separated from my arm, along with other injuries, including a blow to my head that again challenged function and verbalization. Surgery repaired body damage. But it was being a guest on one radio show after another for months on end that forced my brain to rally and my mouth to produce a coherent flow of words. There's nothing like putting one's self in the "hot seat."

I'm still writing, redoing some books, reprinting others, finishing my theoretical model of how one can use near-death states to better understand transformations of consciousness. I'll complete it someday soon. In the meantime, look for *The Near-Death Experience—A Single Sourcebook That Tells All,* due out later in 2007. Is there more? Of course—that sheriff's deputy was right. Writing is in me. It is part of my soul. It is how I express my passion, my truth, my dedication, my faith, my love for this wonderful world God has given us. It is my discipline for research and my determination to share what I have verified so you may verify it for yourself.

Who would have thought I would ever have become a writer? Not my family, certainly. I was born in the reclaimed deserts of southern Idaho. My goal as a youngster and as a young woman was to live life the best that I could so someone could write on my tombstone, "Well done." I had no other ambitions.

Still, opportunities to do otherwise kept creeping into my life, tantalizing me with possibility and "what ifs." Life's hardships have only served as fodder to instill in me a desire to work harder and do more. Sometimes life is like that—sneaky. Although my route to becoming a writer is unique to me, it stands as recognition, proof if you will, that the craft, our craft, is really about life and how we express it. Life is art, fine-tuned by the artisans who have chosen to understand it and develop what they experience. I am so grateful my handwriting clarified more than my mind that one fateful day so long ago, I opened up and spread out my arms and said, “I’m going to do this. I don’t know how, but I will do it. You’ll see.”

"From Fiction to Film: Crafting Screenplays from Books"

by Rosa Turner Knapp

As anyone who's seen the film *Adaptation* (written by Charlie Kaufman and based on the book *The Orchid Thief* by Susan Orlean) might gather, adapting a book to a movie can be no picnic for a writer. Conversely, it can prove a creative feast, if you're the type who enjoys an artistic challenge. Nonetheless, these projects can seem daunting, even for the most ambitious scribes. How does one take a 450-page fiction manuscript and turn it into a 110-page screenplay? Judiciously, I've learned.

I've had modest experience of writing both books and screenplays and very recently engaged in the task of transforming one of my own unpublished novels into a script suited to feature film. I've therefore been asked to share something of what I've gleaned from the process. While nonfiction books, magazine articles, and other literary properties can also be adapted for film, please note my primary focus involves the conversion of fiction to screenplays, because therein lies my "expertise." For more authoritative data on the subject, I greatly encourage you to consult your local library or favorite bookstore, where information on all sorts of writing abounds. What I offer here reflects only my personal perspective as a somewhat published, sometimes paid, ever-hopeful writer.

To better understand the procedure involved in going from fiction to film, an acknowledgement must first be made that, while a novel is a finished product, a screenplay is merely a transition piece providing the basis for a full-blown production meant to be absorbed visually and auditorially en masse rather than consumed solo. A screenplay is therefore primarily written for its viewers (or the "camera's eye"), versus a reader, which leads to the development of several stylistic differences between the two creative works. Most obvious of all is the discrepancy in page length. Screenplays tend to be less than half as long as novels, sometimes a fourth to a sixth as long, when the novel is hefty! That's a lot of cutting, with no pasting allowed.

While the time required to privately read and enjoy a novel is highly personal, viewing a movie is a communal experience determined by a preset time frame. This time frame can be predicted, more or less, in accordance with a script's page length, with one page in proper screenplay format translating into roughly one minute of screen time. Hence, a 115-minute movie likely comes from a 115-page script, which is significantly shorter than a published novel.

Another major difference between these two genres involves structure. In novels, chapters rule, each conveying a ministory within the book's overall framework, while moving the plot along. A script's momentum is maintained by independent scenes, generally a maximum of three pages each, which are more visual than literary. In the movies, pictures are paramount. Excepting the use of witty or poignant dialogue, the dense "weight" of eloquent language necessarily gets left behind. The action on the screen, expressions on the actors' faces, or what they do versus what they say, are just as important—often more so—than any scripted lines.

These separate movie scenes ultimately hold together to form a script's relatively equal-in-length three acts. Adhering to Aristotelian principles: act one serves as an appetizer, setting up the story and introducing its primary conflict; act two represents the "main course," which culminates in a climax; and act three rewards us with dessert, presenting an overall resolution and (hopefully) leaving the audience satisfied with either the proverbial happy ending or at least one that befits the tale, as well as character motivation, and leaves its viewers more acutely able to reflect on a particular theme.

The third primary difference between screenplays and novels is one that is apparent to the naked eye. Compared to their literary cousins, scripts contain a plethora of white space. While some novels, especially thrillers, incorporate sparser dialogue and shorter descriptions, often this is episodic, occurring periodically between lengthier expository passages. In contrast, screenplays contain consistently shorter scene and action descriptions, as well as concise dialogue, generally without the inclusion of any internal monologue ("thought" cues) via voice overs.

With screenwriting, the formula's rather straightforward. Scenes are labeled and introduced, larger action sequences are laid out (such as car chase scenes in a thriller), and then dialogue reigns, with very little scripted interpersonal action, because much of what actors *do* during the course of speaking is up to their (and the director's) individual art. Screenwriters generally only include detailed descriptions or character actions ("beats") when these are critical to the script's accurate interpretation. For example, a seemingly inconsequential prop might be specifically named in an early scene when its appearance is elsewhere reinforced or when it becomes useful, either literally or symbolically, to the story's development later on.

Similarly, if a character's written dialogue is in opposition to what she or he is thinking or feeling, small body language beats might be included to alert the script's reader (hence, ultimately the movie viewers) to any underlying motivation. In general, however, scenes are restricted to presenting location, portraying larger action, briefly describing new characters, and delivering dialogue.

Given this "tightness" of form, it's easy to see where all that white space comes in! So, how *does* one go about the business of toning down a tome of fiction (bursting with black ink) into a stripped-down screenplay? It all depends on what the intent adapter is able to bring to—and take away from—the table.

For the book-to-screenplay adaptation process to succeed, the screenwriter must first and foremost possess one essential tool: an open mind. Nearly everything in the work can, and is likely to, change. With an understanding of a script's basic bare-bones format, it's easy to see the need for eliminating excess exposition. Because a picture is worth a thousand words, this is not as difficult to accomplish as it seems, as most sensory and emotive information, which may take several paragraphs—or even pages—to describe in a book, can be quite directly conveyed with a skillful shot (or series of shots) in only a few seconds on camera, because, again, a script is principally a means to an audiovisual end.

Important changes regarding the number and nature of characters may also occur. When moving from a book to a screenplay, for example, the total number of story characters often drops, with any personas seeming to be too similar or duplicative in purpose either becoming consolidated or entirely written out. Alternately (sometimes simultaneously), new characters might be added in. This is especially true when they contribute to the development of a primary, or significant secondary, character.

As most films don't contain a high degree of internal monologue expressed as voice overs on the screen, another "confidant" type character, with whom the primary character can overtly share that information, must be available for the audience to become privy to those thoughts.

Surprisingly, adding new characters, or even wholly original scenes, can actually help *decrease* the story's overall screen time by streamlining and sequencing events so that only the most important information is portrayed in as succinct a manner as possible. The screenwriter is then free to discard pages (sometimes chapters) from the source material whose significant messages have been alternately transmitted. What's critical is getting the point across, while staying true to the tone and intent of the original story. How an adapter retells that story is highly individual.

Other transformations that may occur during the adaptation process that don't directly affect the length of a piece but may affect the efficacy of filming or a project's marketability include altering the ages of the characters to suit a targeted audience demographic or changing specific scene settings to better accommodate a film's budget and/or its producer's preferences. Producers, in fact, may offer enormous contributions toward shaping a film's evolution from its foundation as a book into an all-encompassing visual and auditory extravaganza.

Producers don't only initially option scripts or other literary properties on which scripts are based; they also then go on to develop those projects by collaborating with writers to establish workable screenplays and securing talent (that is, actors), directors, and funding, typically via a studio willing to foot the bill for the whole shebang and pay the screenwriter his or her balance due. The "option" amount is the percentage of the final take the screenwriter receives up front upon signing a contract, which may detail everything from high- and/or low-end caps on a script's sales price to the dimensions of lettering assigned to the screenwriter's name on movie advertisements. Although it may fall within a predetermined range, a script's final sales price is generally between 2 and 5 percent of the film's total budget, with the advance option amount equaling anywhere from 0 to 10 percent of that, depending both on the financial strength of the producer and the reputation—as well as the negotiating power—of the writer.

Most important for writers, experienced producers have a genuine "inside" understanding of what makes Hollywood tick and also possess the business connections and good gut instincts to see a saleable project through. They can offer stellar suggestions as to a film's direction, and most will eagerly encourage the writer's feedback in return. Together, these entities can form a blockbuster partnership that might actually land a project on a marquee, at the video store, or on television.

This prospective positive end result notwithstanding, many writers, novelists-turned-screenwriters key among them, may find so many storyline upheavals maddening, particularly when they tend to recur from one version of the script to the next—and there are typically several drafts, with collaborative conferences calls or meetings scheduled in between. Novelists who are keenly tied to the expressive authenticity of their carefully chosen words and who prefer to work alone may not find themselves drawn to screenwriting at all. Others, open to having their work adapted for film, would much rather someone else tackle the process for them, rather than risk transforming their own work after having it torn apart then reconstructed in public view. At the other end of the spectrum lies that group of slightly unbalanced, perpetually optimistic individuals (yours truly included) who enjoy the unique qualities inherent to writing in both genres and rise to the pleasant personal challenge of accomplishing the tumultuous transition.

Because of my background, I'm often asked whether it's "easier" to sell a book or a script, which is a little like asking whether it's simpler to scale Mount Kilimanjaro or Mount Everest. The truth is that both feats are extremely hard, and most folks aren't up to the climb. I've seen statistics that show fewer than 2 percent of all submitted fiction manuscripts get published.

The good news for novelists is that those fortunate few able to secure book deals generally will see their work in print within a year. Occasionally, books are "sold" that never get published—as a result of the death of an editor, cancellation of a line, or an in-house reorganization at the publisher. This happened to me, initially with a volume of poetry then again with a contracted novel, and both situations were very disappointing. Yet, once I'd accepted the probability that I likely wasn't cursed and doomed for all time as a writer, I gratefully understood those occurrences to be the rare exceptions to the rule that they were.

In screenwriting, the odds are almost opposite. Optioning a screenplay, or even selling one to a studio, guarantees virtually nothing in the way of the project's eventual production, distribution, and box office. Of the many projects picked up, a relatively small number get made. Far fewer are widely distributed, and only a charmed handful ever make it to the Oscars. Nonetheless, signing an option agreement, detailing a screenwriter's working obligations as well as eventual financial rewards, can still be a heady, sought-after experience. Hollywood's an extremely competitive town, overflowing with aspiring screenwriters, several of them highly talented. So, having a script selected by a reputable producer is indeed an excellent show of faith, as well as a soothing balm for a writer's tortured soul, because so many wordsmiths struggle constantly with maintaining artistic confidence and persistence.

Although it sounds clichéd, the fact remains that the ultimate success of any project, whether it relates to fiction or film, or perhaps even ties in with both, is just as dependent on luck as it is on the writer's skill and determination. Sometimes the very best opportunities for writers occur when they're not so ardently looking, not too unlike finding the right romantic partner once one has given up on love. And, when it comes to writing of any kind, it certainly holds true that scribes must love what they do or all hope is lost. For it's the satisfaction of a well-turned line that lets us sleep soundly at night, and the adventure of awakening to improve on it further that rouses us eagerly in the morning. Getting paid for our efforts besides is like finding that elusive pot of gold. None of us really expects it below the next rainbow, but we certainly won't turn it away if and when good fortune comes.

"Some Smoldering Questions on the Publishing Process"

by Gary D. Kessler

As if the time and effort involved in writing a book-length manuscript aren't enough of a hassle for a prospective published author, the process of finding an agent and/or getting the book in print and in the hands of the reading public can be even more frustrating and confusing than writing the manuscript was. The decisions that need to be made at this point on how to get from "here" to "there" in getting published are many and are risk filled. This essay provides basic discussion on just a few of the more fundamental and immediate questions on getting published that typically haunt writers.

Why Not Just Self-Publish?

Those who tout the advantage to self-publishing your book as being that you maintain control of the process and can realize a larger percentage of the profit, which can be true—in the same context that playing the lottery can be profitable—are also pointing to the disadvantages for most of self-publishing. The writer will likely have to spend more time producing and marketing the book than writing it. Additionally, the writer becomes solely responsible for making the most quality- and cost-efficient decisions in the production process and for the marketing functions as well, skills the writer may not be trained and networked for, in an extremely tough market. And a large percentage of no profit or less than no profit—when the cost of producing and marketing a self-published book outstrips the sales profit—is still little or no profit—or, more likely, significant loss.

Unless you are a trained and experienced professional in book production and marketing in addition to being a good enough writer to produce highly salable books—and you must try not to kid yourself through wishful thinking on this issue—it almost always is to your advantage to leave these functions to the experts. A mainline traditional publisher will have production and marketing experience and access to economies-of-scale services targeted markets and will produce and market books at their own expense.

There are different ways to get your work before the public in a printed book. The traditional royalty-paying publisher still exists. But that institution has been joined by a whole range of subsidy presses, vanity presses, and self-publishing services as well as the option not to print the book at all but to have it set up and available on the Internet for download electronically. What then are the relative pros and cons of going through the process of contracting with a traditional publisher and just self-publishing the book yourself?

• Traditional print publishing still provides the aura of (relatively) high-quality books that have weeded out the now-considerable chaff. In self-publishing, no one but the author has decided the book is worthwhile—and both bookstores and readers will know this and will not appreciate a self-published book as they would a traditionally published book.

• Traditional publishers will not charge the author for anything in the publishing process (beyond costs associated with producing the manuscript, which would include the author-borne cost of permissions to use copyrighted material and images). The self-published author has to bear all of the costs up front and also bear the risk of selling enough books to clear a profit.

• Traditional publishers will pay the author royalties, and, if they determine they will make a tidy profit from the venture, they often will pay the author an advance as well. The self-published author must realize sales covering the entire cost of producing and marketing the book before a penny of profit is realized. There may be about five cases out of several hundred thousand self-publishing ventures where the author has financially benefited from self-publishing (and these are mainly with nonfiction).

• The traditional publisher also will cover the costs of copyediting, cover and interior design, printing, advertising, and distribution—and will do so with a professional staff trained for industry-standard work and with cost-effective economies of scales (that is, it's almost always cheaper to produce groups of products subject to the same production process than just one product). The self-publisher will have to subcontract all of these services at the author's own cost and own risk of being able to meet and maintain industry standards.

• In terms of marketing, a traditional publisher will be able to put the book on shelves in a broad range of bookstores. The self-published author will have to negotiate with bookstores one by one and is unlikely to be able to meet the adoption criteria of most bookstores (for example, low retail prices, fast and convenient distribution, deep discounts, and returns policies—most of which can't be supported by self-published books at all). Traditional publishers can usually get the book reviewed; self-publishers have difficulty finding reviewers who have any impact on a significant number of readers/book buyers. Traditional publishers have targeted buying audiences they can directly sell to (and being able to do this is key in their decision to publish your book). Self-publishers have to find and solicit these targeted audiences on their own. Traditional publishers have established book distribution systems; self-publishers have to establish such systems just for the book(s) they are producing.

• Traditionally published books are normally a building block to future publishing. If an initial book does well, it is much easier for the author to publish subsequent books—and at an increasing anticipation of reward (money and fame). In most cases, each succeeding self-published book project is a "back to square one" proposition. The publishing industry doesn't even accept self-published works as having been published unless they produce significance buzz or profit—which is an extremely rare occurrence, especially when the book has been marketed by someone without professional expertise in book marketing.

If you ignore or underappreciate these basic differences, you place your pocketbook, your time, and your emotional well-being at serious risk.

But, then, is there no circumstance in which self-publishing is a good idea? Yes, there are limited circumstances when you might consider it. First, if you can't get a traditional publisher interested in publishing your book and you still want to see it in print, you might consider self-publishing if the following factors also intersect: you have modest goals for the book (that is, you accept a limited distribution in which the project usually will cost more than the sales it produces) and you have a sufficiently sized target audience for direct distribution of the book (for example, the book supports a specialized group or business plan, such as a family reunion book or a textbook for a business seminar).

Do I Need an Agent?

If you are self-publishing or submitting to academic presses or small or even medium-sized trade publishers that aren't known for giving advances, or if you have a short work to place (for example, a newspaper article, a poem, a short story, a magazine article), not only will you not need a literary agent, but also literary agents will not be interested in representing you. They will only be interested if there is enough money in the publishing deal to make the time and effort they put into finding a publisher for you worth their while.

If you are trying to be published through one of the big, New York publishing houses, get a reputable literary agent to represent you, if you can—if for no other reason than this level of publisher usually will not look at unagented work. The difficulty in finding an agent will be a good index to the difficulty in finding a publisher.

It is very beneficial to have a good agent if you can get one. The good literary agent will target the search for a publisher on the best fit for the author; will fully understand the provisions of the contract offered by a publisher (to the extent that most lawyers can't, because most lawyers don't specialize in publishing terms) and will be able to explain the terms to the author; will negotiate the best possible terms and advance for the author; may edit—as part of the basic service—the manuscript to make it more marketable; will run interference for the author during the publication and marketing processes; will help take the best-possible advantage of the rights; and will handle the business matters for the book, including the collection and disbursement of royalties. And, if the agenting experience was mutually satisfactory, the author doesn't have to shop for another agent for the next manuscript.

The responses of several literary agents to the question of what part they play in the publishing process after a book is sold can be found at <http://www.authorsontheweb.com/features/0105-literary-agent/0105-literary-agent-qe.asp> and at <http://wordsmitten.com/diana_interview.htm>.

Literary agents work through networking. They network publishers and other agents to determine what is on demand—and at what general price. They usually make their offers of representation based on this knowledge. They also network to determine what publishers will fit best with the clients they are representing.

Reputable agents will charge a standard rate on the advance and royalties from all uses of rights—most generally 15 percent currently (or 10 percent if the author has already found a publisher and wants representation from the time of contract signing)—plus a reasonable fee for copying and postage for manuscripts they send to prospective publishers—all of which generally is collected out of the money as it comes in from the publisher(s), although increasingly agents are requiring reimbursement for such costs as expended, which the Association of Authors' Representatives condones. Most generally, all such moneys come through the agent to the author, so agents usually take their cut out as it passes through their hands. (The well-worn adage that all money flows to the author, by the way, is a myth—money realized from a manuscript sale flows in all sorts of directions, with much of it going to pay the expenses the author incurred in getting the manuscript sold to begin with.)

A large number of businesses and individuals only pose as serious literary agents, but, in reality, use the publishing hopes of neophyte manuscript writers to prey on them. Thoroughly check out prospective agents, and if the literary agent asks for money up front, or says there is a reading fee, or has someone to recommend to you to improve your book in any way for a fee, run for the exit.

Why Do Agents Take So Long Deciding Whether to Offer Representation?

It will take an agent anywhere from five minutes (for an electronic query) to never to respond to an initial query. Responses to most initial queries probably fall between two and four weeks, which allows time for the query to transit and to work its way up the incoming mail backlog at the literary agency. Agents request a look at far more material than they are going to offer to represent, so they will usually determine fairly quickly whether they are interested in seeing partials or full manuscripts. As far as the time taken to an offer of representation, reviews of and decisions on partials and full manuscripts can take from six weeks to six months or more depending on the agent's review workload and the complexity of the internal decision-making process within the literary agency.

In many cases, a long wait time for a response from an agent primarily means the author is trying to enlist the services of an agent who is good enough that lots of other prospective authors are also trying to sign with her/him. In fact, if an agent gets back to the author quickly and offers a contract, this often means that the agent either doesn't have a lot of business (and therefore might not be all that good at it) or that the author's pocketbook is of more interest to the agent than the author's manuscript is. (Granted it could also mean the author wrote a whambang of a book, the significance of which came across in a stellar query letter.)

Agents have more on their plate than just reading that one author's query letter/partial/full manuscript, contemplating whether/how their work fits in with the type and quality of work the agent is able to place, and then writing out and sending a response. First, the author probably isn't the only one who submitted a query to the agent today—and there are all of those query letters that came in yesterday, and the day before that, and . . . . In addition to query letters, the agent most likely has asked for partials and full manuscripts from a good many authors and must spend time reviewing and winnowing those down to the ones the agent wishes to represent (and then contacting those to offer contracts as well as sending "no thanks" rejections to all the rest).

Also, if the agent is any good, she/he already has clients to attend to—a set of clients whose work is being polished up before it can be submitted; a set of clients whose work the agent is actively trying to sell to publishers; a set of clients whose sales are in contract negotiations; a set of clients who have publishing contracts and the agent is trying to sell subsidiary rights for; a set of clients who need support in the book promotion field; a set of clients whose royalties are coming in and require management; and a set of clients who need to be told as tactfully as possible that an end to the author-agent partnership is looming. If the agent is going to give each one of these concurrently happening activities the attention it deserves—including whatever submission the author now has added to his/her desktop—the agent is going to need considerable time and energy—and patience from all of those who are either working with her/him already or who would like to be working with the agent on the book projects.

How Do Publishers Select Manuscripts for Publication?

Traditional publishers are not selecting manuscripts to publish in isolation. They specialize in a set of book genres/categories, which is based on the sets of buyers they sell to. Their semiannual catalogs typically are a delicate balance of the books in their specialties—something for everyone and not too much of anything for anyone. So, your manuscript is not being assessed for purchase on its own merits alone. Publishers generally are looking for very specific manuscripts, not the next best manuscript of just any sort that crosses their desks. The timing of the acceptance process is greatly controlled by the size and formality/informality of the publishing house. Those involved can run from a one-person operation to a big New York publishing house. The larger and more complex the publishing house, the more individuals there are who are involved in the selection process.

A book manuscript usually gets selected as a possible purchase by a topic-specific acquisitions editor and then has to go to a combined selection committee, where the offerings for a future catalog season are all compared and contrasted to determine what the publishing house's optimum offering in that season would be. In preparing for this selection process, the acquisitions and manuscript and production editors, the head of marketing, and, often, the director of the press have to become at least familiar with the content of all of the books being considered. The editorial and production staffs have to do a rough estimate of the production costs of the books being considered, and the marketing team has to consider how each would fit—in relationship to other possible offerings—in a promotional campaign. For many nonfiction manuscripts and most academic press books, the manuscript also has to go through a peer review process in which it is read and critiqued by experts in the field and the author is asked to adjust the work for any significant academic shortfalls. This usually is not a book-by-book "I love it; let's do it" decision, and, except for small presses, the decision to publish does not come quickly.

What Does a Publisher Do to My Manuscript?

The total time for the actual production process (manuscript acceptance to bound books) in the typical publishing house usually takes at least nine months, although a month or so can be shaved off this if the book's release is being expedited to pair release with a particular promotional event. In fact, however, publishing houses typically release their books in two catalog seasons (fall and spring), and a book does not just drop into a conveyer-belt-like production schedule on the day the manuscript is accepted. The books are scheduled for particular future catalog seasons, and their production schedule can be accelerated or, more typically, elongated to meet a target release season. It thus is typical for a book not to launch in bound form for a year or eighteen months after the manuscript has been accepted.

In many nonfiction book cases, of course, the first thing that has to be done after the author signs the publishing contract is to actually go off and write the book. In the case of a completed manuscript, however, the first thing that happens to it in the publishing house is that all material is checked over to ensure the manuscript is complete. If new graphics—photographs, tables, figures, charts, maps, or illustrations—are to be included or written permissions are needed for existing graphics or to use quotes from previously published books, copies of use permissions for these either need to be in hand at this stage, or the author needs to be committed to a drop dead date on providing these. (It almost always will be the author's responsibility to obtain and pay for use permissions). At this point a tentative production schedule is drawn up for the book—and, contrary to what the author might think and probably would like, this schedule is driven by the release season that has been chosen for the book, not by a "first in/first out" service rule. If it is now winter, and the book is slated for the spring catalog of the next year, the production schedule will be expedited. But, more typically, the book may be scheduled for the fall catalog—or an even later one—in which case the manuscript will just be shelved until its production schedule becomes a priority.

After the production schedule is established (and approved by all departments)—and it has been decided that production can commence—the acquisition editor often will do a substantive edit of the book and return it to the author for explanations and rewrites based on issues surfaced with the content. When the author has finished responding to the substantive edit, an updated electronic disk is returned to the publishing house. The editorial department then cleans up the electronic disk, making it compatible for the specific publishing house's composition machinery, and the managing editor assigns copyediting of the book either to an in-house editor or to a freelance copyeditor. This editor, in turn, sometimes returns the edited manuscript, showing the edits and flagging queries to be addressed, directly to the author. But sometimes the time is even further elongated, because the publishing house's procedure may be that the editor returns the edited manuscript to the publishing house for review before it is sent back to the author for comment and approval. When the author has responded to the suggested edits and queries, the manuscript is either returned to the copyeditor for file corrections and cleanup and hence back to the publishing house's editorial department or returned directly to the publishing house's editorial department for in-house cleanup.

In the meantime, the production department is "casting off" (determining layout and the number of final pages in the book) and designing the format of the book and the cover (often farming cover design out to a specialty design company or freelance designer). The author will be consulted about the cover design, but in a traditional publishing house, the author will not have veto power over the cover design. The marketing department is devising a promotion plan for the book and folding this into the house's overall promotion campaign. (Books rarely are marketed individually; they usually are involved in combined ad campaigns with other books from that season's catalog.) The author usually will either be asked to provide a marketing plan of their own or, more typically, will be asked to fill out a marketing questionnaire. This is designed to find out any and all connections to paying readers the author may have to aid sales and to help target promotion.

When the edited book comes back and is checked over by the editorial department, it's sent to the production department to be composed in the design that has been selected for it. The production department then sends it to the selected printer. (Based on the figures obtained from the earlier "cast off" procedure, the production department has put out bids to the various printers used by the publishing house and received these along with a confirmation of a period during which the printer can schedule press time for the book, and has identified the winning bid—and to the apparent surprise of many writers, no, publishing houses usually don't do their own printing.)

The composition files for the book, including the cover and any graphics, are sent to the printer, which produces at least one round of "blue lines"—a paginated dummy of the final copy. These come back to the publishing house, where the editorial department scans them for various problems that might have crept into the content and the production department scans them for flaws in adherence to design. This is when both the acquisitions editor for the book and the marketing department are writing up the jacket copy and trying to line up endorsements and prime book reviewers—which they often will ask the author to help acquire—and, often, are sending blue line copies of the book to the most important reviewers who have agreed to consider reviewing the book.

Having noted any problem areas on the blue lines, the editorial department then sends them to the proofreaders, which in today's world almost always means the author. Book proofs are rarely more than scanned—really for production problems—in house anymore. If there is to be an index, this is when one is constructed. Typically this is a responsibility delegated to the author or to a professional indexer the author hires.

When corrections to the blue lines are finished, these are sent to the printer for final corrections, and the book is printed. In most cases, the printer distributes copies of the books (based on order information provided by the publishing house) directly to the big distribution clearing houses in time for a release date, at which time the book moves from the production to the marketing phase.

For an amusing, but pretty accurate description of the publishing process itself by a top literary agent, Sheree Bykofsky, go to <http://users.rcn.com/sheree.interport/process.html>.

About the Authors and Editors

P. M. H. Atwater, L.H.D., is one of the original researchers in the field of near-death studies, having begun her work in 1978. Today, her research base covers nearly four thousand adult and child experiencers and comprises a contribution to the field that is considered one of the best. Her findings are contained in eight books. Some of her work has been verified in clinical studies, both in Holland and in Florida. She has received three lifetime achievement awards, has lectured around the world, and has been a guest on many television and radio talk shows.

Kurt Ayau (anthology fiction editor) is a graduate of the University of Southern California with a dual degree in English and Drama, and holds an M.A. in English from the University of Virginia, an M.F.A. in Creative Writing from Warren Wilson College, and a Ph.D. in English from the University of North Carolina at Greensboro. His novel, *Nana's House,* won a Virginia Prize in Literature in 1988 and also won the Great American Novel contest of the Virginia Festival of the Book in 2003. He has published short fiction in *The Villager,* the *Michiana Creative Arts Review, City Magazine,* the *Roanoke Review,* the *Front Range Review, descant,* the *William and Mary Review,* and the *Red River Review.* Writing with David Rachels, he has published the novel *What the Shadow Told Me* (Eastern Washington University Press, 2005) and short stories in nearly a dozen literary magazines. He is an associate professor of English at Virginia Military Institute in Lexington and lives in the foothills of the Blue Ridge Mountains with his wife, Kathleen, and daughters, Julia and Leah.

David Baldacci is the author of twelve consecutive international bestsellers: *Absolute Power, Total Control, The Winner, The Simple Truth, Saving Faith, Wish You Well, Last Man Standing, The Christmas Train, Split Second, Hour Game, The Camel Club,* and *The Collectors,* as well as his Freddy and the French Fries children's series. His books are published in over thirty-five languages in more than eighty countries, with nearly forty-five million copies in print worldwide. He's also the cofounder, with his wife, of the Wish You Well Foundation, a nonprofit organization dedicated to supporting literacy efforts across America. He and his family reside in his native Virginia.

Coy Barefoot is a best-selling and award-winning author, journalist, and radio talk show host. His books include *The Quixtar Revolution, Thomas Jefferson on Leadership,* and *The Corner: A History of Student Life at the University of Virginia,* which won the 2003 Nalle Prize for Outstanding History. He has written and reported for magazines and newspapers around the country as well as a long list of online publications. Coy is the director of communications and alumni relations for the Sorensen Institute for Political Leadership at the University of Virginia. He is also the host and producer of *Charlottesville—Right Now,* a public affairs radio program broadcast throughout Central Virginia each weekday on NewsRadio1070 WINA.

Romney Brand is the grandson of the nationally known artist Frances Brand (deceased) of Charlottesville. Romney was born in Charlottesville in 1959. His poems have been published statewide. He is currently concentrating on painting a series of portraits begun by Grandma Fran in 1976, called "Charlottesville Firsts." Romney lives with his wife in Charlottesville and has a grown son.

Rick Britton is an award-winning historical journalist, whose work has appeared in the pages of the *Washington Times,* the *Richmond Times Dispatch, Virginia: The University of Virginia Alumni News, Civil War Magazine,* and *Civil War Times Illustrated.* Having published over two hundred articles—most of them on the history of the Old Dominion—Britton is the editor of the *Magazine of Albemarle County History* and a well-published map artist. He resides in Charlottesville with his wife, two step-sons, and four felines.

Julie Chan was born in San Francisco, California, taught third grade in Berkeley, and currently lives in Louisa County. She is a member of the Friday Poets' Critique Group led by Elizabeth Doyle Solomon in Albemarle County.

James Culmer was born in Philadelphia in 1975 and lived there until 1995. He started writing at age thirteen. His writing is characterized by spiritual and political themes. He lives with his wife, Kamika, and young daughter in Charlotesville, where he is a maintenance technician.

Kurtis Davidson is the author of the award-winning comic novel *What the Shadow Told Me*. Download the first chapter for free at http://www.kurtisdavidson.com.

Rita Dove, the Pulitzer Prize recipient for 1987 in poetry, served as Poet Laureate of the United States from 1993 to 1995 and as Poet Laureate of the Commonwealth of Virginia from 2004 to 2006. She has received numerous other literary and academic honors. In 2006 she received the coveted Common Wealth Award of Distinguished Service. Her published poetry collections include *The Yellow House on the Corner* (1980), *Museum* (1983), *Thomas and Beulah* (1986), *Grace Notes* (1989), *Selected Poems* (1993), *Mother Love* (1995), and *On the Bus with Rosa Parks* (1999). She also wrote a book of short stories, *Fifth Sunday* (1985), the novel *Through the Ivory Gate* (1992), essays under the title *The Poet's World* (1995), the play *The Darker Face of the Earth*, and the song cycle *Seven for Luck*. She is the editor of *Best American Poetry 2000,* and from January 2000 to January 2002, she wrote a weekly column, "Poet's Choice," for the *Washington Post*. Her latest poetry collection, *American Smooth*, was published by W.W. Norton & Company in September 2004. Rita Dove is Commonwealth Professor of English at the University of Virginia in Charlottesville, where she lives with her husband, writer Fred Viebahn, and daughter.

Margaret Edwards was born in 1930 in New York City. She grew up in New England and moved to Virginia in the mid 1960s. She has been writing for fun ever since she grabbed a pencil and paper and has been published in *Poet's Doman* and other anthologies.

Herbert F. Frisbie has worked in both the private sector and for the federal government in various engineering, design, procurement, and contract administration functions. After he retired in 1979, he and his family moved from Northern Virginia to a house they built in Madison County. His family lived there until his wife was killed during the rains and flooding in the spring of 1995. Living alone and with time on his hands, he resumed writing as a pastime. He is an Ogden Nash fan, so most of what he writes is humorous or satirical. He also writes narrative poems for children. To date he has written nearly four hundred poems and stories in verse, some of which have been published. He lives in

Aroda with his dog and cat.

George Garrett, retired Henry Hopes Professor Emeritus of Creative Writing at the University of Virginia and 2002–2004 Poet Laureate of Virginia, has written some thirty books, including seven published volumes of poetry and the trilogy of historical novels based on Elizabethan England, *Death of the Fox, The Succession,* and *Entered from the Sun*; edited nineteen books; and written Hollywood screenplays. He helped found the Associates Writing Programs, the national organization for university writing workshops. His awards for writing have included the PEN/Malmud Award for short fiction, the T. S. Elliot Award for Creative Writing, a 2000 individual (Virginia) Governor's Award, the American Academy of Arts and Letters Award, and, most recently, the Aiken Taylor Award for poetry.

Lucille (Kim) Grimm spent her early childhood on a farm in Illinois, with her two sisters and one brother. She always had a keen sense of adventure with a fearless nature, which at times created quite a challenge for her parents. While living in Iowa, she married a young man she had known since childhood. They later moved to Virginia, where they welcomed a daughter into their home. When her daughter had become a teenager, Lucille took the challenge and started to write.

Seth F. Hartman was born in 1974 in Appleton, Wisconsin. He grew up in Allentown, Pennsylvania, where he attended Emmaus High School and simultaneously worked in his family's tree-trimming (lumberjack) business. Following high school, he moved to Montana and joined the U.S. Air Force, initially serving as a medic and then commissioned as a Space Command officer. He was honorably separated from the military and is attending the University of Virginia to prepare for entry into a creative writing master's degree program.

When **Enrique Herrera's** parents were rural teachers in Argentina, his life consisted of reading children's stories and hunting with his dad. After high school, he studied philosophy at the University of Cordoba, followed by some military training and then by the study of economics at the University of Buenos Aires. Enrique became a professor and worked for the Argentine government, research institutions, and the Bolsa. He also was a consultant of the IDB Bank in many countries in Latin America. When Argentina exploded in a crisis, he came to the University of Virginia. He is now happily retired in beautiful

Charlottesville, where he travels, reads, and writes.
The fiction of **Sarah Collins Honenberger** (1st place fiction, Charlottesville VWC and state VWC, 2005; contest fiction editor) has won first place awards in the *Antietam Review, New Millenium,* and the *HooK.* The recipient of a Virginia Creative Arts Center Fellowship and the 2005 Virginia Writer's Club statewide Fiction Award, she appears regularly on literary panels and has taught writing skills for a decade. Her novel, *White Lies,* was launched in November 2006. She writes at the foothills of the Blue Ridge Mountains, inspired by vineyard views, three brilliant children, a patient husband, and twenty-five years of rural law practice.

Heather Hummel resides in Charlottesville. A graduate of the University of Virginia, she is working toward her masters and Ph.D. in metaphysical sciences. Her work has appeared in *Albemarle Family Living, Messages of Hope and Healing,* and *PetTails.* She has finished her first novel, *Touch of a Feather,* and is working on her second, *Coffee with Middle.* Heather is an active member of the Virginia Writer's Club, the International Women's Writing Guild, and the James River Writers. She's an avid cyclist and lives with her dogs, Julie and Stephan, whose photo appears in *PetTails.*

Gary D. Kessler (1st place, both fiction and nonfiction, Charlottesville VWC, 2006; 2nd place for fiction, State VWC, 2006; anthology volume editor), a former news agency managing editor, U.S. diplomat, newspaper columnist, and movie consultant, is currently a freelance book editor. Published author of a short story collection, *On the Downtown Mall,* and two espionage thrillers, he conducted a worldwide, online editorial workshop, which resulted in the two-volume *WritersNet Anthology of Prose.* He coauthored, with Carol Kluz, a publishing reference, *Finding Go! Matching Questions and Resources in Getting Published.* His latest book is a Bible study, *(Re)Tell Me the Stories,* coauthored with his minister sister, Carole Stockberger. He hosts the www.editsbooks.com and www.publishingquestions.com Web sites.

Charlottesville area writer **Rosa Turner Knapp** has published fiction, nonfiction and poetry, and optioned screenplays to television and feature film producers. She currently has a movie project in development with Cosa Bella Films of Los Angeles and New York, based on her unpublished Latino Romantic Comedy novel "Getting Lucky."

Liz Kollar attended the Newark School of Fine and Industrial Arts, married during WWII, taught art for some years, and had four sons and a daughter. Now retired, she teaches writing at the Senior Center in Charlottesville, where her Writing for Pleasure class meets every Friday. A thousand thoughts gleaned from the pages of her life have found their way into many stories, some real, some fictional.

As a child in Norway during the occupation, **Inger Kretsinger** (3rd place poetry, Charlottesville VWC, 2006) gained alternate perspectives on basic human conflicts and emotions. Now, in a different language and context she has explored alternate modes of expression. In her fiction, she has examined the nuances of these relationships. In her poetry she merely offers hints, hoping the reader will connect, as she employs images from the physical world. Fundamentally, Inger believes, poetry is trying to express verbally what exists only subliminally. Hence, mood or strong emotion resonates in images of natural phenomena. Poetry is like momentary perception, whereas fiction embodies the ongoing saga of human life.

Laurie M. Lawson resides in Charlottesville, where she attends the University of Virginia and is pursuing a degree in science education, with an emphasis in biology. Besides reading and writing, Ms. Lawson enjoys hiking, polo matches, and playing with her rabbits: Snooky, Nibbles, and Sneakers.

Linda M. Layne (anthology production editor) is executive director of the Virginia Writers Club and secretary/treasurer of the Charlottesville Chapter of the Virginia Writers Club. She is president of Cedar Creek Publishing of Bremo Bluff, Virginia. Prior to forming her publishing service company eighteen years ago, she developed and served as an interim manager and designer for two corporate in-house printing and publishing divisions.

Linda Levokove has a degree in art and interior design and a Masters degree in psychology. She heads her own interior design firm and has worked on projects in the New York Metropolitan area, Florida, and St. Martin. She has lectured on design and antiques at Florida Atlantic University and the Boca Raton Museum of Art, where she also served as chair of docents. Linda paints in acrylics and began writing poetry three years ago. She's new to the Charlottesville area and loves her new home.

Sharon Leiter, a former president of the Charlottesville Chapter of the Virginia Writers Club, is the poetry editor of *Streetlight,* Charlottesville's journal of literature and fine arts. She is the author of a volume of poetry, *The Lady and the Bailiff of Time* (Ardis) and a literary study of the Russian poet Anna Akhmatova, *Akhmatova's Petersburg* (University of Pennsylvania Press). Her poetry has appeared in *The Georgia Review,* the *Virginia Quarterly Review,* the *Atlanta Review, Cimarron Review,* and many other journals. A recipient of a Virginia Prize for Fiction, she has published a number of short stories. Her latest book, *A Critical Companion to Emily Dickinson,* was published in 2006.

Sigrid Miribella was born into a Long Island, New York, working-class community, surrounded by estates, field, and woods. She grew up admiring splendid mansions, picking wild flowers, and playing inside a forest that no longer exists. Sigrid raised her daughter in a neighboring fishing village that was just beginning to burgeon. Later, she moved to Central Virginia, where she had spent summers as a child, visiting relatives, riding horses, and exploring. She has always expressed herself through writing and visual media. Today, she lives with her husband, also a writer and sculptor, on a small farm with two dogs, an iguana, a horse, a pig, and a cat. She works as a pet behavior consultant and pet rescue advocate.

Stephen Mirabella is an artist, writer, and teacher who moved to rural Virginia from Long Island, New York, in 1994. His artwork has been seen at many art institutions, including the National Museum of American History, Washington, D.C. A lifelong love of art and poetry merged in the fall of 2000, when his John Milton Memorial sculpture, depicting Eve, Satan, and the serpent from *Paradise Lost,* was installed at SUNY Oneonta. Today, he writes metaphorical poetry in voices of fictional or historical characters. He writes alone and with his wife, Sigrid, on weekends at their Amherst farm. He teaches history at St. Anne's-Belfield School in Charlottesville.

Sheila Moore was born in Pennsylvania in 1939. She began composing poetry and adventure stories at age eight and has continued writing ever since. Her poetry and short stories have appeared in numerous literary magazines. She coauthored the *Little Boy Book,* now a Ballentine paperback. A Montessori teacher, she has written on educational topics for *Parents' Magazine,* the *Washington Post,* and *Instructor* publications. *Samson Svenson's Baby,* her first book for children, received a starred review in *Book List.* Her most recent published book is *Abadaba Alphabet,* which helps young children read better. She has four children and five grandchildren and lives with her husband, Harry, in Charlottesville.

Brenda Morris is a retired special education teacher who is currently a Home Bound instructor. She has four stepchildren and two grandchildren. She lives with her husband and youngest stepdaughter in Palmyra. Brenda writes poetry, memoirs, and young adult fiction. She has been published in the anthology *9-11: Maryland Voices, Scribble,* the *Village Voice,* and the *Creative Writers Notebook.* In addition, she has won contests from *Writer's Digest,* the Maryland Writers Alliance, and the Philadelphia Writer's Conference.

Catherine Gorey Peaslee, founder and publisher of Charlottesville's weekly *Observer* newspaper, received fellowships with the Virginia Foundation for the Humanities and the Virginia Center for the Creative Arts while writing a biography of Virginia novelist Ellen Glasgow. Widow of Foreign Service officer Sandy Peaslee, she has published her nonfiction in China, Taiwan, Brazil, and Canada. *Iris* and *Richmond Magazine* have published her articles. As a research assistant after WWII, she worked for columnist Walter Lippmann and the Senate Postwar World War Committee. She holds degrees in political science from Miami University and George Washington University.

Deborah Prum's short fiction has been published in many literary journals, including the *Virginia Quarterly Review, Folio,* the *Journal of*

Graduate Liberal Studies, and *Lifeline* (at Dartmouth College). Her short story "Triage" was given first place in a fiction contest sponsored by the *HooK.* Her articles, essays, and book reviews have appeared in the *Virginia Quarterly Review, Ladies' Home Journal,* the *Writer Magazine, Southern Living,* the *Writers Handbook,* and *Albemarle Magazine.* She is the author of *Rats, Bulls, and Flying Machines: A History of the Renaissance and Reformation* and also has contributed to history books for children. She received an MALS from Dartmouth College.

David Rachels (anthology fiction editor), an Alabama native, earned his Ph.D. in English from the University of Illinois. He is editor of *Augustus Baldwin Longstreet's Georgia Scenes Completed: A Scholarly Text* (University of Georgia Press, 1998) and coeditor of *The First West: Writings from the American Frontier, 1776–1860* (Oxford University Press, 2002). He has published short fiction in journals, including *Tamaqua* and *Sou'wester.* His first published collaboration with Kurt Ayau recently appeared in the *Portland Review.* David is an associate professor of English at Virginia Military Institute in Lexington and lives in the Shenandoah Valley with his wife, Angie, and their two sons, Aaron and Gus.

Priscilla Randolph's work has appeared in literary journals, magazines, newspapers, an anthology, and a book, *How to Write an Uncommonly Good Novel* (Ariadne Press, 1991); also in a self-published book, *Lifehunter: Selected Stories, Poems and Essays* (Beecher Press, 1994). A fellow at the MacDowell Colony and the Virginia Center for the Creative Arts, a contributor at the Bread Loaf Writers Conference, and a grant recipient of a fiction fund at the George Washington University, she has been a press assistant to a Massachusetts governor, a journalist at the *Boston Herald,* and a librarian at the Folger Shakespeare Library.

Elizabeth Doyle Solomon was born in New Orleans in 1942. Her first poem at age eleven was chosen from eight hundred to represent her school in New York, and since then she has written over 550,000 poems, which are published widely. At age fifty-two, she earned a B.A. in English and K-4 teacher's certification from Mary Baldwin College, graduating Magna Cum Laud and selected as Outstanding Student of the Year. She taught in Albemarle County and private schools for ten years and is now tutoring privately. She authored *Seasons,* an illustrated book of nature poems, and has written columns for many newspapers, including her own, the *Central Virginia Leader.* She currently leads a poets' critique group. She has two adopted children and has fostered more than thirty-five others.

Marian Courtney Styles (2nd place, poetry, 2006; anthology nonfiction editor) came to Charlottesville in late 1994 by way of Southern California and Alaska. She has worked as a secretary, employee travel expert, building issues facilitator, newspaper community editor, fund-raising researcher, and multimedia assistant. Her hobbies include hiking, reading, writing, movies, dancing, traveling, spending time with friends, and playing with her hyperkinetic cat.

Jack Trammell (1st place poetry and 2nd place fiction, Charlottesville VWC, 2006; 1st place poetry, State VWC, 2006) lives and writes in central Virginia, where he lives on a farm with his wife and blended family of seven children. He has published nine books, including three chapbooks of poetry, four novels, and two history textbooks as well as dozens of poems and stories. His fiction and poetry credits include journals such as *Virginia Adversaria, Exquisite Corpse, SouthLit,* and others. His nonfiction credits include a regular Civil War column in the *Washington Times* and related articles in various national publications. He recently completed his Ph.D and a new Civil War novel, and is teaching and administrating at Randolph-Macon College in Ashland.

Leonard Tuchyner (3rd place, both fiction and nonfiction, Charlottesville VWC, 2006) "A Time to Die" was inspired by over thirty-five years of experience in the martial arts, and the tale of the "Golf Course Camp Site" by the wonderment Leonard felt in his first encounters in the Blue Ridge Mountains. His professional writing has been mostly confined to the development of character portraits in the clinical counseling realm, including a series of human behavioral articles for local newspapers. He has written manuscripts for three science fiction novels, a local color novella, a spiritual Sci-Fi novella as well as numerous short stories in various genres. He lives with his wife, two and one half cats, two dogs, and parrot in Greene County.

H.E.R. (Hilda) Ward (anthology poetry editor) is a retired RN and health educator, who, after teaching school for twenty-four years in New York, came to Charlottesville in 1996 as coordinator for the Peer Health Educator program at the University of Virginia. She also coordinates the multicultural education program at UVa's Curry School of Education. Hilda has been writing poetry since the year John F. Kennedy was assassinated, and this event was the subject of her first poem. She has written over three hundred poems and has two CDs of spokenword, with musical background by George Melvin. She is a member of the steering committee for, and frequent participant in, the Virginia Festival of the Book. She hosts the local public access television show, *Artistic Expressions,* and is artist in residence for Albemarle County.

Valarie Watersun: **Journalist:** (1st place poetry, 2nd place fiction, Charlottesville VWC, 2005) *Nelson County Times, Charlottesville Observer, Albemarle Magazine, Inside UVA, Emory & Henry, Virginia Review.* Three Virginia Press Association awards. **Editor:** Two published books, SPWAO, VaNOW, Byrd Newspapers, Carden Jennings Publishing. **Novelist:** *The Quality of Blue.* **Author:** Honors from Writer's Digest, *Muse Magazine,* Writers in Virginia, The Virginia Writing Club (VWC), Piedmont Writing Institute, and Writers of the Future. **Poet:** *Lynchburg Magazine, Muse, Witness to the Bizarre, Worlds of Surrealism.* **Judge:** Poetry Society of Virginia, PARC's Young Authors Program. **Playwright:** *Truman's Word,* directed by Maxine Fox, Broadway producer of *Grease.* Currently editorial services coordinator for *Clinical Chemistry,* a scientific journal. www.valariewatersun.com.

Catherine Wolniewicz's passion for writing began when her short story about a six-legged spider brought rave reviews and a coveted E+ from her sixth-grade teacher. Inspired, she began scribbling daily in an old denim binder the fragile beginnings of a novel about an eleven-year-old girl. Little support at home for this creative obsession, however, forced her to abandon the binder and protagonist for more "practical pursuits." Twenty-five years later, while attending a creative writing course, her passion was rekindled. She has since written songs, poems, short stories, and a play. "Us" is her first published piece.

Lauvonda Lynn Meade Young's love of books and creative writing began in elementary school, when teachers asked her to read her work in class. Her first poem, "Spring Plowing," was published in 1962–63 (*Young America Sings—National High School Poetry Anthology*). Additional publications or recognitions include: (1) First Place in Poetry; poems "Searching," "In a Dark Place," and "Endings and Beginnings" (American Society of Aging and the National Council on Aging, 2002); (2) Poetry Guild's, Editor's Choice Award; poem "Flowers"; *Shelter in the Storm,* 1998; (3) "Best in Poetry" (Piedmont Virginia Community College, 1989).

Michael S. Zbailey (2nd place nonfiction, Charlottesville VWC, 2006; 1st place nonfiction, Charlottesville VWC and state VWC 2002 and 2005) is a freelance writer with a concentration in nonfiction. His articles have appeared in the *Providence Journal Sunday* magazine, *C-Ville, Blue Ridge Country* magazine, *Albemarle* magazine, *Keswick Life,* and as a feature in the Sunday Style Section of the *Washington Post.* He is in the process of completing his first book. He has his undergraduate degree from Pennsylvania State University and an MBA from the University of Pittsburgh. Mike is based in Keswick.

ABOUT OUR COVER ARTIST

A graduate of the University of Virginia and Pratt Institute, **Frederick Nichols** has been exhibiting his paintings and silkscreen prints in galleries and museums throughout this country and abroad for over twenty-five years. Since 1972, Nichols has had twenty-six solo exhibitions, including shows at the Rich-Perlow Gallery in New York; OK Harris Gallery in Scottsdale, Arizona; Capricorn Gallery in Bethesda, Maryland; and the Columbus Museum of Art in Ohio. Nichols has won numerous awards for his work, including a purchase award at the 1991 International Triennale of Print in Osaka, Japan. In 2005 his work was exhibited at the International Biennale of Contemporary Art in Florence, Italy, and in an exhibition at the Hygo Prefectural Museum of Art in Kobe, Japan, commemorating the tenth anniversary of the post-earthquake restoration. Frederick Nichols maintains a printmaking workshop and painting studio in Barboursville, Virginia. www.frednichols.com.

The Charlottesville Chapter of the Virginia Writers Club, Inc. is a 501(c)(3) nonprofit organization serving both aspiring and published writers in the following region: the City of Charlottesville and counties of Albemarle, Augusta, Fluvanna, Greene, Louisa, Madison, Nelson, Orange, and Rappahannock.

Membership benefits include: programs and activities planned around the needs of members; opportunities for interaction between new and veteran writers, as well as industry professionals who serve writers; hosted and/or cosponsored events to serve and/or promote Virginia writers; support of a teen division - the Young Virginia Writers Club (YVWC); writing contests and publication opportunities in the Chapter anthology; and a monthly newsletter.

The Blue Ridge Anthology is a publication of the Charlottesville Chapter VWC intended to showcase the diverse talent of member writers in the Central Virginia region. Funds generated from the sale of this anthology help to fulfill the Club's mission of supporting and stimulating the art, craft, and business of writing, as well as being an advocate for literary arts in the communities served by the Chapter.

For more information about the
Charlottesville Chapter of the Virginia Writers Club, Inc.,
or to obtain additional copies of
The Blue Ridge Anthology
please e-mail VWCMail@aol.com or visit
www.virginiawritersclub.org/cville.html

Printed in the United States
71994LV00003B/94-249

9 780979 020544